GRANT ME VISION

GRANT

A Journey of Family,

ME

Faith, and Forgiveness

VISION

SABRINA GREENLEE

with Tatsha Robertson

HARPER

An Imprint of HarperCollinsPublishers

HarperCollins books may be purchased for educational, business, or sales promotional use. For information, please email the Special Markets Department at SPsales@harpercollins.com.

FIRST EDITION

All photographs courtesy of the author unless otherwise noted.

Library of Congress Cataloging-in-Publication Data

Names: Greenlee, Sabrina, author.
Title: Grant me vision : a journey of family, faith, and forgiveness / Sabrina Greenlee.
Other titles: Journey of family, faith, and forgiveness
Description: First Harper hardcover edition. | New York, NY : Harper, 2024.
Identifiers: LCCN 2023053916 (print) | LCCN 2023053917 (ebook) | ISBN 9780063291232 (hardcover) | ISBN 9780063291249 (ebook)
Subjects: LCSH: Greenlee, Sabrina. | African American women—South Carolina—Clemson—Biography. | African Americans—South Carolina—Clemson—Biography. | Blind—South Carolina—Clemson—Biography. | Victims of violent crimes—South Carolina—Clemson—Biography. | Hopkins, DeAndre, 1992—Family. | Clemson (S.C.)—Biography.
Classification: LCC F279.C6 G74 2024 (print) | LCC F279.C6 (ebook) | DDC 975.7/2300496073 [B]—dc23/eng/20240312
LC record available at https://lccn.loc.gov/2023053916
LC ebook record available at https://lccn.loc.gov/2023053917

24 25 26 27 28 LBC 5 4 3 2 1

To my parents, to my children and grandchildren, and to Steve

Foreword by DeAndre Hopkins

Millions of football lovers know me as "DHop," an unstoppable force on the field. But for me to be an NFL star, to stand where I am today, there was a lot my family and I had to get through.

As many know, my mother, Sabrina Greenlee, was the victim of a heinous attack that rendered her blind. July 20, 2002, was the day that changed our life forever. I was ten years old.

I remember returning home from school that day to find our yard packed with relatives. Mama loved putting on a good cookout, but I could tell something was wrong, that this wasn't that. As I walked through the crowd of adults, I felt a stillness; there was no laughter, no celebration. I found my grandmother, who simply said, "Your mama's been hurt." But then when she told me Mama had been airlifted to a burn center in Georgia, was fighting for her life, and might not make it, I began to cry. I dialed my mother's number on my cell phone. That day I remember I just kept calling Mama's phone over and over and over again, wanting to just hear her voice. As I listened to her voicemail recording, I became more and more frightened that it would be the only thing I had left of her—her voice.

Me and my siblings weren't allowed to see my mother during her stay in the hospital. But when Mama finally returned, she was no longer the feisty mother we knew: she had hit rock bottom, hiding away in her room, depressed. When I found the courage to enter her room one day, I'd see fifty different bottles of pills—some she needed to go to sleep, others to stay asleep, and others for the pain—on her nightstand.

Family members, who despite their own demons, issues, and bad habits, did their best to help us while Mama was hidden away in the bedroom. But none of them could replace her; she was our mama. And so, us kids were mostly on our own until about a year later, when

Mama began moving around again, trying her best to get back to being a mother to us.

At that time, as Mama was coming from this very dark and hopeless place, she began to sell crack in a last-ditch effort to support us all. Me, my two sisters, and brother could barely sleep because of all the addicts knocking on our door from sunup to sundown. Because Mama was blind, she'd unknowingly drop crack rocks around the house, and I'd pick them up, returning them to her stash behind her nightstand, because I knew selling the drugs would be the only way we'd have enough money to eat. I was also terrified that the police would one day burst into our home and arrest my mother and split my family apart.

We struggled so much during that time that I made a decision when I was thirteen to never ask anyone for anything. I tried to take care of myself. I'd find a way to pay for my own shoes and school clothes, and stole Hot Pockets with my friends from the grocery store for my meals.

But I'd also lay in the bed and think: *Is this what life is now?* I knew there had to be more.

Even as a child, I had a big chip on my shoulder, but especially when I played sports. It was my release and saving grace, an escape. I was good, but I think the real reason I was better at sports than everyone else was because of the emotions built up inside of me. And my own struggles, too. A relative once told me to take that anger and aggression out and put it somewhere good: I did that, and I left it all on the field. As a result, my success is linked directly to my mama in many ways.

You see, Mama and I have a spiritual connection that's very hard to explain. During my senior year in high school, Mama and I made a pact, though we never verbalized it: she would stop selling drugs if I went to school someplace far away from the troubles of our hometown. On the day I left for college, on a full athletic scholarship to Clemson University, I later learned Mama had flushed the last of the crack in her stash down the toilet. And while I chose to attend Clemson to be closer to her, we both did what we said we'd do. In the meantime, I would survive off the cafeteria food at school and take care of myself. Any extra money I made was to help my sister and my mama any way I could. We survived together.

When junior year rolled around, I decided I would leave Clemson early to try out for the NFL. In my small hometown, it's frowned upon to leave school early; if you had the privilege of attending college, you were expected to finish. I asked my mother what to do, but she reminded me that it was my decision. Many people today call me a leader for many reasons, and it's really because my mama raised me to be one. I always did my own thing, even as a little boy. I know it's all because of her.

Mama also had a profound effect on others around her. Despite being blind, she'd somehow whip up four-course meals of meatloaf, mashed potatoes, collards, and macaroni and cheese. It's something I've never seen before or since. People were always coming to the house, and she'd make them meals, providing them the support they needed at the time, along with a little bit of love. At times, I would come home to find the house packed with women. And there was Mama, in the center of the kitchen, giving all these ladies lessons on how to strip! All my mama's friends, who couldn't make ten dollars stripping if they tried, were focused intently on Mama's moves! But that was Mama: always trying to make the best of a day. Even today, women love to be around her, not because her son is an NFL star, but because Mama is funny, a real character, and someone who never stops helping people. People loved coming to our home, because even though my mother couldn't see anyone, she took care of everybody. I had four friends who lived with us throughout the years; Mama took care of all of them. She's someone who is always looking for and giving love.

Despite the challenges, there was a lot of laughter in our home, too. I guess it was just my family creating our own happiness within whatever environment we found ourselves in. Kesha, my oldest sister, played basketball; my older brother, Marcus, played football. We were all good at what we did and would play together, outside all day, on a slab of concrete my cousin laid down. That was enough excitement for us; we didn't need much except each other.

In 2013, there was no doubt in my mind that I was going to be drafted by the NFL. I was confident I did well in the combine, but I didn't know which team might select me. A draft party in my honor was put together by my mother, who spent several weeks tasting the food, being sure to include lots of shrimp tempura, my favorite dish. She wanted everything to be perfect, not just for me but for all the people who came out to support me. Mama knew those people were going to see something they'd never see again: a hometown boy getting drafted in the first round by the NFL.

Draft Day was a day I'll never forget. Reporters and television lights were everywhere. At the table were my two sisters, my brother, my godmother, and Mama. We also had photographs of other athletes in my family, including my mama's two brothers and my father. When I say everyone in the town of Clemson, South Carolina, came out, I mean *everyone*. When I didn't get drafted toward the end of that first round by the New England Patriots, I whispered to Mama a bit nervously, "I might go in the second round, so what we going to feed all these people tomorrow?"

My mama, who's a comedian in her own right, shook her head and said without missing a beat, "They going to get chicken fingers."

But, soon enough, I eventually became the first-round pick of the Houston Texans, the twenty-seventh player taken in the draft. As soon as it was announced, everyone in the room went crazy—everyone was patting me on the back, laughing, shouting. I put on my new Texans hat and looked over to Mama, who said just one sentence: "I knew this day was coming."

Hours after I was drafted, I was on a plane to Houston with Mama. I slept with my head on her shoulder the whole way, and as the flight descended into Houston, we wondered what the future would now hold for our family. I wanted her to embrace it all, as best as she could, to not miss the moment, to take it all in, even though Mama couldn't see. I wanted her to feel it. After we got off the plane, we were greeted by Texans coaches and took a tour of our new home. I looked out the window of the SUV and instructed, "Mama, look to the left . . . there are all these high-rise buildings. And Mama, look to the right . . ." And, although blind, she turned her head left and then right, imagining what she thought I saw.

"Mama, you can't see this, but we're going over a bridge. Everything is so beautiful. I wish you can just see this." Then I looked at my mother, dressed in white and her hair in a perfect updo. "Mama, we made it," I said to her. "You'll never have to struggle again. We made it out."

She just smiled and said, "Son, yes, we did."

* * *

The things Mama went through—from helping to raise her brothers when she was young, to later selling drugs, to losing her sight in the most violent way—most people could not even understand that, but in this book Mama will lay it out to you honestly, and tell you things even I didn't know. I'm happy that she's evolved to be a person who can help people and lead them to change their lives through her life experience. In fact, I believe God wanted her to be where she is for this very purpose. I don't think if she was able to see, and she didn't carry her scars, that people would listen to her testimony.

Although Mama has never had the chance to see me score a touchdown, all through college at Clemson and to this day in the NFL, I bring her the football after I reach the end zone. I deliver it to her when she sits in the stands so she can touch it, so she can feel that I scored. And that together, we won against all odds.

Yes, her assault left her blind, but my mother survived to put four children through college. She's done the most unimaginable things, though I do believe Mama had to first go through the most unimaginable difficulties to become the woman she is today.

GRANT ME VISION

CHAPTER 1

Easley

Easley, South Carolina, is where my only good childhood memories reside. I was raised in the center of the town, at a crossroads, and on one corner of that intersection was where my grandma Zona Ladd, my daddy's mother, lived. It was a pretty, two-bedroom house with a small kitchen and dining room and big, manicured rosebushes outside that grew larger than me. And there was always this scrumptious aroma coming from Grandma's house, where she'd be cooking up three meals a day—oyster casserole, green beans, fried chicken, or delicious lemon and chocolate pound cakes, especially if someone from the Easley Union Baptist Church passed away. "Y'all children take this to auntie or miss so-and-so's house down the street," she'd say. That was the type of neighborhood it was: everybody looked out for each other.

There was a full-length, screened-in porch at the side of Grandma Zona's house, with very pretty steps that no one ever used and with a view out toward the town's big water tank. Behind that was the cemetery. People used to walk through the graveyards to get to downtown Easley, which, looking back, should have been an omen for me. If you came around back then, in the early 1970s, you'd see my stepgrand-daddy there—he pretty much lived on the porch, stuffing and smoking his pipe. A small white house next to theirs opened up, and eventually my daddy and mama—Terry and Rosa Nett Smith—rented it and moved in.

They were just teenagers then, having met as middle-school students at Clearview High School. That was the school all Black children in Easley went to, regardless of whatever grade they were really in.

"Truth be told, I was not attracted to him till I seen him with another girl who had on his jacket and hat," said Mama. "I got kind of jealous of that—him giving another girl attention."

Daddy played football with Mama's brother Louis and started a life-long, close friendship with Ottie, my mother's first cousin, which is how Daddy knew about Mama. Ottie would grow up to become something like the pride of my mama's wild side of the family. At the same time, Uncle Ottie would end up changing the trajectory of my family's life, spinning my mother into a deep, dark abyss and sending the rest of us into a hell that has taken us years to dig out from.

Like Ottie, Mama was from Clemson, which Daddy derisively called "country"; Daddy was born and raised in Easley, which, of course, was just as country. While Grandma Zona created a quiet, sheltered life for her only child, my mama grew up plum poor in an area in Clemson called "the Hill." Mama's kin living on the Hill were loud, wild, and always raising hell. I heard Daddy say a million times over, "It's something in the water down there."

* * *

Daddy was six feet tall, light-skinned, and very good-looking. He was also a basketball and football star in Easley. To this day, if we go out to eat at Smitty's Smokin Soul Food in Easley, somebody's going to call him "a living legend."

He started playing basketball in the ninth grade because the Black children in Clearview didn't have a junior varsity team. At that young age, Daddy was voted Best New Athlete, averaging 26 points a game while also starring as the MVP of the football team. During his first football game in the ninth grade, Daddy got severely injured. It was fourth down when he was clipped from behind as he tried to stop the punt returner. Daddy fell face down, breaking his cheekbones and shattering his jaw. He was in the hospital in Greenville for more than a week. Grandma Zona was in the bleachers the night of the accident and saw the whole thing. From then on, she only listened to the games on the radio.

By around 1969, the year before I was born, the schools in South

Carolina became integrated. Daddy was sent to Easley High and Mama was sent to Daniel High School, where she was a cheerleader. Mama was beautiful, with dark eyes, a big butt, a tiny waist, and curvy hips. Her pretty smile was accentuated by a gold tooth. She once told me two of her cousins were playing and accidentally knocked that tooth out. The dentist replaced it with a gold one, which became her signature. I've always thought it looked good and made Mama Mama.

Mama was always a hell-raiser. It never took much to push her buttons, which meant she was always getting into a fight, even when she was pregnant with me during her junior year. Her teacher would say, "If you're pregnant, you need to quit fighting before you get hurt." Mama would shake her head. "I'm not pregnant," she'd lie.

Mama says one of the reasons she kept fighting was because the white kids would call the Black students "nigger." Between the racism and Mama's upbringing in the Hill, it was the making of a troubled woman. Truth is, she never really had a chance to be any different, because fighting was all Mama knew; violence is how she was taught to handle things in the Hill. And the tragedies awaiting her in the near future would only bring out her worst.

Regardless of why she got into the fights, some school official would always call my poor grandma and say, "Come pick up Rosa because she just got done fighting; she got to go home." Grandma Frances, Mama's mother, would have to leave her job at the laundry on campus at Clemson University to pick up her daughter. And by the time Mama got big and pregnant with me, she just never returned to school.

Mama tells a story about how, after I was born, she took me to Easley High School to see my daddy. While she had dropped out of school, Daddy had become a star quarterback. That day, a white girl Mama said "your daddy was fucking" wanted to hold me. Mama cussed the white girl out. Daddy, on the other hand, he insists "none of that ever happened." That was how their relationship often went: two people always at odds, with the only thing in common being me.

* * *

At first, Daddy hated that integration had shut down all the formerly all-Black schools, because his old school, Clearview, was much nicer than the larger Easley High. Still, the newly integrated schools were exciting for mostly everyone else, for the Black boys and girls as well as the white students. To this day, some of Daddy's best friends are his white football mates. Of course, that doesn't mean being the first Black quarterback in a white school in South Carolina was easy. During the games, some of the fans—even on the Easley side—would call him a nigger and taunt him with animal noises. They'd shake the fence like they were going to break it down. Daddy would egg them on—"Come on! Come on!" and brush off the monkey calls, pointing to the scoreboard whenever he'd make a touchdown. He'd say, "Now, just look what that nigger has done!"

One night, he got caught sitting in a car with a white girl. They were parked at the foothills of the mountains when a car full of white kids pulled up, their headlights glaring in Daddy's eyes. From afar, the Ford looked to Daddy like a police car. As the approaching car tried to block them in, Daddy revved up the engine, intentionally bumped the car, and drove off. The riders in the Ford gave chase, hollering threats. Eventually, he swerved off into the parking lot of a Black juke joint. Daddy knew they were not crazy enough to pursue him there.

* * *

To this day, Mama describes me as a "beautiful, bald-headed baby" who looked just like her Daddy. "I had her spoiled," she says of me. "I couldn't set her down or she would cry for me. I dressed her like a baby doll. Growing up, I had five or six baby dolls, and she was one of them."

In April 1970, Daddy was still a senior at Easley High School. He had been admitted to Johnson C. Smith University, in Charlotte, on an athletic scholarship and would be starting in the fall. Of course, my arrival changed everything. In fact, Daddy only married Mama because I showed up, and back then it was the "right thing" to do; Mama herself admitted she only married him because I was born.

I was three months old when they got married in Daddy's biological father's living room, which was very small, with one couch and several chairs. On my mother's side, only my Grandma Frances and two cousins attended. Daddy remembers about ten people squeezing into the house. The preacher had them stand in a tiny hallway to say their vows.

There's a picture of Mama in her pink prom dress cutting a cake with Daddy. So few of Mama's family showed up—they all believed she was too young to get married. During her own wedding, that's how Mama herself felt, too: dumb and too young to be marrying someone else when she was still growing up herself. But, at the time, Mama didn't care much. She knew she didn't want to raise me on the Hill with all the fighting. And with Grandma Zona pressuring her to get married to Daddy, proclaiming, "I want to able to see my only grandchild," Mama thought getting married was the best thing to do.

With only thirty dollars in his pocket, Daddy was scared as hell of everything that was coming at him: college, a new family, and a baby! "I was thinking, how am I going to make this work?" he recalls.

And for a while they tried. Daddy arrived at Johnson C. Smith University that August but was back home for good that same month. He said he had to quit school because of me, which is something, for some reason, he never lets me forget.

"They didn't have a lot," Daddy has said about Mama and her people. "So I felt it was my responsibility to do what I could. I'd go to work or do whatever I could do to make sure you had what you needed, which included marrying your mom. I would have never married your mother if she had not gotten pregnant with you."

Were they ever in love? Sometimes I think so and other times I don't. I refuse to believe you can have three children and go through so many struggles without having *some* feelings for each other. Truth is, they were two kids trying to figure it out back in the days of segregation and de-segregation, during a time when it wasn't popular to be Black, let alone Black and in love. Mama insists the reason she didn't like my daddy is because she never got over the white girls who he'd show interest in. Daddy swears the second he got my mama pregnant he stopped "all of that" and did everything he could to please Mama, but nothing was ever enough. I suppose Mama was just not capable of letting it go, but she should have in order to receive love and give love another chance. And so, as far as I can tell, this is why she started cheating on Daddy, eventually breaking up our home.

I do think my daddy tried, in his mind, to do the right thing, because this is what they did back in the day: if you got a girl pregnant, you were told you had to marry her. And you had to take on your responsibilities and do the right thing. Regardless of whether they ever truly cared for each other, one thing I *do* know is that I wasn't conceived out of love.

I lived and breathed my daddy, though. I just didn't think my daddy ever did nothing wrong, although there is one thing he did that still hurts. All my life, he'd throw in my face that *I* was the reason he never finished Johnson C. Smith. He'd say: "I quit because your mom was calling me, telling me that she needed help with my baby."

He'd tell me, "You was a baby that *only* drunk Carnation milk. And I had to get you cans and cans of Carnation milk. So I went ahead and married your mother."

Can you imagine growing up hearing that your entire life? I am almost certain he was just ignorant of the hurt he was causing, unable to realize the pain those words caused me. But he had recited this mantra in his head so much—and would say it to me all the time—that he didn't even see the harm in the words: *If it wasn't for you, I would have finished college.*

Right after the wedding, Mama and Daddy moved in with his father and his stepmother. A few months later, though, they moved out of there and into a trailer near Grandma Zona, which is when my brother Terry Allen—affectionately known as Hummie—was born. I might have been a Daddy's girl, but Grandma Zona was the one who really doted on me. She'd buy me all these expensive clothes and would never let me get dirty—she was always washing something off me. My mama says I was used to getting my way with Grandma Zona, and I never liked hearing the word "no."

Our small family eventually moved to Clemson—to the Hill—with Mama's parents, but Daddy hated every moment of it. "Them people," he'd start, meaning Mama's wild kin on the Hill. "They were always fighting," he said. "I found myself having to fight, too."

When Daddy got a job at a plant in Easley, he commuted thirty-two miles for a spell, and eventually moved the family back. In retrospect, this must have been hard for Mama. Here she is, a teenage wife with babies, who now must move from the Hill, where all her close relatives resided, to a home next door to her mother-in-law. She did get lots of help from Grandma Zona, but Mama and Daddy argued a lot during this time, and I imagine it was a strain.

They were just two strangers: one seventeen, the other eighteen, both trying to raise children. Before they knew it, there were three children to feed, born in rapid succession: me in 1970, Terry in 1971, and lastly, Russell Bernard—who we affectionately called Dilly—in 1972. Mama says, "I was having children like doorsteps."

Before moving next to Grandma Zona, we lived in a brick house Daddy bought in a subdivision called Marshal Heights. During that time, Mama was always going back and forth to Clemson, which caused fierce arguments. Things got so bad between her and Daddy that Mama became deeply depressed, even suicidal. Her family put her in the hospital, and when she got out, she moved us to Connecticut to live for a year with a relative. She eventually returned to Easley because Hummie—who was especially close to our father—began to miss him deeply. Soon, Daddy, Mama, and us three kids again moved next door to Grandma Zona.

*　　*　　*

We lived in the Black section of Easley, near a popular café called the Brown Derby. Back then, all the Black communities had their places to go—some legal, some illegal. This was a legal one: they sold beer, hamburgers, hot dogs, sandwiches, and they even cooked soul food on the weekends, like chitlins and collards and sweet potatoes. Crowds of men would gather to hang out near some pool tables they had there.

Our house was very small. You'd walk into the living room, and if you stood there you could look right to the kitchen. If you took another couple steps into the hallway—it was kind of like a little square—you had a room to the right and a room to the left. My room with Hummie and Dilly was to the left. If Mama or Daddy were to walk out of their bedroom, they could take less than three steps before they'd be up into ours.

But my fondest memories were next door over at Grandma Zona's home, which was always pleasant and a place that made me feel tucked in. The two of us made magic in a kitchen that was so tiny that if you took a couple of steps forward, you'd bump into the refrigerator. You take another step, and you were right there in the living room, where my granddaddy had his big chair in front of the floor-model TV. He was always watching wrestling, which was really big back then. In fact, the stars of wrestling, Ric Flair and Wahoo McDaniel, would often perform at the Memorial Auditorium in nearby Greenville.

Right on the other side of the big TV was the real living room, which had nice furniture my grandmother covered in plastic and a coffee table where Grandma laid out mints that would melt in your mouth. However, the only time people were allowed in the room was when the women from the church missionary board arrived for their biweekly meetings.

My granddaddy RL—who was really my stepgranddad, but we called him "Granddaddy," else Grandma get offended—was a deacon. Meanwhile, Grandma was busy on the usher board. They were both very active at Easley Union Baptist Church and took two separate cars every Sunday. Me, Hummie, and Dilly always rode with Grandma Zona.

As soon as you walked into Baptist Union, you knew you were in a Black Baptist church. The ushers, who wore all white, including white gloves, gave you the eye as if to say, "I know that's your grandmother, but you bet not be in here cutting up."

They were always putting a gloved finger to their lips, which meant everybody needed to be quiet, especially the children. They rarely smiled, and always gave us kids a stern look. Although they terrified me, the ushers were just executing a cardinal rule in Black churches: Children must be still and very quiet.

Grandma Zona, a beautiful light-skinned Black woman with green eyes, was the only usher I wasn't afraid of. The moment she walked into the church, everybody acknowledged her. One of my favorite things to do was to roll Grandma Zona's hair the night before church. She taught me to cover the pink Styrofoam with tissue to prevent hair breakage. I'd take my time, because I wanted Grandma to look her best. The next day, she'd take the rollers out, comb her fingers through the curls, and go.

We always sat in the pews in the order we were born: me, Hummie, and then Dilly. Everybody said we were polite kids, but at church service we didn't dare make a move. The three of us kids sat like three stiff little boards throughout the service, even as the choir performed.

Me and my brothers would always sit on the first or second row because it was easy for Grandma to get up and perform her usher duties. At some point each morning, Grandma Zona would hand us a handkerchief and would snatch it back at the end of the service. If you looked around, all the grown-ups were handing their kids napkins, just in case they sneezed or had to cough.

Stepgranddaddy RL sat with the rest of the deacons on the first row near the pulpit. On Sundays, Reverend Cruell and his family would come to eat at Grandma Zona's house. The reverend was stocky and very good-looking. As he preached, he'd constantly wipe his brow and mouth. He wasn't a tall man but knew how to command attention. For some reason he reminded me of Martin Luther King Jr. Maybe it was the mustache or the suits. When he started humming and singing his words, we knew service was close to ending.

* * *

The cemetery in Easley was about thirty feet away from ours and Grandma Zona's house. People walked along it every day. Despite it being a mostly white cemetery, it was smack in the middle of downtown, surrounded mostly by Black neighborhoods. Aunt Dora, who was really just a cousin of Grandma Zona, lived down the street and often would give me a dollar to walk with her to the flea market. We had to go through the cemetery to get to there, which made it not worth the dollar, because Aunt Dora walked so slow. I just hated walking with her. I would think to myself: *Darn, I hope she doesn't come get me tomorrow to go to the flea market.* We'd get there, and she'd never know what she wanted. I now believe Aunt Dora was probably walking slow in the cemetery because she rarely got out and wanted to take in the scene, but to me she was just ancient and slow.

The cemetery and the water tank, which were right beside each other, separated the white side of town from the Black side. Any- and every-body trekked through the cemetery to get to downtown Easley, and as they walked past our house, they always waved and spoke, which is as Southern as cooking fried fish and grits. We could be outside playing, and no one ever bothered us. We walked through the cemetery so much, the tombstones were never scary to us kids.

One day, I hid myself in the cemetery, hoping my parents would go searching for me, afraid that maybe some weirdo had grabbed me. I didn't hide in the walking path but leaned between a few tombstones. As I sat there, I'd played a math game that Hummie and Dilly and I always played in the cemetery: I'd choose a tombstone and subtract the death of the deceased with the birth date and say, "That person died at sixty," or "Darn, that person died at eighteen." That day, I stayed in the cemetery as long as I could, waiting to see when someone would notice me gone. As much as I loved my father and mother, I knew after Hummie and Dilly were born, it wasn't about me anymore; I had this inkling. Truth be told, Daddy, who already could tell Hummie had the build and the ability to be a great athlete even when he was a tiny boy, cherished the ground Hummie walked on; and Mama loved herself some Dilly. But me, I believed no one really cared what I did or what I said or who I was and where I was. I was not anyone's favorite. This is not something I made up in my head, but something later in life my parents admitted to be true.

I could feel it growing up, which is why I clung to Grandma Zona. She definitely loved me; I felt it. Sometimes I thought she loved me more than the boys because she needed me to do things, and I saw that as a special kind of love.

That particular day I hid in the cemetery, I wanted to cause a ruckus and was risking getting a whipping. I imagined Mama crying and Daddy hugging her, telling her it would be all right. Finally, Dilly or Hummie would say, "Let's check the cemetery," and everyone would head down there and look for me, calling my name, relieved when they finally found me.

But hours after sitting alone between a whole bunch of dead white people, I realized no one was coming. It was dusk dark, and I was starting to get the creeps; I walked back into the house, and it was like I was never gone. Mama was cooking, Daddy was watching TV, and the boys were wrestling in the bedroom. To this day, I've never told anybody in my family what I did.

* * *

We were not allowed to gather with the other children in the neighborhood, so we stuck to ourselves. We'd play hide-and-seek, and we'd go sit on the bench outside Grandma's house and draw each other, draw Mama, Daddy, and Grandma. Out of the three of us, me and Dilly were very outgoing and always talking, with Hummie being the laid-back one. We'd draw together and occupy ourselves, just sitting outside by ourselves in our own little world.

We were allowed to go to the local recreation center, however. I thought that was just the biggest thing because I got to see boys. I remember thinking, *Oh God, they* do *exist.* I had the biggest crush on one boy in particular, Johnny Hill. Johnny was dark-skinned, tall for a boy his age, and he was always making me laugh. As a little child, probably seven or eight, I had a recurring dream that me and Johnny were the King and Queen of this dreamland packed with children called Kid's World. I realize now it was likely just a subconscious reaction to how I was feeling—alone and unloved by my parents. Kid's World, on the other hand, was a place I was seen, loved, and respected.

* * *

Us siblings were allowed to have one playmate, a mixed-breed collie and Lab named Chang. He was a beautiful light-brown dog, but I was scared to death of him. It wasn't anything wrong with Chang per se—Chang never did anything but love us—but I just never took to animals; I never even wanted a goldfish.

I remember one day, we had to take Chang to get some shots. Me and my two brothers were in the back of the car with Chang, while Mama and Daddy were in the front. Something came over me. I began to think Chang was going to attack me. I started kicking and screaming.

I remember my mama and daddy were so mad. "Brina, stop that right now!" they said, but I wouldn't stop. My fit was so bad they had to pull over and get Chang out of the car. The dog bolted. Hummie and Dilly began to cry. When we got home, Mama said to me, "You better hope Chang come back, or I'mma whoop yo' ass."

He returned three days later, and everybody was happy, but I remember thinking: *What about me?*

* * *

One day Hummie was sitting at the table in the elementary school lunchroom, so shy and quiet. He wouldn't even touch his food or pick up his fork or put his straw in his milk. So I went over there and sat beside him and opened his milk. I put his fork in his hand. "Hummie," I said, "it's okay, you can eat." And he began to eat.

He reminded me of this moment many years later when he was married with children. "Brina, I never forgot that you came over there to me and kind of told me it was okay to eat. "Go on now. Eat. You are good," he recalled me saying.

Back then, I didn't even realize what I was doing. That was just my maternal instincts I had for my brothers kicking in. As things began to change, and our lives became more volatile, those instincts would kick in more and more.

Along with my two younger brothers, we'd be in our room hearing everything: all the shouting, Mama and Daddy fussing and fighting. I'd just shut the door and get the three of us under the mattresses, crammed below the little bunk beds we had. I didn't know what else to do. We'd pull the covers and make a fort. That was our safety net. I learned very early on how to distract my brothers from what I heard in the other room, and we would sit there in our own little world for hours.

But we'd still hear bumps on the walls and floors and a lot of cussing, and even Daddy saying once, "I done told you to stay away from that motherfucker!" Mama shouted back defensively, "You don't know what you're talking about, you fucking crazy! What about that white bitch that you was sleeping with?" Back and forth, back and forth. In the morning, Daddy would come out with a cut under his eye, and Mama had bruises.

One day they had a huge argument, a fight that changed my life. I was about seven years old. Mama had taken me earlier in the day to what I learned later was a boyfriend's house. That man there was living with a woman, but he was always tugging on my mama. He'd put me with some other kids living in the house, and he and Mama would sneak off. But this particular day, Mama wanted me to stay with her. I remember this man pouring liquor on the ice cream all us kids were eating. Now I didn't like this man, and I'm crying, saying I'm going to tell my daddy what he did. And when we got back home that's what I did. But I didn't mean for all hell to break loose.

The next morning, after fighting with Mama all night, Daddy got this gun and ordered us all to get in the car—Mama, me, Hummie, and Dilly. Daddy had the gun to Mama's head; he's saying he's going to kill her and himself.

We soon stopped at a gas station. When we pulled up to the pump, Daddy told Mama to go inside to the attendant to pay for gas. She grabbed my hand to go in there with her. While we were walking, she said, "Tell the people in the store to call the police, that your daddy got a gun."

Instantly, in my head, I thought, *I'm not going to tell on my daddy.* What I realize now is that my mama had to be scared to death. Here she was with me, but she could not run or scream because her other two children were in the car with him. After we paid for the gas, I didn't mention anything to the cashier. Mama and me looked at each other, neither of us wanting Daddy in trouble, but also neither of us knowing what was in store for us when we entered the car again.

Even to this day, in my mind, my daddy can't do no wrong. And so I still try to think of how he must have felt. I was the snitch who answered his questions and fed his doubts. He was at his wits' end.

Once back in the car, Daddy started driving again, cussing, one hand on the wheel, the other pointing the gun at Mama's head. We all drove to nearby Pickens, to the house of the man my mama had gone to see.

As soon as we got there, we noticed the man's wife on the porch. Daddy hollered at the man to come out. He yelled to the man's wife, "Get your husband—you need to know he's been fucking my wife last night! He can have her!"

Shortly afterward, the man came out the door. Daddy said, "You a coward, motherfucker. You want her? You can have her."

While recalling the incident years later, Mama said the man replied, "Well, let her and the children all out the car first."

Daddy was waving the gun, and we were hollering in the back seat. The two men stared each other down, cussing in broad daylight. They started back arguing but the wife rushed in the house to call the police once she noticed the gun. Daddy jumped back in the car, and we swerved out of there real fast. Using a back road, Daddy drove us straight to Clemson, about thirty minutes away, pulling into my mama's parents' home on the Hill. A cousin pulled in and blocked the car while relatives poured outside the house, asking us what was wrong. Me and my brothers jumped out the car crying, and Mama started crying and screaming. Daddy managed to pull off, and Mama got my aunt to bring us three kids with her to a police station.

I had never been to a police department before. Everything I knew about the police was bad, so my guard—even as a little girl—was up. Me and my brothers sat still in our chairs while these big white police officers with guns hanging at their hips bent down staring at us, asking us questions: "Have your parents ever hurt you? Did your parents fight in the house?"

We knew not to say nothing while they probed us about our home life. I cut my eyes at Hummie and Dilly, shaking my head so they'd keep their mouths shut. I was trying to protect them: I knew already that it wouldn't take a lot for us to be taken away from Mama and Daddy. Later, somebody—I don't remember who—came to pick us up, and me, Hummie, and Dilly, and Mama got driven back to the Hill. That's where we're going to live now—without Daddy—at my grandmother's on my mama's side.

* * *

That all the misfortune and the terrible events that occurred after Easley, that they all happened to one person and one family, *my family*, made me feel cursed. Nothing seemed fair, and I felt deeply unloved.

All that followed, the years of fear and feeling sorry for myself, were the culmination of all the destructive paths I went down in my choice of relationships with men. I did not yet have a conscious awareness of why I made those choices, and I made zero effort to challenge the myth I bought into that as long as I had a man by my side, I wasn't alone.

CHAPTER 2

The Hill

I did not want to move to the Hill. It was in a lousy part of Clemson and worlds apart from Easley, where I had my bed and where Grandma Zona was. And why should I have to go? I'm a daddy's girl; he was not moving to Clemson, and so I felt I should be staying with him. But then when I asked, Daddy said no, and he was keeping Hummie with him—he didn't choose me or Dilly. For the life of me, I couldn't understand this—I was his only baby girl.

Daddy favored Hummie because he was into sports, and so Daddy lived vicariously through him. Although Hummie lived with Daddy for only two weeks—Mama would eventually "steal" Hummie off the play-ground at school one day and return him home because she couldn't stand to see her children separated—I still felt betrayed by Daddy's choosing Hummie over me. It hurt. I didn't know it then, but it was the start of my abandonment issues. As an adult, I'd beg men to stay when I should have let their asses leave. When Daddy left me, I felt so much resentment—this was the first time that I didn't like him. How could he let me go with my mama? She's the one who whooped me, and Daddy never did. Mama was in her own world—she acted like she didn't know me, and from the beginning, complained that Daddy favored me. I was even the one who told him what Mama had been doing with the other man!

Once Mama took me to the Hill, I barely saw Daddy for a long, long time. He almost never came down there. It was only on the rare occa-sions when Mama brought me, Hummie, and Dilly to Grandma Zona's house for a visit that Daddy, who still lived next door to her, would come around. But even then, it wasn't because he planned to—he'd just happen to be dropping by to say hi to Grandma Zona. At least Mama would drive us to see Grandma Zona occasionally and make an effort to keep Daddy's side of the family in my life. Daddy also provided Mama with very little money to support us.

So, here I was, living with my grandparents on the Hill. I never liked visiting Mama's parents, Grandma Frances and Granddaddy Edgar, not even for a weekend. All my bad cousins were there. The kids called me Olive Oyl because I was so skinny. And because I was light-skinned, and the rest of my cousins were darker, they would throw dirt on me and laugh and treat me like I was different. Grandma Zona had me so prissy that I was scared of dirt, which I guess to them was funny.

In Easley, us kids would play hide-and-seek, but on the Hill, we played hide-and-go-get-it, where the boys chase you and hunch on you. They'd say: "Let's get the 'white girl.'" Of course, I wasn't a white girl, but my skin was lighter than the rest of theirs, and most of my cousins hadn't even been around white kids, so I was the closest thing in their minds. And me, Dilly, and Hummie were always picked on because we were the clean kids, or the bougie kids, whatever they called us. I remember at night some cousins would put cockroaches or hot sauce in Hummie's mouth or ears. The cousins saw Hummie and Dilly as weak and would bully them. But I just wouldn't allow it, so I'd stay up all night to protect my brothers. Maybe I sensed that they were vulnerable; even as a child I felt it was my duty to keep them both safe.

No one had their own bed, and we often had to sleep on the floor with other relatives, sometimes up to twenty of us. And there were roaches everywhere; a run-down house, especially when compared to Grandma Zona's. The house used a kerosene heater, so everyone smelled all the time. There was a big freezer outside where they kept all the food, but it was never defrosted, so the food was always trapped in deep ice. There weren't too many actual walls—the "bedrooms" were divided by hanging sheets, so it was easy to see the person laying right next to you.

My grandparents slept in two different beds because Granddaddy would often come home drunk. He'd carry a piss bucket around the house because he'd get up in the middle of the night and have to pee. It didn't matter who was in the room or how old you were; if he had to pee, he'd just go, because he never could make it to the bathroom. You could play around the house, but you had to be sure to avoid Granddaddy's piss bucket. It was always sitting around there, too easy to accidentally kick over.

The bathroom had a tub, but nobody used it because it was always filled with clothes. At some point, someone cleaned it out, but I don't think anyone ever used it. We just washed up in the sink, which I learned later was called a "hoe bath."

Somebody was constantly patching up the toilet. If you sat on that commode, you could look down and see the ground and various creatures like roaches with wings below. My cousin Missy and I would always go to the bathroom together—someone would use the toilet, and the other one would stand guard. It was frightening when I had no one to guard me—I'd do the fastest pee I ever forced out of my body and run back out of that bathroom.

There was also a big ol' rat in the house the family called "Big Ben." Whenever there was an unseen ruckus, somebody would say, "That ain't nobody but ol' Big Ben."

Grandma was sick a lot, and I gradually became her caretaker, because, even then, that was my nature. I was taking care of Dilly and Hummie because Mama would hang out with her relatives once we arrived. It's not to say she didn't feed us or take care of us, because Mama was always there for us, but she was going out now more than we were used to. I'd wake Hummie and Dilly up for school in the morning, get them breakfast, and make sure they were out the door with their homework in their book bags. A few times, I had to feed them dinner at night, making use of whatever we had on hand—usually some rice, hot dogs, or canned stew.

I have to think that Mama just wanted to be free—free of her husband, free of her family—and could now roam around with all these aunties we had on the Hill. Mama had loved two of my aunties in particular—Auntie Sylect and Aunt Louise. Aunt Sylect was tall and thin and cool. She was Grandma Frances's younger sister, so she was really my great-aunt.

Grandma was one of the oldest of the sisters, but Aunt Sylect was only about ten years older than Mama. Aunt Sylect was always dancing and talking about men. I remember coming outside with a short dress one day and all the aunties telling me to go back into the house and change.

Aunt Sylect chimed in, "Y'all leave that girl alone," I remember her saying. "She ain't doing nothing wrong."

Mama was crazy about Auntie Sylect, and Auntie was always in Mama's ear, telling her to leave Daddy alone and that she could do better.

My other favorite aunt was Louise, my mama's older sister. I couldn't imagine any of the women in the club being as beautiful as Mama and Aunt Louise, who to me were the essence of beautiful Black women. Aunt Louise was thin, with long hair, and loved to dress in the most beautiful clothes. Mama and Louise wore big Afros, and Mama fancied dark lipstick, which only enhanced her gold tooth.

Whenever my great-aunties went to go do something, whether it was shopping or going to Bottom's Up, their favorite club, Mama attached herself to them. Now when I mention they went shopping, what I mean is they'd go "boosting"—stealing clothes from the stores and malls and then coming back to the neighborhood to sell them for a discount.

None of them had anything on Aunt Louise. She wasn't any old shoplifter; she was brilliant, a highly organized and skilled booster who'd started her "trade" in Germany, where her husband was stationed in the army. She'd proudly share that she used the money she got from boosting to put herself through beauty school, to buy a hair salon and a home, and to renovate Grandma and Granddaddy's shotgun house, adding a modern toilet and bathtub.

I recall Grandma warning Aunt Louise to be careful and not get arrested, but she knew Louise would never get caught boosting. "You gonna get enough stealing them white folks' stuff," Grandma warned, then she'd shake her head. "You will steal stank out of shit." In other words, Grandma was saying Louise would steal anything.

Mama wasn't good at stealing; she was more of a pocketbook booster—she'd take what would fit in her bag. But once, Mama caught herself using one of Aunt Louise's techniques with little success. That day, she took me, Hummie, and Dilly to Sky City, a local store, and informed us that we'd have to steal our own school clothes. She ushered us into the dressing room, where we layered on our boosted pants and shirts and nervously attempted to exit the store. Of course we were stopped by the store manager, and after a long lecture, we returned the clothes and the manager let us go. I guess he felt sorry for Mama for having three children who needed clothes for school badly enough that they had to steal them.

Louise never got caught because the police just couldn't catch her. One day I was out playing in the front yard of Grandma's house when Aunt Louise flew by in her car, slowing down to wave her arm out the car window. "They can't catch me!" she yelled as she sped up, trying to lose the cops who were tailing right behind her. I remember everyone getting in their cars to follow her; we were worried Auntie would be killed by the police, but Auntie disappeared into the woods and eventually outran the po-po. When she returned, free and with her latest inventory, I was in awe.

To this day, Aunt Louise, who is in her early seventies and no longer boosting, takes pride in the fact that she dressed all of us in the neighborhood throughout our years of school.

"I didn't want none of these children on the Hill to be going to school with these white people looking all shabby," she told me once. "These children, not just my kin, were dressed just as good as those white children."

* * *

Some mornings I remember waking up and not seeing Mama there. But so many other cousins and relatives were getting dropped off, and there were so many other adults around to tell us what to do, that I almost forgot she was supposed to be home.

Everybody came over on Sundays. They had these big, huge pots cooking, and by noon I could smell the food, but no one ever invited the kids to eat until nine or ten o'clock at night. Instead we were being told to stay out, all day, to go outside and get out of the grown folks' faces.

But it was always better for me to be inside, because I was safe (from the dirt and the teasing) with Grandma, who would have a rag in one hand, and the other hand she'd used to wipe sweat off her brow. I was the one who helped her cook, and I knew when she needed to sit down and rest. Grandma cooked with fatback and lard. And us kids knew better than to touch the blue-and-white Crisco can that sat by the stove, because sometimes we were told it could be filled with hot grease and that grease needed to get recycled over and over.

The two of us, me and Grandma, would take a minute in the midst of chaos, waiting on the collards and pinto beans, which boiled over on red-hot burners that were always on high in my grandma's kitchen. Meanwhile, the gospel sounds of Mahalia Jackson's strong voice would blare from the tiny radio on the counter. To this day, I find myself playing Mahalia some Sundays. No one sings "Amazing Grace" like her.

*   *   *

During those Sundays on the Hill, the family was all together, but it wasn't like everyone was happy to see each other. In fact, we spent a lot of time just mad at each other. I remember Mama and Aunt Louise even duking it out once—on their tippy-toes, literally popping each other in the mouth until someone started bleeding.

"I'mma stomp a mudhole in your ass," Aunt Louise said.

"That'll be a cold day in hell," Mama replied.

At one point, they were circling each other while the men in the family sat watching like it was an Ali-Frazier bout. But eventually the two would get tired of swinging at each other, allowing the men to break them up. There was always tension in the air; you just knew something was about to pop off when my family got together. There was this unspoken thing, an unspoken code of behavior among the adults, it seemed: if you stole someone's stuff, or if you said the wrong thing, there would be a fight, whether we're kin or not. And if you got the best of someone, they'd be back to get the best of you next time. Nothing in the house was ever solved peacefully. My family must have been bred to fight, and on the Hill, we saw fights at least once a week. Sometimes though, it wasn't physical: you'd just get a good cuss-out and that would be that.

The Hill wasn't the Wild, Wild West, but it was darn close to it. Still, sometimes my relatives could act civil, especially when we headed for a Sunday outing at the Twin Lakes. We'd never leave on time because Grandma would be in the kitchen frying chicken and cooking up macaroni and cheese. I don't know if it's a Black thing or not, but we weren't allowed to get into the water immediately after we ate; they made all the kids wait an hour, so I'd hustle to finish up any meal.

Even though my cousins were mean, I'd play with them, whether we were at Twin Lakes or home on the Hill. Outside on the Hill was an old, abandoned well that had everything in it you can think of—except water. There was so much stuff down there—furniture, mattresses, all types of things—that there was never any worry of anyone falling in.

Only recently did I learn from Aunt Louise that the adults threw stuff in there to prevent us children from plummeting to our deaths. There was also an old tree beside the house that had been struck by lightning and caught fire. Its big trunk had a body-shaped cutout in the middle, like someone ran clean through it and kept on running. All the kids liked to play under this tree, its branches brittle and bare.

Farther up the hill, right by the well in the next house, is where Granny—Grandma Frances's mama—lived. Rumor had it that Granny had fourteen children (with two sets of twins to die at birth, which wasn't uncommon back in those days). To the left of Granny's was a garden, and no one wanted to get caught there. If you did, you'd see her shotgun. At times, Granny would babysit us, during which, we'd be subjected to being called a "bastard." To Granny, everyone was a bastard; that was a favorite word. Mama would complain, telling Granny that the kids were saying she'd been calling them bastards all day. She'd just look at Mama with a straight face and say, "Them bastards are telling a lie."

When you stayed with Granny, you had to sit there on the couch and watch this little, itty-bitty television set up across from her; it was so little you had to squinch up your eyes to see anything. Granny always sat by the heater, crossed her legs, dipped her snuff, and drank her corn liquor—all at the same time—and you were not allowed to get up till she said so. I hated staying there.

* * *

Then there was Granddaddy Edgar, my grandfather with the piss bucket. He was called Nine Lives because sometimes he came home in his car, and sometimes he didn't, just like a cat.

Aunt Louise described her father like this: "Daddy was handsome, long faced. Most people say I looked just like him. Like me, he didn't have much butt. And loved to dress. He loved to have his clothes matching. When he gets ready to go on his raids, he'd clean his car up and ride until it got dirty. The roads were dirt roads back then. During the week, his car was filthy, but on the weekend when he was ready to go on a raid, he'd clean himself, clean the car up, and just ride."

A raid is when Granddaddy would go drinking and want to fight. He loved to drive and was very good at it. Police would be sitting in their car, hiding out somewhere they thought drivers couldn't see them, but Granddaddy always spotted them. Then he'd rev up his motor, a signal for them to chase him.

"They could never find him 'cause he'd go through all kind of woods," Aunt Louise told me. "When they did get him, that was only a couple of times, they'd beat the shit outta him."

Aunt Louise said that was usually when he'd already settled down and was already in bed asleep. "The police would come in the house and drag him out of the bed. Back then, white police would beat your ass."

If he didn't get home with a car, Aunt Louise said that meant he was drunk, and there was a good chance the police would show up because he had wrecked the car somewhere and walked home.

One day, a Sunday, he drove up the Hill to the top of our driveway, near where all us kids were playing around the old tree.

Mama was yelling at us, "Y'all kids, get out the way, Daddy up there acting damn stupid again!"

But we were confused and looking around—it was just Granddaddy, of course he wouldn't hurt us. But the next thing I knew, he revved the engine, hit the gas, and drove the car straight into the house.

Earlier that morning, Grandma Frances had had the radio on, playing her Mahalia as she was cooking. Granddaddy came down to the kitchen, and she was telling him she wasn't feeling good, asking him to get out of the room.

A typical exchange between the two went something like this: Grandma would be busy mixing up her crackling cornbread to put in the oven. Meanwhile, Granddaddy would walk up and snap his fingers in Grandma's face. "Frances, you got the food ready?"

Grandma would say: "Hell no. You been out here drinking all night with the whores; go get the whores to feed ya."

Granddaddy would start stuttering. "Got damn it . . . damn it. I'mma turn this house upside down!"

Grandma wasn't educated but she liked to talk proper. She called Granny "Mother" and sometimes called Granddaddy Edgar by his full name. "James Austin, I told you to get out of the kitchen and leave me alone."

He'd snap his fingers at her again. "You feeding everybody else, but when can I get my food?"

She'd put her hands on her hips. "Go on, James, I told you to go now."

But when he didn't cooperate, when he didn't listen to her, she'd get angry—like when she picked up a Mason jar of tomatoes and hurled it at him.

The way Aunt Louise told it, "Daddy started pouting, playing like he been injured to get sympathy." Aunt Louise always starts to laugh as she imitates Granddaddy. "Ohhhhhh Frances, you done hurrrrrrt me," she'd mimic.

That morning before Granddaddy drove the car into the house, Grandma Frances had hit him on the head with a big iron skillet. So he'd left all mad, though of course he came back—and what he did was drive through the living room wall.

My uncle Jimmy lived in a trailer down the hill from Granny. He rushed over after hearing the crash and snatched Granddaddy out the car, backed it up, got out, and started beating the crap out of Granddaddy. "I done told your fucking ass!" Jimmy shouted.

Mind you, all the kids had stopped playing and were watching this. By this time, Mama and Aunt Louise decided they were going to take turns jumping on Granddaddy, too. He kept trying to get up, and he was mumbling something—"Hope God may kill me." That was his way of swearing he's going to do something to you later.

Soon enough, Granddaddy left. We kids couldn't wait to get inside to see what had happened. But it turned out he'd busted his car through the wall that was our room. After that disaster, the men in the family put up a big plastic sheet up where the outside wall used to be, until it was eventually rebuilt.

* * *

There was a path to the left of our house on the Hill that went past an old shed, crossed a creek, and then leveled out. At the end of this path was where Reverend Lottie Davis lived with his wife, who we called Aunt Floreen. Reverend Lottie was in his sixties and no longer running a church, but everyone still called him Reverend and spoke of him as a good man. He was bald, with a mustache and dark skin, and he'd always stare at people through these thick glasses. He had a strange habit of smacking his lips, like he was eating without eating.

Reverend Lottie had two big refrigerators set up next to his house, and that's where he sold sodas for a dime. So every Sunday I was told to go down to Lottie's to get sodas. By the time I was ten years old, I was very familiar with this task. In fact, I'd volunteer for it because I'd be tired of playing outside with lizards and all the other creatures and bugs the boys were catching. I'd go down the path for the sodas and wait for Reverend Lottie to see me standing at his door. He'd come out and always kind of touch my shoulder or hold my hand a little extra longer than I was used to. But it didn't matter much to me, because I was usually with my cousins. We'd pick up so many sodas that we'd have to cuff our shirts up and make a knot at the top, just to carry all the cans back up the path.

A lot of the time, especially if I had run down for sodas by myself, Reverend Lottie would make excuses to get me to come into his house. He would say, "I got something for you," or "Come give this to Cousin Frances." I knew enough that he was making stuff up to get me in the house. I remember him sitting in his chair, telling stories. He would always want to tell stories to the kids, whether it was boys or girls. It's like he wanted kids around him. Anyway, sometimes I'd go in there, sometimes I wouldn't.

Still, he would single me out. "You know, you're so pretty," he'd say. Or: "You look just like your mama." Or he would say little stuff like that, but no matter what he said, he'd be looking at me. Even if he was talking to somebody else, he was looking at me. I would just be polite because I couldn't go home without the sodas. And he'd take such a long time to get to it. I'd be sitting there and he'd just talk and talk. Sometimes I could even hear people calling down from Grandma Frances's house because he'd take so long. Reverend Lottie made me feel a little weird, but at the time I couldn't say I was really scared.

I should've been.

* * *

Later that summer, Grandma started feeling ill. For a spell, she was sickly and in and out of the hospital, so everyone knew not to come down much on Sundays. But for whatever reason, it was on one particular Sunday that Reverend Lottie and Aunt Floreen decided to stop by the house for a visit with Grandma.

That day, I was in my room—rather, the very small area divided off from the living room by hung sheets. Mama was getting ready to run the streets with my aunties again, and I was crying because I didn't want to stay back to take care of Grandma—I wanted to go with her. But Mama was determined not to take me. "Go back inside with your grandma. I'll be back," she said as she pushed me back toward the house. I knew that meant she'd be back in a couple of days. That's just how my mama was— she wouldn't come back until she was ready.

After Mama left in the car with the aunties, I headed back inside, angry at being abandoned again. Reverend Lottie was out there on the porch, while my grandma and Aunt Floreen sat and talked in the living room. By now I'm back in my "room," behind the sheet, sitting on the bed. I'm mad, I'm pouting and I'm stomping. I was calling my mama all kinds of crazy things under my breath.

In walked Reverend Lottie. While I was stomping around and cussing Mama, Reverend Lottie saw that his wife and my grandmother had gone back out to the porch. What he also knew was that Grandma was sickly, and that they'd be out there for a while. He sat beside me on my bed, saying, "It's okay, you know, your mama will be back." "I know, I know," I replied and attempted to stop sulking.

"You got some really pretty brown eyes," he said. "What grade you in now?" I was sitting there, not even weighing eighty pounds, and he put his hand on my leg. Even in that moment, I still didn't fear him. My grandmother was right there, on the other side of the sheet, I reasoned. I could hear other people speaking outside.

But then Reverend Lottie took my hand and he put it down on his lap. I hadn't even noticed or looked down the whole time we were talking, but he unzipped and pulled his pants down. He took my hand and forced it on his privates. He had an erection, and he started stroking it with my hand.

Now I was terrified.

He had the tightest grip on me, but I still didn't scream. I was just sitting there thinking that Grandma was about to walk in. Meanwhile, he was talking to me the whole time, and he had that smacking sound going on with his lips. At some point, he pressed his lips together, and he was moving them without smacking—like he's contorting his face and lips. I was staring at him, trying to pull back my hand. But I couldn't do it. The next thing I know, he was on top of me, ripping at my clothes and fighting to penetrate me. He was a big man, breathing hard and sweating, and was able to pin me down on my back easily. I tried pushing him off, but he wouldn't move. He wasn't able to stick it in—as they say where I'm from— but that didn't stop him from hurting me. My family was right *there*, just on the other side of that hanging sheet—until I realized that they weren't.

Finally, he got up off the bed, and I scrambled up, too. He zipped his pants back up and started talking to me again: "You know, this is our little secret. Don't tell your mama, don't tell your grandma. You can't tell nobody."

I just stood there, in shock. I didn't say yes or no; I didn't say anything. Then he left. I heard the screen door pop. I darted out to the porch, but for some reason, Grandma wasn't out there. Reverend Lottie was just sitting there on the porch, relaxed, as if nothing happened just moments before. I went back to my bed and cried.

While the rest of the day was a blur, what happened left a question in my mind for years. There was no doubt I was violated, but was I *raped*? Until recently, I called it a molestation. I didn't think I was raped because he didn't penetrate me, although he tried. Now, as someone who has lived for five decades, I'm 1000 percent sure: the second he tried to enter me, it was rape.

At some point, Reverend Lottie and Aunt Floreen left. Mama came home and then went back out again. I just lay there in my bed, numb. Why did he pick me? I didn't say anything for a couple of days—I was sure that I'd done something very wrong. And my body felt different now. I didn't understand what, but something wasn't right.

After a few more days, I worked up my nerve. I was sweaty and panicky, but I told Mama and Grandma what had happened. I told them Reverend Lottie hurt me. I don't remember which one of them said it, but after I was done speaking, I was told the following: "Go somewhere and sit your fast ass down." She paused, as if she was the one shocked by me. "That man is married! You're not about to mess up his life."

Not only did Mama and Grandma accuse me of lying, but they sent me back down there again and again to get sodas. I'd cry, begging them not to send me to Lottie's. But they would insist and threaten me to "pick my own switch." In the South, this was a common form of corporal punishment—kids were told by an adult to go outside and find a tree limb (usually nothing thicker than a hickory branch) and bring it to them to be whipped with it.

They did not believe me. And that was the beginning of me not trusting anybody.

I did not want a whooping with a switch, so I'd go to Reverend Lottie for more soda. I was so terrified that first time after the rape that I peed my pants on the way there. I remember so clearly the look on his face that day—he would make this smirk. And no matter who I would recruit to accompany me after—everybody, every boy I could get to go down there with me—Lottie would grin like he had gotten away with murder.

All the subsequent problems I've had with men sprang from this traumatic incident. There's something about a little girl who walks in a room after she's been brutally touched or tampered with. She somehow, for some reason, believes that men want her. After my rape, I'd look at any man, convinced that they wanted me, as if I had some sweet stone inside of me they had to have. And in a strange way, that excited me. So I began to walk differently and think differently. Reverend Lottie destroyed every bit of who I might become, who, at ten years old, was still developing inside me, and he left me only as prey—simply an object of sexual desire.

And it's not that I would think I was pretty—it was the opposite. After Reverend Lottie, if someone said I was beautiful, I thought they were trying to be funny.

But at that age, I couldn't make sense of it. All I knew was that something in my mind was no longer right. It was like Reverend Lottie took a piece of my soul that I could never really grasp or even identify. Something was now missing, and whatever was gone impacted my decisions and behavior from that day forward. I would not be able to grow into the woman I was truly meant to be. In every relationship I would have with a man over the next few decades, I was that wounded little girl, trapped in an inner world that I lived in all by myself. I now know that I was carrying years and years of shame, and that same shame would fester within me for decades to come.

CHAPTER 3

Death Valley

Where we lived, everything fell under the shadow of Clemson University, and specifically, for us, Clemson football. The campus was less than five miles from where we lived on the Hill. With Granny dipping snuff and me staring down roaches in the toilet, Clemson was a paradise, an entirely different world.

To this day people somehow think there are no Black neighborhoods in the vicinity of the university, but that is simply not true. There's Vista, Red Hill, Calhoun, and of course the Hill, were my family lived. After all, a lot of the original campus was built many years ago by Black labor crews, so there have always been Black folk around Clemson from the beginning.

Death Valley, the legendary football stadium that's home to the Clemson Tigers, was built on the western part of the campus, and seeing games there was an experience of a lifetime, a series of core memories that began when I was a child. From when they were about six or seven, my brothers Hummie and Dilly spent the summers working the grounds of Death Valley, picking up trash and painting tiger paws on people's faces for ten dollars. Dilly was especially good at drawing the faces because he had small, nimble hands, and he was very artistic. When they first started making money doing this, my brothers were so excited to show me. But I wasn't moved. "I would never paint no tiger paws on nobody's faces," I'd say.

Of course, I was envious of the money they made, but still had no interest in working in the stadium. Instead, I wanted to be part of the excitement: Imagine eighty-five thousand people cheering so loud you can't hear the person next to you speak! The energy, the smell of beer, everybody screaming at the top of their lungs for the home team—I've been to a lot of football stadiums in my life, including NFL arenas, but there's nothing at all quite like Clemson.

For us kids, the next best thing to a home game was Tigerama, which were the celebrations all over Clemson's campus before Homecoming game Saturday in October. In fact, Tigerama could even be better than a home game because our parents never said we couldn't go. As long as we stayed together, we were good. So, every year, we'd run all up and down throughout town, or sneak into campus, or march right out onto the Bowman Field, where the sororities and fraternities worked on these giant floats that would be judged during the Homecoming game. Tigerama was where we'd see all of our cousins and friends. It was a chance to just run around town feeling free.

While my brothers were downtown painting on white people's faces, I was downtown, too—walking around and being "fast." My first crushes were on some of the football players, who'd smile or say little things to me—"Hey girl, come talk to me" or "Damn, you fine."

Being around the university as a little girl could be dangerous. Attention from college boys—all young men, really—is everywhere, and they're looking at you and catcalling even when you're only in elementary school. Being constantly told that she's cute or pretty can overwhelm an impressionable girl, and I was no exception. It's not like I had to go looking for boys; male attention was everywhere: at the grocery store, at restaurants, standing outside the bars and pizza parlors. I never got enough attention at home, at least not since Daddy left, so I felt like *somebody* when I was interacting and flirting with college students. One minute I'm on the Hill hanging with some stupid cousin or avoiding my mama, and the next, I'm rubbing shoulders with a "sophisticated" college student. My experience with the older kids trained me to switch between two different worlds as needed.

Even though I was raped by Reverend Lottie, life for me continued on as usual. I was ten, Hummie was nine, and Dilly was eight, and though we didn't know it, our little world in the next few years would soon explode. But until then, we basked in the calm of a storm, where Clemson University was a lifeline for the entire town, especially for young boys like my brothers. Hummie and Dilly were always together, usually with our cousins Poopie (whose real name was Larry), who was Aunt Louise's son, and Squeenchie (whose real name was Louis Jr.), who was my uncle Louis's and Aunt Pumpkin's boy. Calling themselves the Four Horsemen—a term that's both from Notre Dame football and the Book of Revelation—they spent hours running the streets, or over at the house of Aunt Viney, who was Grandma Frances's sister-in-law. Aunt Viney had a big field, where the boys would play tackle football all day in the hot sun. Often it would be the four of them, or some older cousin would come and play, or they'd compete against the neighborhood kids. Most of the big plays were made by Hummie, Squeenchie, and Poopie. Dilly, like the rest of my family, was a good athlete, but he was the youngest and not on their level yet. He was smaller, too, and so he was also the one who often got hurt or ended up in a fight, which meant they all were fighting because, like Poopie still says to this day: "No one better not hurt Dilly."

The four of them all shared the same big dream, to one day play football for Clemson. They'd sit and talk about the number they'd wear on their jersey, or what they were going to do for their parents once they made money, what kind of houses they were going to buy.

Clemson University was everything to us. Not unlike the steel mills that once ruled Gary, Indiana, or the movie industry in Los Angeles, Clemson University was and still is the dominant presence and a saving grace for my hometown. Grandma Frances spent four decades cleaning laundry at Clemson—Mama would share tales of Grandma taking her to work with her as a baby and her coworkers taking care of her. We knew scores of friends and neighbors who made their livelihood through the institution. Later on, Hummie would become a huge football star at Clemson who'd break records, and Poopie is still a respected coach there. But as children, we just felt lucky to be in its proximity.

Morrison Elementary School was five minutes away from Clemson, which meant all of the Clemson professors and coaches' children went to Morrison—those parents were going to make damn sure the academics at the schools were up to par and that their children had the best teachers. As a result, average Black kids like us got swept up into some good education and experienced incredible things. For instance, once a year, students at Morrison Elementary would stand outside the school waiting for a charter bus filled with Clemson football players. The bus would pull up across the street from the school, and the football players—like gods from some other planet—would step off the bus and wave to us. You couldn't imagine the excitement we felt seeing the people we watched every week on television; it didn't matter that there was a wide road between us. To this day it brings chills down my spine as I can still see, in my mind's eye, me and my brothers standing outside, waving in awe. Years later, Hummie himself would be one of those players stepping off the bus, waving to a new generation of students at Morrison.

If you were a boy in our hometown, you couldn't help but want to play football for Clemson. When we were in elementary school in 1981, they were national champions. So the thought of going to Clemson, basking in that glory and making everybody around you proud, is something boys like Hummie and Dilly longed to achieve.

I barely ever missed my brother's home games, but Hummie was the love of my daddy's life, so Daddy wasn't about to miss *any* of his games. Daddy had a friend named Al Wilson, a white man who was also a huge Clemson fan. Whenever Clemson was playing an away game, Daddy and Al would load up Al's van and off they went—they hit the road to wherever the Tigers were playing.

There's a tradition in Death Valley worth seeing at least once in a lifetime. During every home game, the football players get on charter buses, which roll a few feet away up a hill. All eyes are waiting on the players as they approach a famous rock—they call it Howard's Rock—brought over from the real Death Valley in California in 1966. The team takes off running down the hill to touch the Rock for good luck, as eighty-five thousand fans frantically cheer them on. The shouts, and seeing orange everywhere, gets the adrenaline rushing, but trying to describe what it feels like, the pulse of powerful excitement in that moment, is hard to do. Daddy loves telling anybody who will listen the story of how he almost passed out seeing Hummie in Death Valley for the first time. "I think it was 1990, that was his first game, and they were playing, I believe,

Furman University. I saw Hummie's number twenty-four as big as day. Between the crowd, the noise, and all the excitement of that moment, and then looking up there seeing that number twenty-four step up and rub that rock the first time, that's when I liked to nearly fainted."

In 1993, Hummie caught the winning touchdown pass against the Kentucky Wildcats in the Peach Bowl, a major college championship game. I'd driven to Lexington with Mama and a few cousins, and Daddy was there with his new wife and other relatives. Luckily for Daddy, he happened to be seated in the stands directly across from the end zone where Hummie caught the pass to win the game. During his four seasons at Clemson, Hummie had 162 receptions for 2,691 yards.

My brother gave Clemson everything, and then some. At times he gave them what he didn't have. His roommate once told me that my brother would sit in the dorm room after each game and literally put his body back together, popping his fingers and his back into their proper places.

Hummie was always trying to do right by Clemson. In my hometown, people expected athletes to complete four full years of college and not leave early to chase the NFL. So instead of entering the NFL draft his junior year, Hummie listened to Daddy, who told him to stick to tradition, stay, and get his degree. Unfortunately, Hummie hurt his knee his senior year, which meant he didn't get drafted. He was, however, signed as a free agent for the Indianapolis Colts. After four weeks in Indianapolis, he decided to return home after growing homesick, missing his wife and children in Clemson. A year later, he contacted the Indianapolis Colts again. Daddy drove to Indianapolis to watch him in a preseason game against Cincinnati. "He did really good," Daddy insists. "You knew he was going make that team. There was no doubt about it."

But the next week, in practice, Hummie reinjured his knee. And it was all downhill for him after that. He did end up signing with the Colts but didn't play even one game in two years. He attempted to get a coaching job back at Clemson University, but Clemson said no. It very well could have been one person who made that decision to say, "We don't have room for you right now. We can't give you a job," but, in my mind, it was Clemson—the institution. We all took it personally, me, Mama, and

Daddy. We didn't know who exactly made that call, who shut the door on a young man who was not long before that their star, but we resented it because here was a hometown hero who had returned in hopes of serving a university he loved.

So, I loved Clemson until the day I didn't.

And I believe this is when Hummie lost hope. Can you imagine being a little boy growing up within an athletic program focused wholly on Clemson University, becoming a proud product of that program, devoting four years of your youth to it, and then that one place you look up to your whole life turns its back on you? I believe their rejection broke him when he needed them most, and eventually it led him to make some serious mistakes. Clemson touched the fate of so many people in my life, but especially Hummie. He stuck it out to his senior year, which turned out to be the reason he didn't get drafted. If he had decided to go into the NFL draft his junior year, like my son DeAndre did, things might have worked out better for him.

Even now, Daddy says the worst decision he ever made was telling Hummie to stay his senior year. DeAndre, knowing his story, decided he wasn't going to take the chance, which is why he entered the draft his junior year, understanding he could always go back to college if he wanted.

Shortly after Clemson rejected Hummie, things would not turn out well for my brother. As a result, I had developed an even stronger hate toward the university, refusing even to watch a game. And it was hard, but I had to release that hate when years later DeAndre decided to attend, of all places, Clemson University.

* * *

By the time us kids had graduated from Morrison Elementary to Edwards Middle School, our interests had shifted from hanging around Clemson's stadium to being "downtown."

In the heart of the university is a strip of restaurants and bars where all the Clemson students hung out, including the soccer, football, and basketball stars. Every Friday and Saturday, the strip would be packed with young people, including kids from nearby cities like Pendleton, Seneca, and Greenville, who we called "the locals."

Then there was us: me and my girlfriends—which included Missy, who was Aunt Louise's daughter and Poopie's sister—were only in middle school, so the college students by now had gone from interesting to exhilarating. We'd come back to Edwards on Mondays telling stories and bragging about talking to a football player we had just seen on TV. That really was the draw, that we might see our football crush in person if we hung out downtown.

Even for Hummie, Dilly, and my cousins Poopie and Squeenchie, going downtown and seeing their favorite football superstar was everything.

Chanello's Pizza was the meeting spot for all the Black kids. There was a whole room filled with nothing but games. All you heard was ding, ding, ding. We had *Pac-Man*, *Ms. Pac-Man*, *Centipede*, and *Speed Racer*, where you'd sit down in a car and play by controlling the steering wheel.

None of us usually had any money to buy pizza, though sometimes we'd put our money together and buy a small pie. Truth be told, we didn't go down there for the pizza, but to bring some excitement into our country lives.

At thirteen I was tall, and I looked older than my age. I told the college men I was much older than I really was, but I believe they knew I wasn't in college yet. By the time I was fourteen, me and my girlfriends had graduated to Clemson parties. Before every party, we'd put on some mascara and lip gloss. The best dorm-room parties were put on by the Omega Psi Phi fraternity, a famous Black fraternity better known as the "Que Dogs." There'd be a lot of barking and eventually the fraternity boys would do one of their famous "steps," which was a synchronized dance made popular by Black fraternities, especially the Ques.

If at some point one of my friends couldn't get past the door because they looked too young, that person knew to hang out until we came out, because there was no *if you didn't get in, we were not going to stay in*. Inside the party, we circled the room, which we called "making the rounds." Eventually, some young man would grab my arm and we'd end up making out in a corner, with me promising to hook up later, which never happened because none of us girls were having sex—at least not yet, but soon. Still, getting that kiss from a star football player was always the goal, because whoever was kissed was the popular one the next day in middle school. At fourteen, I was starting to get more promiscuous, entering the dorm rooms with my friends, which often led to me and a Clemson football player kissing and grinding with our clothes on.

Mama would eventually come looking for me downtown. The last thing I wanted was to run into Mama, but if I hadn't cleaned up, or done my chores, or I had snuck out without her permission, she was coming. To Mama's credit, sometimes I'd get home on Fridays, throw down my books, and catch a ride with friends to downtown. Mama would park right in the front of Chanello's, the pizza joint, and ask everyone, "Hey, have you seen Brina?"

I was embarrassed mainly because I didn't want to be seen getting in her car, which was this large white Pontiac Catalina, with a picture of a black cat winking on the front tag. But that wasn't the worst of it. The car was like a roving bomb waiting to explode, because Mama never got oil changes or maintained it in any way, shape, or form, which meant the muffler dragged on the ground, causing red sparks to shoot up the back pipes.

It was so embarrassing. Me and Mama reminisce about it today and laugh, but it wasn't funny back then. Here me and my brothers were in the back seat, choking off fumes and watching flames shoot out the back of the car. We had to sit at the edge of our seats because the seat was too hot if you dared lean back. Meanwhile, Mama would be up front bobbing her head to Millie Jackson's "All the Way Lover" on her 8-track sound system, like she didn't have a care in the world. On the other hand, we were in the back, our asses damn near sizzling like bacon.

Recently, I asked Mama, "Weren't you worried about us back there being engulfed in fumes?"

"It's all I could afford," Mama explained simply.

When she came looking for me downtown back then, I had two goals in mind. First, I was determined not to let anyone see me get in that car. Second, I was trying to buy a few minutes to be seen or to talk to some cute athlete walking along the strip.

Lucky for me, all the Black kids had my back. After Mama asked had anyone seen Brina, someone inevitably would say, "She went that way," and someone else would say, "No, I seen she went that way," but I was never in the direction they were pointing.

If I caught a ride home, I knew Mama would be hot. She'd threaten to put me out, but she never did. I would just have to hear her raise hell until she went to sleep, and the next weekend it started all over again.

CHAPTER 4

Russell "Dilly" Bernard Smith

Even today I find myself at times scared to ask my parents some important questions, which means I, too, have been tainted by this generational trauma of ours: not talking about painful things and letting them fester like old sores. When there's emotional or physical abuse in a family, everyone involved begins to treat it as the status quo, the way things just *are*. Of course, back then I was just a kid, so for all I knew everything that was happening to me—the chaos, the fighting, the instability—was normal. I guess all the adults around me then were too busy with their own dramas to engage with me the way any child needs to be engaged. It's no wonder that, deep down, I felt unlovable.

But now, not only do I want other people to know the truth, *I* need to know the truth so that I can heal. And that required asking very tough questions of the adults in my life during that time—namely, my parents. Whether they screamed or cursed me out or hung up on me, getting answers to some very important questions was, and remains, very important to me.

While Hummie was my daddy's boy, Dilly was Mama's heart. At age twelve, my youngest brother, Dilly, was charismatic and affable; everyone loved him. He was a skinny boy with curly, dark hair, and even when we were little it was obvious how good-looking he would grow up to be. He believed he was Michael Jackson—he didn't think it, he *knew* it. He would walk around with a white glove; its beads would fall off frequently, and I always had to help him glue them back on. He kept his pant legs folded up and wore a black jacket everywhere. He was always dancing, always listening to music.

Dilly was two years younger than me and, like I said, a real mama's boy—my mother loved him like crazy. Dilly loved her right back, but he also loved me, too, and was always asking me what I was doing, forever wanting to know what I had going on. In turn, I adored my brother and was his protector. We were as close as a brother and sister could be, and it would be no stretch to say he was my only real friend on the Hill. Still, although charming, Dilly could be a pain; even Mama would admit that. If he wasn't teasing me, pulling my hair, or getting Hummie in trouble, he was showing out in the classroom, cracking jokes or teasing some student to get attention. The teacher would pull him outside the class, and he'd cry, "But I pass every test, so why you want to put me outside the class?"

Mama would get a letter outlining what he'd done, but by the summer of his seventh-grade year the teachers had enough of him. This time the principal didn't send a letter but called Mama to come to school. Dilly, they said, wouldn't be allowed to attend the class dance that weekend or the football game on Friday because he had been acting up. As Mama was talking to the principal, Dilly was making faces behind the principal's back, which a teacher saw and shared with the principal. That's when Mama knew Dilly had done everything they said he'd done.

When they got home later that day, Dilly, clever and anticipating Mama's punishment, cozied up to her, all coy and cute, and said, "Mama, what you gonna do to me?'"

Mama turned to stare hard at him. Her defenses were weak against her favorite child. "What do you think I need to do?" she replied.

Dilly thought about it. "What you really need to do is take me shopping. Me and you just should hang out."

And Mama smiled, hugged him, and that's exactly what they did.

* * *

By the end of that school year in 1984, downtown Clemson was still the place to be for me and my brothers. One particular Friday in May the boys and I headed to town. Hummie and Dilly wanted to go to Chanello's Pizza to play in the arcade, but me and my cousin Jacine had other things in mind, specifically boys. I was fourteen and had graduated from just grinding and kissing Clemson athletes at parties or in Chanello's to now hanging out in their dorm rooms or apartments.

That day, everyone was at my cousin Larry Jr.'s—Poopie's—house. His parents—Aunt Louise and Uncle Larry—had this really nice, double-wide trailer where everybody hung out, where we all went to eat and see friends. That day was like any other day when the family gathered at Aunt Louise's house to cook a big meal. Just before dark, I walked from the Hill to their house, and was standing outside with Jacine waiting for a ride downtown.

Soon thereafter, Uncle Ottie, pulled up in front of the trailer in his car. Ottie, if you recall, was my mother's first cousin and my father's best friend, who attended Johnson C. Smith University with Daddy. Ottie was probably the most respected person in our wild family at that time. He was in the navy, and he drove around in a nice car with a sunroof. Poopie, our cousin Louis Jr. (Squeenchie), Hummie, and Dilly were all in Aunt Louise's house, but the moment Uncle Ottie pulled up, Squeenchie peeked out the window and saw Ottie's car, prompting the boys to bolt out the house.

I remember the car stereo was blasting Luther Vandross's heartbreak song "Since I Lost My Baby." That should have been a sign of his mental state at the time, but we had no clue that behind Ottie's friendly smile was a man in pain. Not moving out from the driver's seat, Uncle Ottie said, "All right, get on in," and the boys piled in, leaving me and Jacine behind, though we didn't care at all. We'd find our own way.

I remember Hummie sitting in the front passenger seat. Poopie sat in the back, behind Uncle Ottie, Dilly was in the middle on the hump, and Squeenchie sat behind Hummie. The boys were not only excited about going downtown, but they were happy they'd get to cruise in Ottie's car with a sunroof, booming speakers, and electric seatbelts, rather than Mama's raggedy white Catalina.

That night, Ottie decided to take the back way to downtown, which meant they'd ride in the dark on a two-lane little back road called Old Central Road, which leads to downtown Clemson. About two hundred yards from the house was a bridge that everyone in town used to call the "overhead bridge on the back road." As soon as they reached that bridge, from what I was told later, the car began weaving from side to side. They had made it over the bridge, when suddenly Ottie lost control of the car and it flipped over.

Since I wasn't in the car and can't really imagine what happened inside, and maybe I didn't really want to know, I decided I'd have to look to Poopie, who is the only person I trust to tell me exactly what happened.

He recalled the music in the car playing and the car moving fast for about a quarter of a mile across the two-lane bridge. Coming off the bridge, about ten yards up a hill, the car, speeding, careened into a curve.

I could hear Poopie sigh on the other end of the phone as he relived what happened next. "Sabrina, this is when it gets tough." Poopie's country accent had been replaced with the distinguished voice of an educated man long ago, but just then I could hear the boy again. I braced myself and urged him to continue.

"Go on, please," I said. "Be specific."

"All I remember is *boom!*"

The car flipped over three or four times. Everyone's ears were ringing as they tried to collect their senses: they couldn't figure out if they were on their feet or upside down. When they didn't see Dilly, Uncle Ottie got them to lift the car. Poopie also recalls Ottie being mature and adultlike, though I imagined all these years, maybe because of how much I resented him, that he was acting very drunk and confused. Poopie recalled the three boys were quiet and calm as they ran for help, but once they rushed into his parents' yard, they started screaming for help.

Out of respect, I believe his side of the story because he was there, but my fourteen-year-old self recalled things a bit differently.

As I remember, I was out on the street when I heard screeching and then a loud crash. Jacine and I were standing there, trying to figure out what's going on, when down the street came Squeenchie and Hummie, running. It didn't connect yet in my head that they were in some sort of accident, and the car was wrecked. They seemed hysterical, though, as they got closer. I was thinking, why were they laughing? What were they up to now?

But then I realized they were shouting for help. I dropped whatever I was doing and raced toward the bridge, where I saw that some other cars had already stopped to help. Uncle Ottie was there, standing on the road. People were all out, trying to lift the car out of a ditch, but I was looking around, wailing and crying, "Where's Dilly?" Somebody said he's under the car. Finally, some men pushed the car over and there was my baby brother, my Dilly, laying there in the ditch. He was breathing, but his eyes were rolling around like he was there but not there.

I scaled down the ditch to Dilly as quickly as I could, not completely registering that he was badly injured. Just then Hummie came running back from the house, and he's saying we got to get Dilly to Mama. But when I tried to lift Dilly, it was like nothing I ever felt before. He was not himself. He was fragile, like he was broken. His eyes were opening and closing but he wasn't responding. I said, "Dilly, we're going to get you to Mama!" Then an ambulance came, and I was still sitting there holding him, and he just closed his eyes. Someone pulled me off, and they began working on him. By this time Mama pulled up with the aunties, she's screaming in terror. My aunt Louise and everybody else was crying, everybody was shouting. There was so much shouting.

After a few minutes, the emergency workers put Dilly in the ambulance and took off. Then they took Mama to a different hospital, because she was hysterical and obviously under great stress.

I was left standing there, telling everybody who would listen, "Don't worry, when we all get back to Auntie's house, you know, Dilly will be there, we'll all be there." But before long, some paramedics took me to a third hospital—I guess they thought I'd been in the accident too because I had Dilly's blood on my clothes. And they took Hummie away somewhere, too.

Later that night we were all released and back together when, at 1:00 a.m., my mama walks into the kitchen. She was talking crazy, saying, "Why y'all sitting around, the boys are going to be here in a little bit. We still got to cook, we got to cook this food, they'll be here!" But she was having a breakdown. That was when it hit me—Dilly wasn't coming back home.

Dilly's dead.

And this was also the first time I thought: *Mama's done lost her mind.*
I remember just sitting on the bed, by myself.
For the first time on the Hill there was no noise.

* * *

Dilly was one of the first people I saw every morning and the last I'd see at night, since we shared that tiny room in Grandma Frances's home. I was the one making sure he was straight. I was there cooking for Dilly so he never went hungry, made sure his hair was combed in the morning so he looked good for his school photos. And now my baby was gone.

That summer, shortly after Dilly's death, all my white cheerleader sisters came by to see me. The week of the tryouts was the week Dilly died, so I didn't get to try out, but they came to tell me I made the squad anyway.

I got another surprise that summer, a much less welcome one. It's common for Black parents to send their children off to relatives in the North or South, but no one sends their children to crazy-ass Florida. However, my parents did something that to this day I will never understand: they sent me to live with Uncle Ottie and his wife, Rosemary, in Pensacola that very summer after Dilly died—so that they could deal with their grief, I guess. I recall riding to Florida with Rosemary, but I didn't want to go for many reasons. For one, I had just met a young man, who'd later become my husband, and I would have rather spent time with him. The other reason was more obvious: Uncle Ottie had just killed my little brother.

While I was there in Pensacola, Uncle Ottie often drove me while he was drunk. I look back now, and I wonder why my parents, who had been divorced for a while at that point, possibly could think it was a good idea to send me to stay the summer with him. Sometimes I think my mom and dad were still in shock; maybe I might have been a peace offering? Or was I just too much for them to handle that summer? Was I lashing out in anger as I grieved Dilly's passing? Truth be told, I did start resenting everybody around me during this time. And it wasn't just Ottie—he deserved it—but it was everybody else, too.

A couple days after we settled in, I remember Ottie coming into my room. He looked at me from the doorway and asked simply and strangely: "What do you want?"

"What do you mean?" was all I could think to say.

He smiled wide. "I mean I want to take you shopping."

By then, I had been seeing people in Florida wearing Kangol hats made famous by the rapper LL Cool J. "I want a Kangol," I said definitively.

Ottie made this big deal about us going to the store and getting the Kangol. I thought to myself: *Just go buy the damn Kangol without me. I don't want to go with you.* But he dragged me from store to store, in search of the hat I wanted. We eventually found the perfect hat, but I never wore it.

Ottie was trying to be my buddy, but I wasn't having it. Despite how nice he was trying to be to me, I'd ignore him—either I'd stare at him or not answer. I was raised to address adults politely, but the only power I felt I had at the time was to not respond to him.

I was already a good cook, having spent so much time in the kitchen, up under Grandma Frances. I knew how to keep the bottom of the macaroni and cheese moist by adding water in a pan under it. Ottie watched me, beaming. The way he went on and on, you would have thought I was a famous chef. He reared back and grinned. "Man, she does know how to cook. I wouldn't have never thought of that."

He sat down to eat my macaroni dish, proclaiming, "Man, this is good. Who taught you how to do this and that?"

Soon as he turned his back, I rolled my eyes at him. The rest of the trip, I stayed most of the time in my room or on the phone.

A month later, Uncle Ottie and Aunt Rosemary sent me back home on a Greyhound bus. To this day, I have no idea why my parents allowed them to put their fourteen-year-old daughter on a Greyhound bus alone to travel from western Florida back to South Carolina. I was terrified—and for good reason.

I didn't get off the bus to transfer to the second leg of my journey because I didn't know that I was supposed to; nobody told me. Next thing I know, I was in Alabama, sitting next to a pimp who tried his darndest to get me off the bus and to go home with him.

He asked me to come with him about four times, but I remained in my seat. "It'll be no more than five or ten minutes," he'd nudge me. "I'll get you something to eat and we'll be right back."

"You sure?" I said, considering his offer because I was lost and scared. But something ultimately told me to not get off. Finally, he gave up and left the bus. From the window, I watched the pimp walk over and talk to several obvious hookers—one woman was wearing a leather outfit and the other nearly toppled over in red high heels. I began to cry and the bus driver kindly took me into the station's waiting area, where I sat beside a female employee who called my parents. The only bus that was leaving that night was headed to Atlanta, so I hopped on it and met my daddy's brother Reggie, who happened to live there at the time, and he drove me home to South Carolina.

To this day, I can't even imagine the conversation between my parents when they agreed to send their daughter to stay with the man who less than two months earlier had killed their youngest son. I have no idea what they were thinking, but I know during that time they were not equipped to deal with their pain and my own questions and confusion. Going to counseling was unheard-of back then among the Black people I knew, and we never once sat down as a family to talk about the night that changed all of our lives. No one said a damn thing. Instead, we were doomed to just bounce down a hill like a big ball of trauma, which is exactly what happened.

When I got home from Florida, that's when the resentment kicked in. All my relatives would talk about was Ottie and how he was getting his life together and how my parents were right to keep him from going to prison for causing the death of my brother.

As a child, I understood that when someone did something bad, they went to jail for it. Yet Ottie wasn't going to jail—and it was because of my parents. Dilly's parents. While my mother and father never discussed with me the reason they stuck by Ottie, there were plenty of whispers. I would be forty years old—with children of my own at this point—when an aunt and uncle sat me down and told me the "truth."

"Oh, sugar, you didn't know what happened?" they asked.

They recounted: on the day of Dilly's death, Ottie was drinking all that day with my father, because Ottie found out that his wife had been sleeping with a white man she was working with. Ottie had beaten up the man, and later that afternoon, Daddy took Ottie back to his house to drink it off.

Two hours later this man . . . Ottie . . . recklessly killed my daddy's youngest son.

Of course, I had no reason to *not* believe what I was told. Back in the day, especially in the South, and even more so in my family, Black people kept secrets. Nobody said nothing, least of all not to us kids. That's what happened when I was raped by Reverend Lottie. It's what happened when our men beat their women, and that's what happened again when my Dilly passed away.

It's partly because of this culture that Ottie, even though he had been charged with vehicular manslaughter that night, didn't go to jail. I heard Mama and Daddy, at places and times, say that Ottie was actively enlisted in the navy, and because of that, they didn't want to ruin his life. He had a house, he had children in Florida—there was no sense in destroying him or his career. I recalled they both signed papers to drop the charges. Instead, Ottie was ordered to attend AA meetings and complete all the Twelve Steps—which, of course, he never did.

This is what I swore to be true, mostly because it's what's been told to me all my life or what I believed I heard. I've often wondered: how could my daddy still remain best friends with Ottie, the man who killed his son? To this day, they go to high school games together and talk every day. I finally began to recall, decades later, why I hadn't really talked to Daddy about this for so long. It's not only because I figured he wouldn't discuss it, but I also wouldn't dare reveal the words my aunt and uncle said about Daddy getting Ottie drunk before the wreck. I really could have hated my father based on what they told me, but I didn't. My anger and my frustration were channeled in the right place to me—I blamed the person driving the car. As much as I always longed to hear from Daddy what happened between him and Ottie before Dilly's death, I was always too afraid to ask.

Of course, the only way to end a generational curse—which for my family meant burying deep secrets, even when they were really not your secrets to keep—is to confront the people protecting them. Surprisingly, Daddy did agree to answer my questions, questions it took me nearly four decades to ask, and I had to reflect on the fact that the story I knew, the story I believed, was very different from the story my father would tell.

* * *

Daddy said I was wrong about him taking Ottie to drink the day of the accident. In fact, he insisted that Ottie had traveled from Florida to Easley unannounced the Saturday before the accident. Daddy was leaving a grocery store when he saw a crowd of people watching two men roll around on the ground, fighting in someone's yard near the railroad tracks. Daddy pulled over there and realized it was Ottie and a white man who Ottie believed was having an affair with his wife.

Years after the incident, Daddy told himself that he knew what was going on between Ottie's wife, Rosemary, and the white man, but then he recently said, after thinking about it, that he couldn't have, because now he recalled that fight he happened to come upon that day took him by surprise. What he was sure of was that someone was going to call the police, and Ottie, the Black man, would be the one in trouble, so he rushed and grabbed him and threw him in the car. They drove away before the police arrived.

It was in the car, Daddy now said, that he asked him what was wrong, and Ottie told him about the affair. The white man was the director of the local recreation center in Easley and Ottie's wife, Rosemary, worked in the office as an office assistant.

"I just rode him around to get him away from there. I can't remember where I took him, but I know I got him away from that scene right then and there," Daddy would say to me. Daddy also said he never saw Ottie again until the following Friday, the night of the wreck that killed Dilly. But he added that he did believe Ottie was drinking that Friday when Dilly died. Although my parents have expressed their truth, the things they say still confuse me as I shuffle between what is the truth and what is not to me. Mama and Daddy will both take some secrets to their graves, leaving me, their confused-ass daughter, not knowing the difference.

At the time, Daddy was living with his second wife in the same little white house we lived in next to Grandma Zona in Easley.

"Somebody called me. I can't remember who," Daddy recalled. "But by the time that they called me, evidently it was almost dark when Ottie picked those kids up to carry them down to Clemson, because when I got the call from Easley, it was dark. I took off and went to Clemson and I actually got down there before they hauled Hummie away in the ambulance. Dilly was already gone."

Daddy left his car and rode in an ambulance from the wreck site to the Easley Baptist Hospital, with Hummie, who had cuts and scratches.

Daddy said he saw Uncle Ottie a week later. "He was just crying. I had some bad feeling then. I could have shot him. I know he really didn't mean to do it, but I could have killed him at that moment."

I was shocked to hear that, and so I pressed him. "Daddy, did you ever say that to Ottie?"

"Sure, I did," Daddy said. "I told him that at every opportunity." But in the same breath, Daddy added: "He's still one of the best friends I got. He's coming by, actually, to go to the game with me this afternoon."

When I asked why they didn't press charges, Daddy said it was because Ottie was Mama's first cousin. Family don't call the police on family.

To Mama's credit, she wanted to shoot him, too, and wanted him to pay for what he did to her baby, but once again she fell under the influence of her family.

Recently, I called my mama and asked how she felt about helping him avoid prison.

Mama sighed heavily. "It ate me up," she began. "I couldn't live. I couldn't eat. I couldn't sleep. I couldn't breathe. I hated Ottie so bad. I told him, 'If it wasn't for Brina and Hummie, I would've blowed your brains out.' My grandma was the only reason I didn't shoot him."

I just shook my head. "Mama, what exactly did Granny tell you?"

"My grandma said, 'If you kill him it's not worth it; let him live and let God punish him.'"

We were both quiet for a minute, and then Mama started back up talking. "He would be all smiling and grinning every time I see him, and I hated him for seeming so happy. He was controlling my life." I could feel Mama returning to the present as she continued. "Right now, though, I don't let him steal my joy," she says. "I see him, I speak to him, I talk to him, and I couldn't live the rest of my life hating him. But to this day, he never ever admitted to me that he was drunk. He just says he wrecked the car." Mama was silent again. "Brina, your family members can be your worst enemies."

Mama loved her granny but now believes Granny was wrong to encourage her to let Ottie go free. I know now it wasn't Daddy who pushed Mama not to press charges, but her own kin. After all, they reasoned, it made no sense to ruin the life of a man who had things going for him—a career in the navy, a house in Pensacola, and some kids he had to take care of. It was the state—not my parents—who brought charges against Uncle Ottie, eventually finding him guilty. As a child, I was always angry because my fourteen-year-old mind thought my mother said my parents signed papers asking to set Ottie free, but both my parents recently told me they never signed any papers but instead appeared in court to state they didn't want him going to prison.

Daddy said something that surprised me, though: He now wonders if it was the right thing to vouch for Ottie. He also theorizes that if he hadn't stopped Ottie from fighting that day with the white man and allowed him instead to go to jail, Dilly would still be alive today. How does someone live their whole lives with such deep regret? I suppose that the past is done and can never be changed, no matter how much regret anyone has.

I was moved to ask my father some hard questions, but I wasn't going to bluntly ask him, "Did you get Ottie drunk," because my mom and daddy have been through some real shit and I love them and want to be protective of them. Asking them anything is like pulling a scab off of a wound, but at the end of the day, I got his version of the encounter between him and Ottie prior to Dilly's death. I don't think for one second that Daddy is lying, because he will remember that day until God calls him home. However, none of these answers will bring Dilly back, none of them changed the fact of how I feel about Ottie, or that he killed Dilly, but what I did come to understand was that Daddy wasn't complicit in getting Ottie drunk right before the accident. Or was he? Regardless of what was told to me, I was never mad at Daddy, never held any hostility. And even if my daddy himself *did* pour liquor down Ottie's throat, my question still would be why did Ottie drive drunk in a car with four children?

At what point should he have just said no?

I blame Ottie in full to this day.

Eventually, Daddy forgave Ottie. "I've completely forgiven Ottie in my heart," he told me. "If he could have taken it back, he would have. But he was just stupid, drinking and going on because of his wife. He screwed up. He's paying the price for a lot of things that he can't do now because of that. He can't buy a gun. He just got himself squared away to where he can vote, because of that felony."

Poopie, my cousin who was in the car with Dilly that night, also believes Ottie has paid the price for a horrible mistake, and credits the heinous experience of Dilly's passing to making himself, Poopie, the honorable man he is today.

"I can honestly say, and I'm fifty-one now, that I have never so much as drank an ounce of alcohol in any form, wine or anything," Poopie told me recently. "Not even at my wedding. That accident is an experience that redirected a path that people in our family have naturally taken—alcoholism, drugs—a path that has been in our family for generations."

That particular night allowed Poopie to fight off any damaging pressures he came across during high school and college. "There was nothing that would overcome that night to make me even taste alcohol or experiment with marijuana or any of that stuff today."

While he became a college athlete and is now a Clemson coach, Larry didn't play a lick of pro ball. Instead, he earned his master's degree and bought a new house for his mother and father.

I'll be honest—there are still times I cannot comprehend at all how Daddy or Poopie could forgive what Ottie did. As far as I was concerned, karma is a bitch, as they say. Years later, Uncle Ottie's demons finally caught up with him when he became a poster boy for hitting rock bottom and became a crack addict, living in a dusty, nasty trap house. A trap house is a drug house where people caught up in the circle of drugs go to purchase their fix, whether with money or sex. Later, Ottie told me that that trap house he was in was raided by police, but for some reason, they didn't bother with him. If he had gotten arrested, with the felony from Dilly's death, he would have gone to prison for many years. But an officer looked at him and just said, "Get out of here."

Ottie escaped the trap house and never went back and got off drugs from that day forward. "That was nothing but the Lord who got me out of that situation because I was in there high," Ottie told me. From that day on, he had given his life to God.

Daddy still believes Ottie's addiction had nothing to do with his guilt for Dilly's death, but that's something Daddy and I will never agree on. But neither of us hate the man. Mama despises Ottie, and my daddy has shown he loves him, and I am somewhere in between. I don't want him to go to jail, I don't want anything to happen to him, because I believe karma has bit him in the ass several times. What I would love for him to do before my mama leaves this Earth, though, is to apologize to her. He has never done that. I don't know exactly the nature of the conversation that he's had with my dad, but I know that my mom is still holding on to so much hostility because Ottie never told her he was sorry for taking her child. Everybody just assumed that my mama was okay and could handle it. When my mother eventually got hooked on drugs, people would see her act out and call her crazy. My mom was not crazy. My mom was crying out for help because she had lost the love of her life.

There was a point I wished Uncle Ottie to hell because I had to live with my mama and see the hurt in her eyes, I had to sit and hear her cry in the next room at night, wishing that her child was still here. I began to resent Ottie and hate him, but I no longer feel that way. I don't want to be around him, but I'm going to answer his calls and speak to him when I see him. I am going to love him because God says I must love him and forgive him. I also know that if I continue hating him and I die, I would never see Dilly again. Being someone who believes there's a heaven and a hell and that Dilly is in heaven, I know I can't hate someone on Earth and expect to go to heaven and be with Dilly again.

At the end of the day, I finally came to understand that I had to overcome my profound resentments, betrayals, and hatreds not simply because I should be fair to the person who caused them but because these emotions were eating me alive.

There's no other way around it: the only way to do this is to forgive and to find a way forward in grace and in love. But I did it for me because I eventually realized peace and happiness can't reside where there is hate and resentment, so I chose peace on purpose.

CHAPTER 5

The Wrong Child Died

In the days, weeks, and months after Dilly died, no one ever put their arms around me. No one asked if I was okay. Everyone kept hush with each other. And counseling was unheard-of, because talking about your problems with a professional back then meant you were crazy. People just brought some fried chicken to the house after Dilly's funeral, and that was that. After the smoke cleared, we were all left on our own to deal with the invisible emotional scars life had left us with.

When Dilly passed, I lost my daddy all over again, and the little I had of Mama slipped away, too. They were so wrecked by grief that they couldn't see anything else, including their daughter, who'd lost her baby brother and was just as damaged as everyone else. Meanwhile, Hummie had thrown himself into football, and even though we felt closer because it was now just us two, my chances to see him were few. Hummie spent nearly all his time with Poopie and Squeenchie; the three of them were in the car with Dilly when he died, so I'm sure they were together trying to figure things out in their own way. In fact, my whole extended family on the Hill was in shock. You had a hill full of children, and nobody ever died around there, so no one in my big, crazy family could wrap their heads around my little brother's death, certainly not me. All I knew was that I desperately missed my brother; I'm sure Hummie missed Dilly like I did.

We both went through life kind of being up under Mama, but Mama wasn't emotionally there. Every few days her chest was hurting so bad she felt like she was having a heart attack. I didn't know any better other than try to stay away and involve myself with as many activities as I could, just so I wouldn't have to go home. There was no aid for us, no counseling, no talking to a preacher, no family meetings. You soldiered on and internalized the grief. I now know the importance of experiencing the full grieving process at its various stages, but no one knew about that back then.

As for me, cheerleading and running track were my outlets. So was Mark Greenlee. And I latched on to him for dear life.

I met Mark Greenlee the year Dilly died. He was eighteen, and I was still fourteen, almost fifteen. He was tall, but not real tall, had light-brown skin, with a goatee, and was very good-looking. He was a football star and a bad boy, rugged and rough, who drove a mustard-green Pinto. All the girls wanted to be with him; I was no different. I was drawn to him and probably did not realize I was trying to fill the gaping hole in my soul that was only growing bigger and bigger with each passing day. Of course, Mama didn't care if I was with him or not, or even if I ever came home—Dilly, her baby, her favorite, was gone.

I'd seen Mark around downtown Clemson, hanging with the older guys at Chanello's every now and again. I was in the ninth grade at Edwards Middle School, looking forward to tenth grade, which is when I would enter high school. Mark had a football scholarship and was heading for college in North Carolina after graduating from Daniel High School. We'd catch a look at each other, but I didn't know his name until one night in downtown Clemson he pulled my arm.

"Hey, I've seen you around," he said coolly. "What's your name?"

"You know my name," I said, trying my best to sound older and unbothered.

Mark sighed. "I wouldn't be asking if I knew."

"My family calls me Brina," I replied.

We shared a smile, and I stepped closer. I looked up at him and could only think: *God, he's fine.* I blushed. "Where are we going?" I playfully rolled my eyes. "And don't be pulling my arm, who you think you are?"

He held my gaze while his eyes glazed over my thin, lean body. We talked a little bit more, and then he led me to a nearby Presbyterian church.

I heard about kids sneaking into the church to smoke but I never had any reason to go, because well, I didn't smoke, or drink, and I didn't hang out with people who did. I hung out with girls like me, who were "fast" and wanted to kiss boys.

The basement was probably reserved for a quick prayer, which is why the door was always open. The room wasn't very big, with only a few pews on each side of the aisle. At the very front was a podium and behind the podium was a giant mural of Christ, which took up the entire wall. That night nobody else entered the basement; it was just me, Mark, and Jesus.

Like everyone else, I thought my first time would be magical, with music playing, lit candles, and with someone I was in love with, but it was anything but that. Here I am about to have sex for the first time, and all I'm worried about is my hygiene. Because we didn't have a running bathtub at Grandma Frances's place, I had perfected what Mama called the "hoe bath," or simply washing with a towel in the sink. There was no such thing as a shower in that house. You got two rags, that's it; one I'd get all soapy and wet and wash with and the other I'd use to dry off. I picked that up from one of Grandma Frances's caregivers. Using big towels was considered wasteful in the house; in fact, if one happened to appear, someone was bound to rip it apart with their hands to make a bunch of rags.

So, all this was going on in my head that night in the church basement: *Do I smell? Are my panties clean? Did I lotion my ankles enough or are they ashy?*

With these questions swirling around, I lost my virginity on the floor of a church at the foot of Jesus, and I felt nothing but excruciating pain.

* * *

I didn't see Mark again until a couple of weeks later when he'd come sniffing around for me on the Hill or in another nearby neighborhood I used to hang out in with all my friends. I'd never seen Mark anywhere near where I used to be, but suddenly he was coming around, knowing I'd be walking around the area. Grandma Frances didn't have a phone, but Granny did. So every day I'd come home from school and sit until someone from Granny's house called out, "Brina! Telephone!" I would run past the well and blow into Granny's house as fast as I could to get the phone. It was always Mark. But when he didn't call, I just remember this sick feeling; it was the first time that I started feeling uneasy, unhinged, or different. My stomach would curl up in knots, and I would just sit there, moping. I didn't know what was going on with me, but I knew when he didn't call, I felt ill.

He was just being young, but I was even younger and, in the beginning, taking things way more seriously than they were. Mark was so irresistible: his face was chiseled, cheekbones high, and lips perfect. In fact, everything about this man was perfect, at least that's what my silly fourteen-year-old brain believed. The more we hung out, the more obsessed I became. I couldn't believe the finest man in town wanted me. He'd call me just to say he'd be over soon, and I'd get nervous and excited at the same time. He never arrived when he said he was coming, and sometimes I'd sit around waiting for hours, but it didn't matter because it was Mark. All the young girls talked about Mark and his brother Ken because they were upperclassmen and handsome. So, for Mark to get in his car and make his way up the rocky and unpaved road to Grandma Frances's house, just to see me, it strangely felt like an honor.

We'd hang out on the porch, where he kissed me for the first time, which felt so much nicer than the painful sex we had in the church basement weeks before. Although he was courting me in his own way, I was embarrassed for him to come inside the old house, worried Granddaddy might show out or that the sheets hanging from the ceilings would push Mark away—that is, until I visited his home and realized Grandma's shack was a palace compared to his.

Mark and his brothers resided with his grandmother, while his mom lived in North Carolina. They slept in a rickety wooden house that always smelled like kerosene. The area was called Red Hill, and the houses were worn down like the ones on the Hill where we lived, and the people who occupied them survived hand to mouth. The moment you pulled up in Red Hill, and regardless of what time you arrived, there'd always be about five or seven men sitting under a tree, drinking beer or liquor. This is all Mark knew, and I related to him on that level.

I didn't miss his football games because, in my mind, that was my man. Number 44. Mark was steady, telling me I was the only one, which was something I needed to hear. I needed to believe that this man loved me as much as I loved him. What really got me was this one time when he drove me to his father's house in Pendleton. I had no idea where we were going until he said he was delivering to his father a graduation invitation.

His daddy never claimed him, and, in fact, his daddy lived with a woman who wouldn't let him acknowledge Mark—at least that's what Mark believed. Still, Mark took that invitation, found out where his father lived, and then went to the house—all that is what drew me all in. I was on the passenger side of his Pinto while we pulled into these people's yard, and he slipped that invitation under the door and ran back to the car.

He quickly turned to me as we pulled off. "See, this is how I know I like you because you're here with me while I'm doing this."

I was all ears. "We've been through some things together," he continued. "I ain't got my mama, your mama crazy. Your people drink, my people drink. Your daddy ain't in your life. My dad ain't in my life."

I'm still in middle school but thinking, *We together thugging and I am down with you. Whatever you want to do, let's do it.*

* * *

I left Edwards Middle School behind and started tenth grade at Daniel High School in nearby Central. Mark was in college in North Carolina, and Mama already had moved us into Vista Circle, in a house Uncle Ottie gave us out of his guilt for killing Dilly. I don't remember a whole lot other than Mama saying one day that she got approved by the Housing Authority and that she was going to move us into Ottie's house. Even though it was the house owned by the man who killed my baby brother, I recall being happy we were moving to Vista Circle, which was one of several Black communities in Clemson; the difference was everyone wanted to live there. Most of the homes were two- or three-bedroom houses with car porches. None of the houses were the same, but everyone kept their yards trimmed. Some of them had just a little more land than others.

For instance, my aunt Pumpkin's house in Vista Circle had a bigger yard than her neighbors and a larger driveway that led to her house.

If you made it to Vista Circle, living was good. It was where all the who's who of Black Clemson lived, and the one-mile circle was where we all walked, regardless of if you had a place there or not. All the cool Black kids in my high school lived there, and now I was one of them.

The residents in Vista Circle were mostly blue-collar workers, though some were teachers and guidance counselors; others worked at Clemson as supervisors over the food services—but never professors. Since nearby Greenville was still known as the textile center of the world—though many factories had started to shut down and were being replaced by big Fortune 500 companies—some residents held on to the remaining factory jobs, which were good paying.

Vista Circle was always in motion. Everybody drove decent cars—station wagons, vans, and SUVs. In the mornings, cars cranked up as parents headed to work and their children gathered at the bus stop. On Saturday morning, somebody was always plucking weeds out of their flower garden or mowing their lawn. Moving to Vista Circle brought a little light into my dark life. I had my own room, where I hung my New Edition posters up on the wall, and stared at Michael Bivins while singing "Popcorn Love." From the car porch, you walked right into the living room, and then around to the kitchen. All the bedrooms were to the left. Hummie had his own room, and Mama had her own room, too.

Everybody walked the circle until they got tired. Sometimes I'd be sitting with my girlfriends on my porch and people are passing our house all day, which was kind of weird because you'd see the same group passing again and again as they finished the circle and started back.

The only person missing in my life was of course Dilly, but I also longed for Mark, who was away in college. I'd play Atlantic Star's "Secret Lover" over and over only because I thought it was a romantic song. But then I soon found out that I was a secret, too, when it became clear that Mark had a girlfriend, and it wasn't me.

In my head I was Mark's true love, because Mark was paying attention to me, he was calling, and we were having sex, but I soon realized I was wrong.

I was sitting in class one day when somebody rushed in to share some frightening news: Mark had been in an accident in Georgia.

When I entered the science wing of the school, I noticed a crowd of people consoling this girl named Lolita. I also heard Mark's name floating about. I tried to piece together what happened: Mark had been helping a family member move in Georgia, and got on the bed of the truck, on top of a mattress. The wind whipped under the mattress, flipping Mark off the truck and onto the edge of the guardrail, which pretty much sliced his leg off at the knee. It was a freak accident.

I finally got in touch with him weeks later as he recuperated in a hospital in Georgia. He called me at home and I nearly jumped for joy when I heard his voice on the other end.

"I want to come see you," I said.

"Lolita and her mom are down here and taking care of me, but let me see when I can get them out of the room and y'all can come," Mark replied coolly.

And that was the beginning of me being a side chick. I've been one many times after that, but that all started for me at the young age of fifteen.

Lolita. I knew exactly who he was talking about. I so wanted to ask a million questions, but nothing in me could muster up anything other than "Okay."

Eventually, Mama drove me to Georgia, where I saw him all bandaged up with an amputated leg, a stub.

"Are you all right?" I kept asking him as I held the man's hand like I was some old church lady. "Are you good?" Mama took a seat in the hospital room, but then left after a few minutes to give us some privacy. The whole time I was with him that day, my mind ticked off every insecurity I was feeling: *If you had contacted me earlier, I would have been here weeks ago. Why didn't you contact me? How dare you have us wait for Lolita and her mama to leave the hospital? And where are they anyway? Are they here waiting for us to leave?*

Of course, I said none of this because I had convinced myself I was with my man, not Lolita's boyfriend.

When he finally came home from the hospital in Georgia weeks later, we didn't skip a beat. We hung out and had sex. I think I loved him more because he didn't have but one leg. I remember him showing up in front of my aunt's house in his Pinto. He jumped out the car, hopping around all confident. This is, mind you, before he got his prosthetic leg.

It was like he was on this mission to show people that having one leg didn't bother him. And that made me want him more. I would look at him and think, *Oh damn, even with his missing leg, he's so fine.*

Despite losing a limb, he was able to keep me *and* Lolita, and I'm sure he was pulling other girls, too, but we were the main two.

I never observed Lolita and Mark together, but during my first year in high school, I was determined to figure out why he chose Lolita to be his official girlfriend and me his side chick. It just didn't make sense. My whole family knew about him and me. And I was the one he chose to pick up and drop off at school and home when he was a bus driver the year before.

Soon enough, I found out Lolita lived in an apartment complex with her mom in La Vista, which was a drive from Vista Circle. So I stole Mama's big white car and went to Lolita's. I am fifteen with no driver's license, nothing, but I managed to pull up at the apartment complex where Lolita and her mom lived. First thing I see is Mark's Pinto backed in the parking space. I sat in Mama's car, thinking, *I got your ass now.*

Miss Cookie, Lolita's mother, stood outside the front door. "Hey, you're Rosa's daughter?"

I flashed a fake smile. "Yes, ma'am. I'm Sabrina. Is Mark here?"

She nodded. "He up there in Lo's room." She moved closer to me, squinting as if to see me better. "Miss Sabrina, I see the look in your eyes. I know that look. Just don't go in my house and show your ass. You hear me?"

I dropped my fake grin. "No, ma'am, I would never do that. I just want to talk to him."

I entered the house and opened Lolita's bedroom door. There was Mark laying on the bed, his little one leg nub propped up on a pillow. The moment he saw me, his eyes stretched wide, but he didn't seem too bothered. "What you doing here?" he asked.

I crossed my arms around my chest. "Nothing, I came to see you."

Lolita, who was in a grade above me, smirked. "Mark just paid for my cosmetology license today."

"Oh, he did?" I asked, before cutting my eyes at Mark. That Mark would pay for her schooling haunted me because all he had bought me during this period was a burger and fries. Even years later, I'd ask myself: Was she somehow better than me? Why didn't he see my worth? I should have been asking myself, though, why didn't I see my own worth?

I tapped my foot. "Mark, can I talk to you for a minute?"

He shook his head. "No, take your ass home. I don't want to talk to you."

I was so upset, not because of what he said, but that he said it in front of Lolita. I lost it, and the only reason I didn't show out was because I told Miss Cookie I wouldn't. "If you don't come outside in ten minutes, I will flatten all your fuckin' tires and I'll bust out all your windows. I'm not playing with you."

I stomped back down the steps and stood by his car.

In my mind, Mark was the greatest lover, but I didn't have nothing to compare him to. Soon enough, he hopped outside and told me to go to his apartment. "I'll be there in ten minutes," he said.

"Okay," I said and left. Mark always had that kind of effect on me; when he looked at me, or he grabbed me, nothing else mattered. When he told me to go to his apartment, I *knew* he'd be there in a minute. I left him standing out there with Lolita, so I could wait outside his apartment. I must have waited for an hour until it hit me that I was going to be in trouble with Mama. I worried she was about to put me out. So I left and headed home to deal with the consequences of stealing my mama's car. The next day, Mark came to take me to Burger King, and then we had sex. That's how he resolved things with me back then, with a Whopper and fries. And not only did I allow it, but I shifted my anger from him to Lolita.

* * *

High school life was crazy because of Mark. One day Lolita, along with her friends Regina and Leah, decided to jump me all because Lolita had shared with them that I was sleeping with her man, and so her friends figured that if I was sleeping with Lolita's man, then I must be sleeping with their men, too.

The school always placed all of us Black kids' lockers in the same block of the hall, which we didn't even realize was discriminatory. We just thought they put us together with our friends. That day, Lolita and her two friends left their lockers and started whispering as I walked by. I heard one of them say, "Look at that bitch; she's a hoe and she's messing with Mark." Then Regina, who was going out with a guy named Tony, said, "I bet she fucking Tony, too." Then Leah, who was going with Earl, said, "I know she fucking Earl."

When I stopped to confront them, I recognized that they had a game plan: they knew I wasn't the type to let someone talk about me and let it go.

I looked at the three of them. "What did you say?"

And that's when Leah swung at me, and I laid in on her. I knew I wasn't fighting because of Mark but because of the Hill in me. I had seen so much fighting on the Hill by my relatives that I finally wanted to try out their moves. As a little girl, you reenact things in your head before they happen. So, when they swung at me, I already had it planned out. With Leah in a headlock, I yelled, "Your short little ugly ass has the nerve to swing at me?" as I'm kicking at Regina, calling her a little bald-headed heifer.

Lolita stood on the sidelines and watched as her minions got their butts whipped by me. At that moment, though, she didn't matter, and neither did it matter that I was sent to the principal's office after I beat up her friends. What really mattered was that I had fulfilled a goal. I had envisioned a thousand times how I was going to whoop their asses before I did it.

* * *

Compared to my friends, I had the "young mother." Mama was more like a girlfriend to me than a parent. A few years earlier, when I was at Edwards Middle, Mama was the supportive cheerleading mom. And even earlier, it was Mama, not my athletic-obsessed daddy, who took the boys to football practice. Having no money whatsoever, she'd steal clothes or get Aunt Louise, the master booster, to steal school clothes for me. She wanted to be certain I looked just as good as the white girls in middle and high school. Even in the house in Vista Circle, as Mama struggled to deal with Dilly's death, Mama always cooked meals for us and kept the house together. As moody as she could be to me, I still was crazy about my mama, totally in awe of her youth, her looks—the gold tooth, the small waist and big butt—her hell-raising, too.

But things began to change between us by the time I turned sixteen.

Despite our really nice home on Vista Circle, which Mama had decorated beautifully, she wasn't there, not mentally. She was still functioning, but emotionally she had "checked out," as she admits now, still grieving for Dilly. Sadly, it was about this time when Mama started doing crack, developing a lifelong addiction, that our relationship turned truly poisonous.

The day I discovered Mama's drug use was such a low point that I began to see her in a different light.

Mama had begun dating a man named Plug, who was, as his nickname suggested, a drug dealer. One day, I got off the school bus and entered the house to find Plug standing in the living room while Mama was in there with a rag held up to her mouth. Blood was everywhere. Seeing my mother like that made me nervous. My palms were sweaty, and my whole body was on alert.

Plug smirked. "Your mama stole my fucking crack, and I just whooped her ass."

Crack? I was so confused. What was crack, and what did it have to do with Mama?

Mama did not look visibly beat up, but her lip was split wide open. "It's okay," she said unconvincingly. "Everything is okay."

In that moment, I imagined myself slapping this man. I thought about this so many times after that day: what would have happened if I had socked him? I wanted to defend Mama, but for the first time I felt I couldn't because there was nothing I *could* do. Do I go to my room? Do I stand there?

Anything that was confusing in our life, we just allowed it to blow over, and a couple of weeks later, Plug was back at the house. This is what I observed and would mimic later in my own life, seeing this first play out with Mama: she'd allow a man who hit her return to her home and to her bed. This became ingrained in my brain as normal. It never occurred to me until later that this was not right—this was not supposed to happen. Once again, my own mother was in another cycle of domestic abuse. And there was nothing that I could do.

Even though I'd repeat Mama's doings on so many levels, especially when it came to men, the one thing I didn't repeat was using crack.

Still, crack would eventually become central in my life.

* * *

Dilly's death took away Mama's capacity and energy to handle a promiscuous teen like me. Because Mama was out of it, me and Hummie were practically raising ourselves. Once, when I was sixteen, I remembered it snowed, and Mark stayed two days in my bedroom, where we had sex. In fact, he had free rein in my bedroom.

Meanwhile, Mama was always sad and down, and she took it out on me. She never talked to Hummie the way she talked to me. I was probably hurting and being defiant, too, but there was no one saying, *Hey, come home*, or *Where are you going?* There was a thin line I had to straddle, because if I did not know when curfew was and nobody's telling me anything, I figured I'd just come home whenever I wanted. Sometimes Mama just looked the other way; other times when I'd try to sneak in after a day or night with Mark, or I was walking the circle or over at my cousin Wanda's house, she'd lose it or be so overwhelmed and say, "Pssshh . . . I'm going to send you to your daddy's. You ain't shit. You laying around here effing."

Her favorite word for me was "pretty-faced dummy." I'd roll my eyes and ask her what that meant. She'd smile and say, "It's when girls like you let men go out and use them."

I was confused about our relationship because I loved Mama, and I had seen that many times she'd do anything for me, but then the same woman, after Dilly died, made me her number one enemy. On those real bad days, she'd shake her head and say, "I wish it was you who died instead of my baby in that car." Before the night was over, she'd say, "The wrong fucking child died."

I never cussed or fussed back. I started being rebellious to Mama only after I moved out of the house. The whole time on Vista Circle, I just took it. I can't even say it hurt me when she'd say those things because I got used to it.

But it sure didn't help that Mark and Mama despised each other. And the more I became obsessed with Mark, the more he became obsessed with pissing off my mother. Every chance he got, he did something to spite her. At first, I assumed he was just on my side, on my team. If they don't like you, eff them, and all that. What I didn't understand at the time, however, was that it wasn't that Mama didn't like me, but she had lost her favorite child in a most devastating way and was grieving poorly; I just happened to be the person she took her pain out on. Mark understood the wedge growing between me and Mama, and so he leveraged it, stirring the pot between us whenever he could. As a result, I began to think that it would be better to live with him rather than at home with Mama, which was exactly what he wanted.

A year or two later, Mark still was all I thought about. It didn't matter what he did to me, it was better being with him than being at home. Yes, me and Mama were just poisonous to each other, but I didn't know then what I realized later: Mark took advantage of my deteriorating relationship with Mama to fuck with my state of mind. He never said, *I'm all you got*, but he'd show up just enough to make me feel that that was true, which only increased my devotion to him.

I was even with him when he got fitted for his prosthetic leg, which caused him a lot of pain because it produced sores that would create scabs. He would pull the scabs off, and I would even pull the scabs off sometimes for him. And then I'd rub that little nub like it was my own. It was a part of him, so I felt like it was part of me, which is why nothing about his deformity fazed me at all.

In a weird way now, we had another connection that was going to link us for life—at least that's what I believed. He lost his leg; I lost my brother. I'd be thinking, *You got one leg, but I love you even more.* And I imagined him saying, *You lost your brother, nobody else seems to understand you, and I'm going to be there for you for life.*

I realize now this was not love. Instead, it was nothing but codependency.

CHAPTER 6

Homecoming Queen

While I loved Mark, Mama couldn't stand him nearly from the start. But then there were two big things that happened that made Mama dislike Mark even more then she already did. One started when I began to feel nauseous while working at a Burger King to save up money to buy my class ring. A day or two later, my cousin Wanda took me to see Dr. Bryce in Easley, my childhood doctor, the only doctor I knew. After I peed in a cup, the doctor looked straight into my eyes: "Miss Sabrina, you're pregnant."

The room started to spin. "What am I going to do?" I asked out loud.

He looked serious but then shrugged. "I'm going to give you twenty-four hours before I call your mom and your grandma Zona."

By the time I got home, I was terrified. With Wanda waiting in the car, I headed inside where I found Mama in the kitchen cooking.

"What is it, Brina?" she said as I stood in the kitchen doorway.

I lowered my gaze. "Mama," I started. "Dr. Bryce say . . . I'm pregnant?" My words sounded like I was asking question, probably because I was still in disbelief.

Mama's face fell. "By whom?" She pointed a finger at me. "That fucking Mark?"

As Mama began to lose it, I knew I needed to get out of the house; this wasn't going to be a good moment. Mama hadn't been stable since Dilly's death, and by this time, she and I were not getting along *at all*. It took me mere seconds to change into my Burger King uniform and rush back outside to Wanda, who was waiting with the engine running and about to take me to work for my shift. Thirty minutes after my start time, Mama pulled up and stormed into the restaurant in a rage. "Where the fuck does Mark live?" she screamed. She started cursing in front of customers and my coworkers. "So, you just gonna get pregnant by this no-life motherfucker?" That was my mama's favorite name for Mark or anyone she didn't like, "no-life motherfucker."

People in line were gawking at the whole scene. I started crying and looked around. "Mama, I'm at work" was all I could muster through tears.

Mama slung her pocketbook behind her shoulder angrily. "No, you gonna talk to me! How you just gonna tell me you pregnant by this no-life motherfucker and walk out the door?"

My manager cut in, almost apologetically. "Sabrina, just go handle your business; take off or whatever," he said as he ushered me and Mama out the door.

The ride back home was the longest as we sat in silence, quiet rage coming from Mama behind the wheel, and me, scared of what would happen next. We got back to the house, and Mama went straight to the telephone and called all my aunties. "Y'all better come get this bitch, come get this motherfucker before I kill her," I could hear her say into the phone.

Mama began pacing with the phone to her ear. "She's sitting over here smirking and done laid up and got pregnant by this no-life motherfucker." I wanted the ground to open up and swallow me whole. I had just finished the eleventh grade and knew nothing about being a mother. Then the aunties—who were Grandma Frances's sisters—Aunt Celeste, Aunt Marylyn, and Aunt Anne, who was in town from Connecticut, showed up. They all marched through the door one by one, shaking their heads at me saying, "Mmm-hmmm . . . just look at her."

And there I was, sitting with my little bitty, tiny belly. I did not know what to do, but I did know I couldn't talk back and defend myself in any way. Instead, I had to just take their admonishment. I had no other option. When Mama was out the room, I recall one of the aunties—I can't remember which one—saying, "You know we come over here to help you, and we know your mama crazy as hell, so we'll take you to have an abortion."

Another aunt offered to pay for it. "What you want to do? You need to decide soon."

When they left the house, I informed Mama of the offer the aunties had made to me. Although they berated me, the aunts were giving me two choices to consider: keep the baby or get rid of it.

Mama turned her head around so fast, all I could think of was that little white girl in that movie *The Exorcist.* "I know them bitches did *not* come in my house and tell you that," she spat bitterly. She could barely get the words out before she was back on the phone, fussing and cussing. Right then, I knew I had to have this baby.

"They better not come in here and do nothing to my grandbaby," Mama said. "I'll help you."

That was so far from the truth.

* * *

I was seventeen, pregnant, and always sick, but that same year I was also a cheerleader and was voted Miss Homecoming, which was a near-impossible feat for a poor Black girl at a predominately white high school in South Carolina. Despite being popular, I began to change and developed a bad attitude. I resented everyone. I was always cutting my eyes at people, and I treated school like a fashion show—a place to look cute, not to learn. I went to class in heels every day, my long brown hair done up just so. I recall strutting into gym class in heels and the school principal shaking his head at me. "Whatever," I'd mutter under my breath.

I hid my pregnancy as long as I could, but as I walked up and down the halls, I could hear the whispers. Being pregnant and a teenager was a horrible sin where I'm from. Girls in my high school had become pregnant before me, including my own mother, but most of them left school the moment everybody found out. I tried to be defiant and hide my pregnancy, but I was throwing up all the time, and soon everyone knew. None of my classmates said anything to me about it, but everyone either stared at me or averted their eyes when I passed by. Once I overheard the principal talking about me. "They say she's going to have a child," he said. "What a shame to waste all that talent."

By this time, I couldn't take the stress of being pregnant in school any longer. Soon the administration called me into the principal's office and asked my mother to come in. They tried to take back my Homecoming title as some sort of punishment, but Mama lost it. "We ain't giving shit back," she said before stomping out of the principal's office with me.

As we drove home, I thought to myself that the gig was up—the cheerleading, track, the proms, the school fights, I no longer cared about any of it. After they tried to take my crown, I decided that I didn't want to be in school anymore.

* * *

One day, someone in the school nurse's office mentioned Homebound—a program that provided teachers or instructors to a student who couldn't attend school on-site for whatever reason—and I signed up immediately. The first few times the Homebound teacher arrived at the screen door, I hid. I was used to never finishing anything—whether socially or academically—and this was no different. With no real structure at home, I was used to getting away with not trying and doing my best.

But this teacher, a white woman who was famous in Clemson for having quadruplets, didn't give up on me. In fact, she'd continued to return day after day, though I continued to hide from her. One day, she shouted outside the screen door, "Sabrina, if you don't get your act together, you're going to fail out of school!"

She returned the next day and said she was going to keep coming until I let her in. She was one of the few people to show me compassion and to believe in me. As she described how she was raising four healthy, happy children, I began to think that maybe being pregnant wasn't a sin. Before she came into my life, I was isolated and lonely and had given up on trying to finish high school, but she convinced me I could. She eventually got me all caught up, and I returned to school to graduate with my class.

Before then, however, I had to deal with the illnesses that came with being very young and pregnant. Because I was only seventeen, the doctors said I was a high risk, which meant I had to go all the way to Greenville for my checkups, where the doctors were more experienced. After a few weeks of doctor's appointments, Mama convinced me to finally tell Daddy I was pregnant. He came up from Easley and drove me to Greenville, but he wouldn't say a word to me in the car. I kept eyeing him, but he wouldn't look my way. I said to myself: *I know you're pissed or whatever, but how are you not going to say nothing to your child?*

When we entered the health department, Daddy looked around at all the young women sitting in the waiting room, and then looked at me and shook his head. He was disgusted with me, though decades later he'd say he was disappointed because I was such a good athlete and could have been a track star.

After leaving the health department, he asked if I wanted something to eat. He took me to a Burger King and then dropped me back off at Mama's house. My daddy, who I worshipped, never took me to another appointment and, for the duration of my pregnancy, never called to check on how I was doing.

After that, I didn't want him to take me to another appointment anyhow. I had Mama and my friends. There were so many times Mama rushed me to Greenville because I thought I was in labor. I returned to the hospital at least three times because every little pain felt dramatic to me; of course I didn't know what I was or wasn't feeling. One day I was at the house in Vista Circle when I felt the sharpest pain in my life. When we got to the hospital in Greenville, Mama began to walk me up and down the halls and stairs like the doctor told us to, which assisted with the contractions.

Meanwhile, she'd share her own special unfounded medical advice, insisting that I was going to have a C-section because she had had one when each one of us was born. "You can't have no babies natural because I didn't have none of my babies naturally," she said decisively.

All I could think of was a whole bunch of white doctors cutting my belly open, because my mother told me so. I walked for hours, though the medical staff told us not to go too far because my water could break any minute.

A whole two days later, Mama was right there for my natural delivery of Kesha, who was born April 2, 1988. As I held Kesha, Mama began to cry.

Kesha was dark-skinned, a little chocolate drop. "My first grandbaby. Oh, she so pretty. She looks just like me," I heard Mama say. That day, the tears flowed as me and Mama had a moment and held hands; before then, I couldn't remember the last time we'd reach for each other.

* * *

On the day I returned home from the hospital with Kesha, I could hear Mark's Pinto pull up from a mile away; there was something about the way it stopped, the motor piped down, so I always knew when he was coming. That day, my heart kind of did a little dance; he was here to see the baby. Mark blew in, walking fast as usual; even with one leg, his every movement was quick. He grabbed her, holding Kesha high in the air like she was baby Kunta Kinte. My mama came out her bedroom and, in typical fashion, began rolling her eyes, just trying to find something to fuss about. She laid eyes on Mark, and it was on.

"Why you lifting the baby so damn high?"

He let out a sigh; he was not unaccustomed to Mama's antics. "Nett, I'm good," he said to her.

She persisted. "You don't even know how to hold a fucking baby."

He kept his eyes on Kesha. "Go on now, Nett. I said I'm good."

But Mama didn't relent. Soon, Mark handed me the baby and stormed out the door. I was so embarrassed.

Mama followed behind him. *Oh my God, here we go*, I thought to myself. I didn't leave the room, but I heard the Pinto rev up, and then the sudden smashing of glass. Mama had thrown a brick through Mark's back window. Of course she did. Funny thing is Mark never stopped the car, didn't even skip a beat, and just kept driving as if his car window hadn't just been smashed out.

Honestly, I wasn't mad at Mama. Before Kesha's arrival, I hadn't seen Mark in a while; people had been saying he was with Lolita (and other girls). This man didn't come to the hospital when I was admitted, waiting to give birth. So it didn't bother me one bit that Mama threw a brick through his window. In fact, I was thinking, *Good for Mama. She on my side for once.*

That day marked the beginning of an all-out war between Mama and Mark, which left me and Kesha in the middle. He'd say, "I can't come over there, and I don't want to be around your fucking mama."

And Mama would say, "He bet not ever bring his Black ass back in my house."

Now I had to pick my poison: stay with Mama, who may or may not help me, or be with Mark, a man who hadn't been there for me.

Me and Mark continued to talk and sneak around, but he refused to see me at Mama's house.

So, ten days later, on April 12, the day I turned eighteen, we went to the courthouse to get married. We were so dumb—we didn't even know we had to find a witness, so we grabbed someone who was passing by. I stared at the marriage certificate, which said I was married. It didn't feel like a marriage, but I believed it was better to be with him than with Mama. I didn't tell Mama what Mark and I had done, and conveniently, Mama was absent again; she was back to mourning Dilly, and she was going through it. I was the last thing on her mind.

Meanwhile, Mark sold me a dream. He said he was going to be Kesha's daddy, and we were going to be a family. He also promised me that after we got married, we'd move to Greenville. All I knew was red dirt and the Hill, but Greenville was the closest thing to a big city.

What happened, though, was when we got married, he literally took me home to Mama. He never asked me to live with him, in fact, that wasn't even on the table. So here I was, still living with Mama because I had nowhere else to go with a newborn baby. I'd barely see Mark or talk to him, but spent most my time taking care of Kesha. I did what all teen mothers did in Clemson—get the baby dressed all up on Sundays and show her off at church. One Sunday, I'm sitting in Abel Baptist Church with Mama and baby Kesha, when Miss Rodale, a fellow churchgoer, stops by our pew and says cheerily, "Sabrina, congratulations!" I wanted to shrink in my seat because I knew what she was talking about. She continued, "I seen you, I seen you in the papers when you got married!"

Mama turned and gave me a death stare I'd never forget.

The ride home was only ten minutes, but it seemed like an eternity. This was now the second thing that made Mama hate Mark more than she already did. "I know damn well you didn't marry that bastard. I know you didn't marry Mark Greenlee," she muttered in the car.

She shook her head as she drove us home. "You married that no-life motherfucker."

When we pulled up into the car porch, Mama gripped the steering wheel and turned to me. "You got to get the fuck out of here. You can't stay here."

So I called Mark. "Mama said I got to leave."

He arrived the next day, backing the Pinto up to the house. I packed up every picture that I had because that was really all I had of any value. I loved taking photos of myself, including prom photos and my Homecoming pictures, and I'd frame everything, but now I just packed them up with all of Kesha's toys and clothes.

Hummie was there on the porch. Hummie and I made the pact the day of Dilly's funeral to stick together, which we did not completely follow through on because Mama and Daddy began to create a wedge between us: Hummie was treated like the perfect son, the athletic star, and I was the loser daughter who had a baby at age seventeen. But Kesha's birth brought Hummie and me closer again. He'd come into my room and play with her for hours. In a short amount of time, he built a bond with Kesha; he fell in love with his niece, and he didn't want her to leave him like Dilly did.

That day on the porch, he slid his hands in his pockets. "Brina, don't take the baby," he begged me.

I had promised him I'd never leave him and here I was leaving with the baby. I knew Hummie saw Kesha as a replacement for Dilly, but I had no choice but to go. I still remember his sad face, but my mind was racing. "Hummie, I can't stay. Mama ain't gonna let me stay here. I got married. Mark can't come in the house or anything."

He looked down, kicking an invisible rock. "But you don't have to take the baby."

"She my baby, Hummie" was all I could say.

Because Mama wouldn't let Mark in the house, I had to do all the packing myself, and then I got in the car, and we left. It was one of the worst mistakes of my life.

Mark lived in an ugly prefab in Red Hill. When I walked into his place, my heart just sank. I hated it. Compared to our home on Vista Circle, the house Uncle Ottie let us live in, Mark's home was nothing but a tin can. The moment you entered, you immediately saw a kitchen, a living room, and beyond, a giant bed that took up the entire bedroom. I nodded and gave Mark a weak smile. Making the best of it, I quickly set my framed photographs everywhere and laid out Kesha's clothes and toys in the living room, which I turned into a nursery. I had no idea what I was doing; I just wanted to make us feel comfortable. And I did feel comfortable for a minute, but it was short-lived. First, the giant, hard bed had become the bane of my existence. Trying to sleep with a colicky infant and a grown man in an uncomfortable bed is not only cumbersome but terrifying: I worried my baby would die of SIDS or one of us would roll over on her. I started making an excuse to sleep on the couch rather than the bed, and I'd put her in the bassinet next to me.

* * *

I was infatuated with Mark, but once you live with somebody every day, that's when you really get to see who they are. I had been looking at the outside, which was beautiful, but Mark had so many internal demons and was dealing with so much trauma that I had no idea who he really was. I quickly started to believe the man was nothing but pure hatred and evil inside. Add to that, I had a baby but no idea what I was doing, because I left behind the little help I had at Vista Circle.

Mark continued to cheat on me, would leave me alone in the house for days, and when he was there, we fought all the time. He called me bony and swore nobody else would ever want me. He'd accuse me of "whoring around" on him. It was always something: "Why the fuck you had to look at him?" Or, "You're embarrassing me." Or, "Why the fuck you put that on?"

He controlled when I ate and when I could leave the house. I was so tired and longed for Mama and Hummie, and I was depressed. I left all my friends to be with this man. It was just me, him, and the baby. Mark knew he had me where he wanted me: alone and in his grip. Soon, the hold on me turned sinister.

One particular day, a friend had kept Kesha, so I had some rare time to myself. I put on some clothes and tied my hair in a ponytail and walked to get my favorite treat from a store nearby. Mark wasn't home, so that meant I had the prefab to myself. It was one of the few days that I felt good; usually I was sitting in the prefab with Kesha, trying to figure out how I even got to this place in my life.

When I returned home, I noticed Mark's Pinto in the driveway. I barely got through the door before he started yelling, the force of his words nearly knocking me off my feet.

I had taken too long to return from the store. His words felt like a brutal beatdown—all because I had gone to get me a honey bun and some soda.

I cried, "Why would you say that when you weren't even here when I left?"

"It don't fucking matter," he raged at me. "I know that you've been up there looking at other niggas."

Life at the prefab literally became my little living hell. I hated to wake up, I hated to go to sleep. The kitchen at the prefab was not fit for cooking, so Mark would go to Mac's Drive In, a local diner, where he'd buy us hamburgers and fries nearly every night. But there were other nights he'd arrive empty-handed, and those were the nights I'd go to bed hungry. Mark did everything in his power to make my life miserable.

* * *

Mark was messed up, a bad boy who was trying to find himself. He didn't know his father, and his mother abandoned him, which makes me think he resented women. He used and manipulated me and despised my mother so much that he eventually told me he only married me to piss off Mama.

I've sometimes asked myself if Dilly hadn't died, would I have been with this one-legged man, starting at age fourteen? The truth is I don't think so. I didn't know who I was at the time or what was my worth, if any, but I don't think I would have allowed someone to hurt me if I didn't feel so lost during that period. I'm not the same mentally and emotionally now, but back then there was nothing positive going on. My energy migrated from Mama to Mark. That's what I must be careful of even to this day, because I am a nurturer. I am a protector. I am a fixer. I thought I could fix Mark, protect him, but I could barely take care of myself. I didn't know any better because, if I did, at some point I would have just gotten my stuff and left. However, in my mind, I was married, and it had to be better than living at home with Mama. It didn't even cross my mind to leave this man permanently.

How do you leave somebody you're married to? If I left him, where was I going to go? Truth is, I tried to leave him a few times, but he'd always sweet-talk me back. The first time I left him, though, it was for two horrible months with a man I had just met. I went from one prison cell to another. The only difference was that my new cell was an apartment with carpet, a one-bedroom with a giant waterbed, a ceiling fan, and a community swimming pool where white and Black people lay out in the sun together. In my mind, I finally found my prince charming, a fancy man, a used-car salesman who drove a 1988 Camaro and wore a high-top fade and button-down shirts. This man, who I will call "Sir," was twenty-eight, attentive, and charming with a playful side. He was always grabbing my butt and telling me that I was beautiful. He was my hero, rescuing me from a worthless life with Mark.

We met at a 7-Eleven after a football game at Daniel High School, where our flirtations quickly turned into kisses and phone number exchanges. Everything moved way too fast; one minute I was living in a hellhole with Mark, the next minute I was grabbing any and everything me and Kesha owned to go live in Greenville with a stranger. I told Mark that Kesha and I were going to stay with my daddy in Easley for a few weeks. I knew Mark didn't want any part of my big, scary daddy, plus Mark was so consumed with his own life, trying to reconcile that he was now a one-legged man, that he hardly gave my leaving a second thought.

Only Hummie and Mama knew I was twenty-something miles away in Greenville. At first, I wondered how I could be so lucky. Mark promised me he'd take me to Greenville on the day we got married, but he never did. As fate would have it, I was now living in the biggest city I've ever known. Sir and I would talk for hours into the night, and then he'd sit in the bed listening to me about my years with Mark.

He purchased my baby's formula and made sure I felt comfortable, even moving the furniture around in his apartment because he thought it would make me feel more at home. Sir would take me to fancy restaurants often, a far cry from the burgers and fries I would occasionally get from Mark. At night, he would lie with me in bed, reassuring me that the life we'd build together would be better, safer, more loving than the horrors I experienced with Mark.

But my good times with Sir were short-lived. Soon, in just a matter of weeks, he began to become more aggressive. He'd come home from work and complain that I was laying around doing nothing. He'd be rude and quick to interrupt me whenever I would attempt to explain myself. He'd be out late after work, telling me he was hanging out with coworkers. I began to feel like an unwanted guest, like he didn't want me there. Soon the verbal abuse and disregard became physical. One night, Sir came home, acting intoxicated—I'd never seen him drunk before, and to be honest, I didn't smell anything on his breath that night. But he was definitely on something. Several days later, things started to make sense. I was cleaning up the house when I found a plastic bag on the floor with four little white rocks in them. I was shocked and instantly flushed the drugs down the toilet.

I asked God, *Please Lord, don't tell me this man is doing drugs.*

I had questions and I was determined to get Sir to answer them. But when I told him I flushed the drugs down the toilet, he swung around and slapped the shit out of me. I touched my face and ran into the bedroom, locked the door behind me, and grabbed Kesha, who was asleep on the bed. As I cradled her, I began to get angry. Here I was again, with my baby in harm's way, at the mercy of a volatile man. It was as if Sir picked up where Mark had left off, but his abuse would only get worse.

The first time he sent me to the hospital, we were arguing over nothing. The fact that I had dared compare him to another man sent him into a rage. That night, Sir kept hitting me like I was a punching bag. With a balled-up fist, Sir raised his hand and punched me in my eye.

He continued hitting me, nearly busting my eardrum. He then choked and kicked and punched me until he couldn't anymore. I stayed in the hospital for two days with a cracked collarbone, a broken rib, fractures in my face, and scratches and bruises all over my body. He always went for my face. If I covered my face, it would leave the rest of my body exposed, and that's when he'd start kicking. Sir kicked me so much that my body was still tired as I lay in the hospital bed.

What I didn't know yet, but would soon find out, was that his waterbed, that giant contraption I hated, not unlike the monstrous bed in Mark's place, would nearly become my deathbed.

The second time Sir put me in the hospital was the last. I remember feeling especially tired that day; I had been losing weight and was feeling utterly hopeless. Mama had Kesha, so I decided to go to a high school game in Greenville with a neighbor to cheer myself up. When I was dropped off back home, Sir asked where I was. Again. I told him, but nothing I said would have mattered, because he was going to find a reason to beat me just because I wasn't home. He backed me into the bedroom. I jumped on the waterbed, because he was blocking the door and there was nowhere else to go. We were tussling on the waterbed, and somehow, he turned me around and jumped on top of my back, straddling me while he beat me in the back of my head. I was pinned down and couldn't move while he pummeled me, so I tried to flatten the sheet and then do my very best to bite through the plastic because I thought if the bed burst, I could digest enough water and drown, which would be better than dying from Sir's beatings.

He beat me until he was tired. I lifted my head and realized I was still alive. He had the chance to kill me and blew it. I was ready to die, but lived—and this lit a fire under me and shifted something inside. Instead of being afraid, Sir's ass whipping ignited a rage like I never felt before.

* * *

When Sir beat me on the waterbed, I was three months pregnant with Mark's second child but did not know it. What I did know was that if I stayed much longer, Sir would kill me or I would kill him. So I made the hardest choice in my life: I went back to Mark, but this time, returning as a different person, biding my time until I could figure out my next step. I knew one thing was true: I was no longer going to take his shit. In fact, the anger I felt after Sir's last ass beating carried over to Mark tenfold. Once Mark started back his old ways—cheating, telling me nobody wanted me, calling me bony, and not bringing me food—I was determined to get Mark back for his and every other man's mistreatment of me.

I knew I couldn't fight him physically, but I could humiliate him as he had done to me so many times. One day I decided to steal his Pinto while he slept. As I walked out the door, I noticed his prosthetic leg was in the living room leaning against the wall. I grabbed it and threw it in the back seat of the car. I took the two things he depended on, things that gave him power, and I hoped he felt the helplessness that I felt all the time. I rode around with the leg all day, visiting friends and telling them about Mark's leg in the car. When I walked in the door with his leg in hand later that night, I expected him to be pissed off, but I was too fed up to care. However, he didn't touch me, because he saw the fire in my eyes, and that finally scared the hell out of the monster.

*   *   *

I had had enough of Mark Greenlee, and I was ready to take my power back, leave him, and change my life for the better. What that was going to look like, I had no idea; I would do it one step at a time. Within two weeks of returning to Mark's tin can, I found work and applied for a one-bedroom apartment in Creekwood Village, which was the projects near the Hill and very close to Vista Circle, where Mama and Hummie still lived. The only thing that separated my new apartment from Vista Circle was "the pines," a trail of bushes linking a bunch of Black neighborhoods that we'd been walking through since we were kids.

I quickly began to make a home out of this small one-bedroom apartment. I went to Kimbrell's Furniture store and put fifty dollars down on both a living room suite and a dinette set. I got my bedroom set from my mama, and I somehow obtained a small TV, which I propped up on four boxes.

All single moms like me who lived in Creekwood knew this rule of the projects: If you had a man, you'd have to hide their clothes on the day of the inspection, which happened every month. Not allowing a woman to live with her man was just so ghetto, but it was the rule in nearly every housing project in the country. Mark knew this rule, too. While he came around less and less, every time he'd come to Creekwood, he'd do something to show out and bring attention to himself because he wanted me to get kicked out and back with him. During this time, I decided to turn the tables: I began to befriend men behind his back. I became fond of a young man who worked with me at Schilletter Dining Hall, an eatery that catered to Clemson students. We had sex maybe twice but nothing more. One day he decided he wanted to come by my apartment to give me concert tickets. I warned him, "You know how Mark is."

The young man promised to be in and out. And he was, but it was enough time for Mark to arrive, beating on the door. I said to myself: *Oh shoot, here we go.* In my mind, I was imagining him fighting me and my male friend. I didn't know I was pregnant with Mark's second child, eight months after my first pregnancy, which might be why I was so hyperalert. Mark called Hummie, asking him to come by the apartment to visit. Hummie and Squeenchie were chilling at the house in Vista Circle. It would have taken them no more than ten minutes to get to my apartment if they trekked through the pines. Mark thought I'd open the door for them, but he got impatient waiting for them to arrive. Instead, he went down to a dumpster that was only a few feet from my door, where he found an old bed rail. He returned and slammed the rail through my window, not even considering that someone could be standing there. I saw what he had just done and knew he was going to try to kick the window in—that artificial leg could easily smash through broken glass. I was terrified, but at the same time I was thinking on my feet.

I turned to my young suitor with the concert tickets who was looking at me for guidance. "Listen, the door and the window are side by side," I explained strategically. "He can't come through both the window *and* the door, and he's got to kick out the entire window in order to get the door open. When he gets halfway through this damn window, I'm going to open the door and run, and you come behind me."

I had Kesha on my hip, waiting for the right moment. Then I shouted: "Run!" I sprinted out the door and kept running until I got to my uncle Louis's apartment. In fact, I ran out the door so fast that Mark could not have caught me if he tried. I remember him stopping to look at me, but I was gone in a flash. Unfortunately, the young man didn't follow me. Instead, he retreated to the bedroom and hid in the closet. Of course, his nice car with rims was parked right outside my apartment, so Mark knew he was still inside.

Mark calmly stopped messing with the window, stepped in the apartment, and proceeded to beat the shit out of the young man. Me and Kesha were two hundred yards away in the lobby of my uncle's apartment, when I heard sirens rush to my building.

*   *   *

Whereas Kesha had me in labor for two days, my second baby, Marcus, who we call "Boodia," didn't give me time to go into labor. My water broke in Ingles grocery store. I insisted on going home to get Kesha's clothes packed, which meant by the time Mama got me to the hospital, Boodia was coming out of me in the elevator. When I arrived in the delivery room, all the medical crew had to do was clean me up. Boodia, who was nearly nine pounds, emerged into this world on August 1, 1989, looking calm, and he's been like that ever since.

While my defenses against Mark were growing stronger during this period, my relationship with Mama was still poisonous. One rainy day I found myself stuck with the kids in Creekwood. My apartment didn't have much furniture in it, and the place felt like it was closing in on me. So I took the kids to her house, which was just a quick walk through the pines. I had one baby on my hip and one in the stroller. It was a good little ways, but when I get into Mama's house, I immediately went to the living room, because I am now a guest. As I peeled off my children's coats, Mama's boyfriend, Sporty, comes through and sees me. "Hey!" he said to me.

I said, "Hey," but I didn't think nothing of it.

Sporty was nice enough. He donned a curly kit, drove a simple white truck, and had a goatee. Like Mark, he was also an amputee, but unlike Mark, he was a one-legged man who was a drug dealer.

Mama finally came to the living room.

"Hey, Mama."

She stood in front of me and the kids. "It's mighty funny that the only time you come over here is when you see Sporty's truck. I'm not stupid."

Understanding the implication, I felt my heart drop to my feet. "Mama? What? Are you really saying this?" My eyes teared up. I thought, *I will never come back around her, and I will never go around her boyfriends.* I wiped my eyes. "If you want me to leave, just say so."

She smirked. "I'm just saying it's mighty funny," she repeated.

I put my kids' coats back on. I got to the door, but it was pouring. What do I do? I started walking in the rain, but luckily a neighbor saw me and gave us a lift home. That was the first time Mama accused me of messing with one of her men, but it wouldn't be the last.

Truth be told, I barely knew Sporty and was thinking, *Ain't nobody want him but you.* Plus, I had already seen what Plug, another drug-dealing boyfriend of hers, did to his women. But Mama was always suspicious of women and accused them of trying to get close to her men.

* * *

Mama says you know you tired of a man when he starts looking ugly. Mark was a good-looking man, but he was so mean that his ugly inside started showing on the outside, at least to me. One morning, I woke up to a horrible phone call. Mama was in Pickens County jail. News in the projects moves around like a summer storm—it's quick and dirty. I learned she was arrested for conspiracy to sell crack cocaine hours earlier with Sporty at Alfie's Playpen, a popular club in Clemson. Nobody was trying to help Mama but me. I made calls and was able to talk Mark into taking me to our family attorney, who coincidentally was based in Pickens. In my frantic state, I made a huge mistake. Me and Mark were barely speaking, but I let him sit and listen as I talked about Mama's case to the attorney.

As we headed home, Mark said, "You ought to let her ass sit there."

I turned to look at him and thought Mama was right: I knew I was sick of Mark's mess because when he said that about my mama, his entire face turned ugly. It looked longer, like it was sagging, and his eyes seemed bloodshot.

I was at my wits' end at this point. Soon as he started talking crazy about Mama, I jumped out of the moving car once he slowed down to stop at a stoplight, and he left me stranded at a gas station in Pickens.

The last straw had nothing to do with Mark's looks, but it was him touching my child. Mark told everyone who'd listen that neither Kesha nor Boodia were his. Boodia was a light-skinned baby who smiled all the time and Kesha was a beautiful mocha-complected child, but Mark couldn't see himself in them. He often made comments that Kesha couldn't be his because she was dark with "nappy" hair.

One day during this period, Mark happened to be at the apartment, and everything seemed fine; we were cordial. I had Kesha between my legs while I combed her hair. Then this man, this monster, sat down and stared at us, saying, "This bastard got nappy hair, she ain't none of mine no way!"

He then walked up and placed her under his arm and said, "I'm taking her for a while." I pulled her back. "Where are you taking her?"

He only said, "If this my baby, there's nothing to worry about."

He knew he had every right to take his child, but he also knew his words had scared me. In my young mind, those words were a threat. After a while my nerves got the best of me. I called the police, the first time I ever called the law on him, and two white officers showed up. They played high school football with Mark and stood there swearing Mark Greenlee couldn't hurt a fly. Looking back now, I think this is what Mark wanted all along: for me to feel helpless while looking absolutely crazy. In my mind, I just knew he'd hurt Kesha, which is probably what Mark wanted me to think. His words echoed in my ears. "This bastard got nappy hair, she ain't none of mine no way!"

For three hours, I had no idea where Kesha could be. The police officers returned without Kesha, but to tell me everything was okay and Mark had done nothing wrong, and that Kesha was at my cousin Missy's house.

I was so upset and knew that if I stayed married to that man, I would literally stab him to death. I didn't even care. What I regret was that I couldn't press charges. I kept telling the officers I wanted to, but they told me I didn't have the right to press charges because Mark was Kesha's father. How could they arrest somebody for being a sinister asshole who had scared the hell out of me?

But this thing he did, taking Kesha like that, gave me clarity: I knew like I knew my name that Mark Greenlee wasn't going to exist in my presence anymore. My rage was at its peak.

I told my friend, "I could kill this motherfucker and sit in jail, tapping my feet the rest of my life and never have no regrets."

In my head, I was plotting to kill him when he next showed up to the apartment, but he never returned. Instead, he filed a suit for full custody of Kesha and Boodia.

He knew he had lost control of me and now was still messing with me so he could just hinder me from living my life. He knew that he and I were over. He knew I was unfazed by any of his bullshit at this point. So here he comes, trying to take two children he swore weren't his. I worried that after the way he had treated me, I didn't want him getting his hands on my kids.

At the hearing, I pleaded with the judge, explaining Mark was not a good man, but because I did not or could not document any type of abuse, I had no proof.

On the other hand, he had no problem calling me an unfit mother and using the entire court hearing to bring up Mama and Sporty's conspiracy to sell dope charge as proof that I was unfit, though I had nothing to do with it. I was only guilty of being stupid enough to allow Mark to listen to my conversation with the lawyer about Mama's situation and not realize Mark was low-down enough to use that moment against me.

That day in court I learned a lesson: I no longer assumed there is going to be justice if you don't have proof. I found myself in court fighting for these two babies with little or no evidence that this man had treated me horribly for years and years.

Mark had also told my lawyer that I had a man. My lawyer cautioned me, saying he didn't know what was going on, and that he didn't care, but if I had a man coming around the apartment after dark, I had to put a stop to it. At the time, it was true: I had met a man who'd later become the love of my life and my third child DeAndre's father, but there was no second thought, and I told him to stop calling on me until all this with Mark was over. I was not going to lose my children. Daddy gave me two thousand dollars to help me fight the case. It took a year, but I won full custody and was granted a divorce on that same day. Mark didn't let up, though, until he got extended visitation rights, which the court granted him: every other weekend, starting at 4:00 p.m. on Friday; he also got one month during the summer, and we were to split each holiday. It was all for spite, because Mark only took the children for one weekend. Boodia returned from that visit with all his hair chopped off. Mark never came back to get them, and, to be honest, I never sent them back. And that was the end of Mark Greenlee being in my life.

CHAPTER 7

Bonnie and Clyde, Part 1

I first met Steve Hopkins while I was living in Creekwood in 1990. I was sure he'd be my happily ever after. He was kind and good to me—he loved my kids and treated them just like they were his. Most importantly, he wasn't violent to me.

He was also a drug kingpin who wore a fur coat in the summertime.

Right before meeting him, I was trying to put my life together as a single mother and find my independence in Creekwood. Mark was still trying to take my kids at the time, but life in the projects was actually pretty good. I had my new apartment, with decent furniture. I also had a full-time job at J. P. Stevens, which was a factory located between Clemson and Pendleton, on the back road near a farm and a kennel. I worked on the assembly line packaging bedsheets. I was controlling the machine where the sheets hit the warm plastic and sealed them, and then we had to box them. If an order called for three in a box, you added three sheets, but if the order changed, you'd have to change everything up. Most of the people on the assembly line were young like me, because we had to move fast. My cousin Missy, Aunt Louise's daughter and Poopie's oldest sister, was supposed to work with me, but she quit after the first day.

Although a lot of Black people worked at J. P. Stevens, I stayed to myself. There were opportunities in different departments, and if you worked hard and were lucky enough to be considered for a transfer, your salary was above minimum wage. Working meant rent in my publicly funded Creekwood apartment surged, but I didn't care. Most of the girls' rent went anywhere from $9 to $25 a month, and some of those girls even got a utility check to pay their utilities, which went from $50 to $150. One day, I was sitting around with some of the women at Creekwood when I told them that my rent was $250. Everybody busted out laughing at me. "You're crazy as hell," one of them said. "Ain't no way I'm going to pay that much to live in the projects."

My rent was higher because I had a job, but I didn't care what anybody thought. They had no idea where I had just come from, sitting in the prefab with Mark and having nothing. I was determined to keep a job and make my own money. I remember there were days at J. P. Stevens when I didn't have a ride home. I would ask different people for a lift home because I was determined to be independent. People would say, "You too pretty to be in here. Ain't you that girl who won Homecoming over at Daniel?"

I befriended a white girl named Erica, who attended Daniel High School with me. Eventually, she would bring me home and pick me up every day. Missy would take care of the kids, or my mama would.

One night after work Erica and I stopped for something to eat at the Huddle House. On our way out, we noticed two men pull up in a car. Out of the corner of my eye, I saw them trying to figure out who was going to approach me. It was second shift, around eleven at night. Steve Hopkins was the big dog of the two, so he won the battle.

He leaned into the passenger side of the car. "What's up? What's your name?"

I blushed. "What's your name? Who are you?"

This man's swagger had me from jump. He was tall and good-looking. He dressed fine and had a mustache. Steve had a way about himself that commanded attention. We didn't exchange numbers but the very next weekend I saw him at the Anderson Mall. I was with Missy, and he was with his family. We made eye contact before he walked over to me. "Hey, what you doing? Meet me at the What's Happening club tonight."

I gave him a playful side-eyed glance. "I know about What's Happening club," I said, shaking my head. "But I ain't going over there."

He laughed at me. "Oh, you coming."

"No, I'm not." I smiled. "How you know I'm coming?"

"I know you coming."

As soon as he walked away, I found my cousin Missy. "Girl, I'm going to go to the What's Happening club tonight."

* * *

The What's Happening club was in nearby Seneca, and it was the place to be. You were always going to bump into someone you knew because everyone from the surrounding areas partied there. I'd been there many times before, but this night was different because I was going to see what this man was about. I sat on the benches with my girls so I could see everyone on the dance floor. In the back was a bar and some tables, which is where Steve was hanging out. He spotted me and led me to the dance floor, where we slow dragged off the song "If Only You Knew."

The connection was instant. I felt like a Black Cinderella dancing with the prince. This man held me close, like I had never been held before. I was fresh out of a toxic marriage, so having someone treat me like I was special was new to me. I understood this man was somebody I wanted to get to know.

Before the night was over, he said, "You going with me."

Someone drove us to a nearby hotel, where we had sex. I didn't even know who he was, what he was all about, or who he was connected to, but I knew I wanted to be only with him that night. That next morning, my body was still on fire. I walked naked to the bathroom and returned to see him standing nearby waiting for me. I melted in his arms and let him lead me back to bed. He eventually called somebody to come get him. I had to call somebody to get me. It never crossed my mind that this man didn't have a car, but rather he just had people doing stuff for him.

I was only nineteen, but old enough to know there was something about this man that got me all nervous and excited at the same time. Again, we didn't exchange numbers, but I knew I had to see him again. Several days later I told my mom, "I met Steve Hopkins."

"I don't know who that is," Mama said, but she asked around. A few hours later, Mama had discovered a piece of the puzzle. "They say he one of the 'Hop boys,'" meaning the son of a man by the last name of Hopkins. She even found out where the Hop boys hung out.

I said, "Mama, take me out there." And of course, my mama was about that life, so we set out to go find the Hop boys. We ended up at his daddy's liquor house in Seneca.

Steve lived in a single-wide trailer with his father and brother, but it was still called a liquor house because it was based in someone's home and because of the way the outside was set up. And like all liquor houses, it was an alternative to a bar. That day, everybody was sitting outside listening to juke joint music and drinking beer.

Liquor houses have been a thing in South Carolina since the olden days. The state has been trying to crack down on them lately because it claims they attract crime, but I always loved them. First, they were packed with men. After clubs, me and my girlfriends would head to liquor houses in Greenville where anyone could buy shots of tequila for one dollar. It was the cheapest liquor you can imagine, in cups the size of a fifty-cent piece. One of my favorite liquor houses was in Clemson, called Tribbles. The owner would cook and sell chitlins and liquor. My daddy said that even my grandma Zona ran a liquor house for a short period of time.

But something about Steve's daddy's spot was different; it was like a scene out of *The Color Purple* but modern day. People of all ages were sitting in chairs and tables outside. Music was playing and women were dancing, while children ran around the yard. I'd never seen anything like it before. We hung outside in Creekwood, but it was nothing like this. This was a seriously loud and crazy party. I got out of the car and knocked on the door of the single-wide trailer.

Someone sitting outside hollered out, "Who you looking for?"

I paused before I said, "Steve."

"He in there."

Steve's brother Anthony answered the door. He was sitting in the living room with his wife drinking coffee and reading the newspaper. He pointed down a long, narrow hallway. At the end of the hall was a room with nothing but a bed. I stuck my head in the room, where Steve was lying on the bed. He rubbed his eyes and looked confused. "Hey, what you doing here?

I stepped into the room. "I just came to see you."

He rubbed his eyes again. "Okay, give me a minute. I'm glad you're here."

Sometimes I think had I not gone over there, we might have never gotten together. A week later, he came to see me in Creekwood. Now he was in my world. Everybody was outside, dope's being sold, people were drinking beer out of red cups—doing what we do in the projects. I noticed he stood taking the scene all in, a bunch of young women out there with a bunch of boyfriends, who were not supposed to be there. Another time he came to check me out, see my little apartment, and he left. He returned and said, "Hey, I wanna come get you when you get off work so we can hang out with my boys. Let's go to Alfie's Playpen."

Alfie's was the same place in which Mama and Sporty were arrested for conspiracy to sell drugs. "There's nothing but old people hang at Alfie's," I said. "My mom and them hang out there. Let's go to Carl's instead."

He shook his head. "I'm cool with Carl's, but I'd rather go to Alfie's tonight."

Before he left my apartment, he handed me a wad of money. "Put this up for me."

It wasn't unusual for a man to give a woman money to hold because it was too much or too dangerous for him to carry. I didn't know him like that, but I also didn't give it a second thought. I instantly put it in my top drawer and never thought anything else about it. I was street-smart and knew he must be doing something illegal, but I didn't feel the need to ask. We planned to return to my apartment, so he'd get the money back later tonight.

A few hours later, we arrived at Alfie's with three of his friends; Steve always had a bunch of men around him. I walked in and instantly I see girls looking at me crazy, and in my mind, I don't care because I'm with him. We go to the bar, but I don't drink. I just get a soda to hold because I'm trying to fit in. Steve left me but would come over a few times to check on me. Nobody else was talking to me, and so I was just standing there trying to look cool, nursing my soda, like I belonged. The crowd was older, and I had no idea who these people were. But I'm sure they were all connected, most from nearby Seneca. If we were at Carl's, me and my girls would be tearing up the dance floor, but people here weren't dancing—they were more like shuffling around. Again, Steve returned, and again he then went off with his friends.

About five minutes later I heard a *bang*, a big commotion, and I looked over—Steve's face was all lit up, and he's holding a gun. He fired three shots. *Pow! Pow! Pow!* Every time I heard a shot, the flash would light up his face. Everyone started running out of the club, but I stood frozen, my legs like lead.

My heart raced. *Did I just roll in here with a killer?!* I stepped over one or two people on the floor, who had been shot and were bleeding. I knew some of them, too. Finally, Missy came to get me. I had no idea what happened to Steve or where he went.

* * *

The next few days I remained terrified, but also intrigued. Every story I heard on television, I wondered if that's him. Every high-speed chase in the news, I was thinking that must be him. I had so many questions: How could Steve do it? He seemed to be so nice. Did those boys die? I didn't know anything.

Then he showed up at my door.

Steve had turned himself in after the shootings, but he was soon enough out on bail. Steve had shot them in their legs and arms, but no major organs were hit. And soon enough, all charges got dropped because none of the injured people would talk to police. Why? Because it was a street beef and it's not something you want the police to be involved in. Even though you might carry that bullet inside you, you'll take it up later.

He came back to see me, and of course he asked about the money I was holding. With Steve was a tall, beautiful woman with meticulous nails and hair. He told me she was his mother, who I'd later learned was a big-time drug dealer in Georgia. She appeared very powerful and dominant. I quickly learned she was the matriarch of her family; everything ran through her, and she took care of everybody. In a way, she was the woman I imagined myself becoming. I later mimicked her on how she handled her family, how fastidious she was, and even how she slept. She slept in a high bed, the type of beds that you had to step on a stool to get on. I had never seen anything like that before, but it felt like royalty. That's how my bed is even to this day. She had those three children, but she was the mama to so many other people, exactly how I am now. But she was also very manipulative.

Steve and I would trade mama stories. There weren't many times when we didn't agree that they were just alike, in a lot of ways. The manipulation, the lies, and even though his mama didn't do drugs, and mine did, they were both cunning and got whatever they wanted by any means necessary. They had that in common. But Steve's mom was a businesswoman, and she was all about getting ahead.

His mother remained outside my Creekwood apartment after Steve entered. I opened my dresser drawer and gave the money to him. He looked at me and said that no one had ever done anything like this for him before—meaning holding his money and not spending any of it for myself. And I'm thinking, *I just saw you shoot three people! I was terrified to touch any of it!*

From that moment on we became closer, with one exception—when I had to separate from Steve during the custody battle with Mark. I told him about Mark.

I didn't want to lose my babies, so I told Steve the whole story. He said, "That's a bet. Call me when you got everything over."

He caressed my cheek. I knew by the look on his face, he was contemplating what he could do to Mark. "I really want to fuck him up for how he treated you."

"It's over, I got through it," I reassured him. "He's not worth your energy."

Months later, on the day I won the custody battle, I celebrated my independence at Ryan's Steakhouse. I picked it because it was cheap and buffet style. I arrived with three of my girlfriends and called Steve, who knew by now that my divorce proceeding was over, and came with his entourage. Afterward, the two of us went to my apartment in Creekwood to hang out, and then we got his clothes from his trailer. That was it. We were together from that day on. It was then that we started our great romance.

I was never in love like I was with Steve.

Steve was a big man who could be rough around the edges to the outside world, but once he stepped into our home, he was a gentle giant, getting down on the floor and playing for hours with Kesha and Boodia until they fell asleep. Then he put them to bed one by one, making sure they were tucked in just so.

Whenever I'd get a little depressed, Steve would sit next to me and say, "Brina, Brina." He stuttered when he said my name. "Brina, it's going to be all right. I'm not going anywhere." Something about that little stutter, which only happened when he said my name, was so cute, and for some odd reason that I can't explain, let me know he loved me.

We spent a lot of time riding in the car, but he loved for us to stop at some country restaurant and get some fried chicken, green beans, and macaroni and cheese.

When we were home, he'd ask me to comb the scabs out of his scalp. While I sat on the couch, he'd sit on the floor between my legs while I separated his hair with the comb, combing out the dry patches and adding medicine to the scalp. I would take extra time because I knew he loved the attention I was giving him.

Truth be told, Steve was a big romantic. Once he gave me four hundred dollars, then he took Marcus and I took Kesha, and we went shopping to see who could pick out the better Valentine's Day gift for the other. When me and Kesha returned home, the living room was filled with teddy bears, candy, and balloons. We laughed about it; I told him I knew he'd win because he was such a dang romantic.

Steve showed me how to love, but he also had a ruthless side of him he got from his mother. I soon found out that, like her, he was a big-time drug dealer. He often told me how he got started selling drugs at age twelve. It wasn't a choice for him, because his mom sent him and Anthony, his younger brother, out to sell when they should have been playing out in the streets with other children. So the drug business was all he knew. Of course, his story drew me to him even more than I already was.

One day he pulled out a bag filled with rocks the color of milk. "This is crack," he said matter-of-factly. The only time I had seen crack was when I found Sir's stash under the waterbed. Missy, who had come to visit me, had to tell me what it was, and I flushed it down the toilet.

Unlike Sir, Steve was not a user, but a businessman. He pointed to the bag. "We're going to make money!"

Now we were inseparable, and we were partners in crime—a true-life Bonnie and Clyde. Steve moved in with me, and we just took over the whole project. I sold crack to the women, and he dealt drugs to the men. Somebody would knock on my door, and I'd deliver the drugs to whichever girl it was. Steve was more aggressive—he'd go out and do what they call chasing cars. In Creekwood, cars come in, they go through the first and second speed bumps, and then they'd go down, turn around, and he'd catch them on the way out.

At home, he took care of everything for me. If the kids needed high chairs, he bought them. If we needed food, he'd go get it for us. He installed a gold bar with barstools in the apartment, and expensive wineglasses and wine—and I didn't even drink. On Christmas that first year he brought so many gifts for the kids that we needed a storage unit to keep all the stuff in. We had the first camcorder in the projects. We had the first mobile phone, back when they were the size of a shoe.

We'd lay in bed and talk about his childhood, and he'd listen to me talk about mine; he was so good at communicating, this was the kind of love where you want to be with each other all the time, where you want to wake up and know he's right there next to you.

But I was also his rider, and our life together was fast and loaded with risks. There were always rumors of a looming drug bust at Creekwood, and you never knew who might rat you out. One day Steve had a feeling something was about to go down, so he grabbed me and said we had to go to Atlanta—right at that very moment. Things like that began to happen more frequently. To this day, I still don't know if he heard something was about to pop off or not, but we jumped in his car, a tricked-out Mustang GTS, the sweetest car in South Carolina, the kind of car people blow their horns at, letting us know it's the baddest thing ever.

One particular time, we pulled up to an apartment complex in Atlanta. I knew he was going there to re-up on dope, which was dangerous because there was always a risk that someone could rob him. That day, he told me to get behind the wheel. "If I'm not back in fifteen minutes, then you need to leave." His words were something I'd never forget.

This was the life we lived, full of danger, but Steve was my man, and so the risk was worth it.

CHAPTER 8

Creekwood

My cousin Missy lived beside me when I was in the two-bedroom apartment in Creekwood. As a child, she was the one who'd stand by as I peed in the bathroom at Grandma Frances's house, and I'd do the same for her because we were afraid of the cockroaches crawling through the toilet. As teens, we'd go together to Chanello's, where we flirted with the Clemson athletes. My family was over her daddy and mama's house on the day Dilly died, and it was her brother, Poopie, who was in the car that night with Dilly, Hummie, and Squeenchie.

Real light-skinned with an athletic build and nice thick hair, Missy has always been the spittin' image of her daddy, who was my extremely handsome uncle Larry. About two years older than me, Missy introduced me to the radio and the night jams. Missy was country like me, but she had lots of energy and influence over my early life, which was both good and bad. She was the girl I looked up to and who I spent hours with doing innocent girl stuff, but Missy was also manipulative in a way where she'd come and "borrow" my clothes, borrow my food and my Barbies, until I looked up and had nothing.

Missy's and my apartments were revolving doors: Mama would come over to my place for a little while and head over to Missy's couch. Missy's mama, my aunt Louise, would hang out at Missy's apartment and then head over to mine. Literally, Missy and I would wake up in the morning and open our individual doors, because we knew our kin would be coming and going from one door to the other. At least once a week, Missy would make this dish of pasta with hamburger and cheese. I'd prepare the tossed salad and the garlic bread, something to complement what she cooked, and the family would stroll back and forth and eat from house to house.

If we didn't want company, we had to lock our doors, but there was always some relative banging on the door to get in. Anyone who came to see Steve never knocked on the door because the door was open, but they knew better than to just walk in, and instead they stood outside the door shouting, "Yo! Yo!"

And one of my relatives would say to me or Steve, "Somebody standing outside the door."

* * *

I had been doing hair as a side hustle for as long as I lived in Creekwood, even while I was working at J. P. Stevens. I'd wash my customer's hair in my kitchen sink but my setup was in the living room. My specialty was pin curls and buns. I was very good at buns and finger waves. I did do Mama's hair and everyone's hair in the projects.

* * *

About a year after Steve moved into the projects to be with me, Uncle Ottie kicked Mama out of the house in Vista Circle because he said his daughter needed it. By then, Hummie was at Clemson University, and was now becoming a star football player, and Poopie was enrolled there as well. This left Mama alone and with nowhere to go. When she lived in the house in Vista Circle, she paid Ottie the remainder of what the Housing Authority did not pay, and although it was a small amount, she never thought he would put her out on the streets because it wasn't like she was living there for free.

I've seen my mother cry over Dilly and her feeling like she was having a heart attack, but this hurt was different because it felt to her like Ottie was inflicting pain all over again, after he had killed her youngest son. She had nowhere to go but to live on the couch in my two-bedroom apartment. She went from a beautiful home in Vista to living with me, Steve, and two babies in the projects. I'd see her sitting on the couch sometimes staring at nothing, as if she was saying, "What the fuck am I supposed to do now?"

It hurt me to see Mama like that, but luckily Steve was cooler than I was about Mama living with us. In fact, Steve loved Mama, and Mama loved him. He'd give her things and just be nice to Mama, which was new to her. He understood Mama because she was just like his mom. He knew how to hype Mama up and calm her down.

We introduced Steve to the Jockey Lot, which was the big flea market where everyone in Upstate South Carolina gathered during the weekend to buy mostly junk. We also introduced him to Bingo, which he grew to love as much as going to the flea market. He'd bring Mama a candy apple back from the Jockey Lot, and he'd make sure she came with us to play Bingo.

And it was Steve who told me Mama was on crack. Steve would give her packs of crack to sell behind my back, so she'd have some money, but instead she'd smoke it all up. When he told me Mama was on drugs, I didn't believe it, but things began making sense: she sold my school ring, and all the rings Steve bought me, and later she'd steal money from me. I also thought back several years earlier when I got off the school bus and walked in on Mama and her boyfriend in the house in Vista Circle. Mama was holding her bleeding mouth. Plug, her drug-dealing boyfriend, said he beat her ass because she stole his shit. At the time I had no idea what he meant, or I didn't want to believe it, but it all started to become clear.

Mama and Aunt Louise were both two beautiful Black women and two functioning addicts. In 1991, we didn't understand the power of the crack epidemic, because when you're in it, you don't really see its true effects. For instance, Steve was selling in Creekwood, but it was a means to an end. Mama and my aunt were using, but they only changed in the way they moved around; now they hung with friends who did crack with them. Mama had a friend she'd get high with, but they'd never come around us high. They'd sit around whispering and scheming to get the next fix, but you never knew what they were up to. You just knew your mama was in the house with her homegirl.

In fact, Mama and Aunt Louise kept their appearance up, even though they were on crack. They'd always get compliments about their beautiful hair and new clothes, and to this day, my seventy-plus-year-old mama still wears tight jeans because she says they keep her shape together.

Aunt Louise was always open about her drug use. She'd say, "I smoke my damn crack and so the fuck what? That's what I do. That's my thing." Mama, on the other hand, was what we called a "closet burner," someone who smokes crack but only in the confines of their own home or somewhere very secretive. Closet burners will even refer to somebody else as a crackhead—Mama would call people crackheads in a heartbeat.

* * *

Steve and my drug business was booming in 1991, but nothing comes easy; risk was always around the corner. Even though Steve was under a court order banning him from his home state of Georgia, he ended up in jail there for three months because he violated probation. He turned himself in, and I drove to see him every week. To keep the business going in Creekwood, I also drove to Georgia to pick up some drugs from Steve's mama, Shirley Ann. They were already prepacked, tiny pieces of crack stored in little ziplock bags smaller than an inch; each little bag was worth twenty dollars. All these little bags were neatly packed in a bigger ziplock pack. All I had to do was pick it up and take it back to Creekwood and distribute it. I didn't need to cut it up or anything, it was already prepared. I about pissed myself driving back from Georgia with all of them drugs in the car—I was so nervous my right leg would shake so bad, causing the car to jerk.

Of course, I didn't make as much money as Steve would have. First, I wasn't going to chase anybody down for our money like Steve did, and at one hundred and twenty pounds, I didn't pose much of a threat. While we had money, lots of it, I still wanted to keep even more money flowing. One day I told Missy we needed to learn how to boost. I wasn't desperate for cash, I told her, but while Steve was gone, I wanted to keep building; I guess I also wanted to see if I had it in me to be a masterful booster like Aunt Louise, who gave us a private lesson on how to shoplift and not get caught.

Aunt Louise was always a hustler compared to Mama. She boosted clothes to pay for her drugs. And Louise wasn't any old shoplifter; she was a highly organized and skilled booster. She had this one blue jean skirt that came all the way down to her ankles and had huge pleats running down it. It was the oldest, mustiest-looking blue jean skirt, but it was her lucky garment. Aunt Louise was a beautiful dresser, and to this day she keeps herself looking her best, but that blue jean skirt was ugly. I don't think she washed it, because she worried she'd wash the luck away.

Under the pleated skirt, she'd put on a girdle. She showed us how she would pull the skirt up in the front and stuff the clothes down, then squeeze her legs together, and then walk out the store. That's how we started boosting. So Missy and I got ourselves the biggest, ugliest skirts that we had, we got a couple of real tight girdles—the girdle had to fit tight on top, but it could sag on the bottom. The more your girdle sagged, the more clothes you could get in.

Over a few times, we did exactly as she taught us. We had gotten so good that by the end of that first or second week, we're in Creekwood with pens and paper, taking orders, trying to be like our mamas. We tended to boost in smaller stores in Easley, because everybody knew us in Clemson, and Anderson and Greenville Malls were too big.

My cousin Missy had befriended a white girl who had two or three kids in Creekwood, and she became our driver and getaway girl. We never walked into a big mall, like my aunt Louise. We were not that good. Aunt Louise instructed us to go through side doors, so that way we could get in and out. And she said always have someone in the car or park your car in a way so people can't see your tag. There were rules to boosting, and we tried to follow them. One day, we got all our orders and headed to Anderson Mall, which was unusual for us because we were starting to get confident. Everything else was by the book: We got everyone's orders, we were parked on the side, didn't show the tag, but that week the white girl couldn't drive, so we recruited our cousin Wanda. We walked around the store, but I decided to boost away from the girls, because I was feeling professional. I had my orders in hand: little kids' clothes.

I got everything I needed while Missy and Wanda were on the other side stealing clothes, when here came this white man, and he was looking at Missy, and then here comes another one, who's looking at me.

The adrenaline that you have when you are shoplifting is nothing I have ever felt in my life. I started rushing toward the door. He said, "Hold up, ma'am." Missy was rushing up behind me.

Outside, I looked at Missy, and Missy looked at me; I could see in her eyes that she wanted to run.

"Don't do it!" I said to her, desperate.

"Fuck that!" Missy said. After all, Missy was Louise's daughter—she had running in her, but the security guards were quicker. They grabbed us and marched us into an office. Me and Missy had over five hundred dollars' worth of items on us, which was considered a felony. Wanda handed Missy a little red shirt, so she was in as a conspiracy to steal. The whole time the security guards thought we were someone else, an actual shoplifting ring that had been cleaning them out.

Regardless, we were arrested and spent the night in jail. I laid on a cot in a fetal position with a headache and hunger pains. At least my cousin Missy was with me.

* * *

In jail, we were provided cheeseburgers, fries, and iced tea. Sweet iced tea in the South is like coffee in France, which I suppose they likely serve in jail there, too. We don't really call it iced tea but sweet tea, though only the northern immigrants from New York and places like that would order tea without sugar. I was so terrified of being in jail that sleep was my only respite, and so I didn't even hear them bring the tea and McDonald's, but I must have smelled it. I was scared and starving, so the smell of the familiar burgers lifted my spirit. I rose from my cot to receive my burger when I noticed a guilty look on Missy's face.

"I didn't think you wanted it," she said sheepishly as she polished the last of my meal.

I was speechless and rolled my eyes at her.

While I was nursing a headache that I'm sure was linked to my fear of being in jail and my hunger, Missy was on the cot across from me playing cards like she's a real thug, like this is our life, but this wasn't our life. All she was really doing was reenacting one of her mama's stories. Aunt

Louise's accounts of shoplifting or outracing the police were renowned. She prided herself for being like her daddy, our Grandpa Edgar, but in truth Aunt Louise was even more of a legend. There was one story of her and a friend being chased by police. Somehow they lost the police and hid in a trash dumpster for hours until it was safe enough for them to come out.

I'd never be like Aunt Louise, but my jail stay did give me one specific thing to brag about: While in jail, I recalled that in the lining of my pocketbook was ten thousand dollars . . . drug money. Weeks earlier I took a needle and thread and professionally sewed the money into my pocketbook, so that Mama couldn't find it. After my arrest, I had a choice: give my pocketbook to my mama or tell them to hold it in evidence until I got out. I chose for them to keep it, because if I gave it to Mama, I knew for sure she would have found the cash. In jail we made little bets. "The police are gonna find your money," Missy kept saying. "You should have given it to your mama."

I shook my throbbing head. "No, it's better off with them."

The police were searching for clothes, and so after they got the clothes out of my bag, they were good. They never did check the lining: My bag was returned to me the next day with the dope money still hidden away.

I sighed with relief. When I got home, I ripped my pocketbook open and showed everyone the ten thousand dollars. I couldn't mess with that money because that was our re-up, which meant Steve needed it to buy a couple of ounces when he returned from jail so that we could keep our booming drug business going.

CHAPTER 9

Bonnie and Clyde, Part 2

Of course, everything's good until it gets bad. Things started to unravel, which only highlighted that living the life of a dope dealer's girlfriend with kids was not always peaches and cream. Steve had a habit of cutting up the crack and placing the white rocks in prescription pill bottles that already had pills in them. To my babies, it looked like candy, because there were three or four pills with different colors. One day Mama was sitting in the living room watching Marcus, who kept saying he was sleepy. She noticed that wasn't like him because he was always hyper, jumping around, but he kept saying, "Grandma, I'm really sleepy."

Mama cradled him but looked concerned. "No, this baby ain't got no business being sleepy in the middle of the day. What's wrong with you?"

He just kept wanting to lay his head on her chest. I drifted over to the bathroom, and I started screaming. "Oh shit, he got into the pills!"

I was so angry at Steve. Marcus was running a fever at this point, and we put him in a tub of cold water before rushing him to the emergency room. My baby stayed in the hospital for three days. I almost lost him. I lied and said that he ingested some of my pills. In my mind, how would they know that it was Steve who mixed up my pills because he needed pill bottles to put the crack in? What really hurt me was that he came to the hospital with two or three of his people, his boys, his workers. "Hey, I lied for you. I almost lost my child!" I whispered to him.

But at this point, he was so consumed with just everything that was going on—for one thing, the Feds had been questioning people about him. As for the fact that he didn't seem to understand he had just put my innocent baby in a dangerous position, well, it crushed me.

There were good times with Steve, but if I am going to be very honest, there were times I didn't want to leave him with my kids because I never knew whether the police were going to show up and grab him. I knew he trusted me to bring half of a key of crack cocaine across the border from Georgia to South Carolina, but I began to understand the risk, and the more I understood it, the more I resented doing it.

I didn't feel threatened at any time by Steve, but there were times during our relationship that I didn't want to sell drugs anymore. So I started putting money aside, because I could see things changing.

After living the life, by late 1991, state charges were filed against him for selling drugs in the projects. There were also federal charges pending for selling to undercover agents in nearby Seneca. By now, he was on the run. Meanwhile, I was pregnant with his baby, DeAndre, who we later called Nuk.

We began to argue more and more because Steve was never at home. At some point, Steve wrecked my car. Then, the repo man took his Mustang—his pride and joy. MC Hammer was one of his favorite rappers, and Steve had the words "Can't Touch This" etched on the back of it. Eventually, he hired a lawyer, and that's where all his money went.

Life was good, and then it wasn't. Although we were still in love, we sometimes had heated arguments. Most of the disagreements were sparked by him promising to do something, or get something for the kids, but disappearing for a day or two. But it was that life we lived, me taking the kids to hotels when he was on the run.

* * *

DeAndre was born June 6, 1992. He was huge, with a face like mine. Steve showed up at the hospital with his goons, and he was only there for a short time. He picked his son up, showing him off to his entourage. "Look at my boy," and then he was gone. I had delivered his ten-pound baby, and this man was only there for two hours.

A few months later, Steve took me with him to his lawyer's office. His lawyer, Mr. Lusk, was a fat old white guy, and he came in sweaty and breathing hard. Steve gave him the last five thousand dollars we had. He told the lawyer that he's done running, but he needed the man's help. We left the office, and we weren't two steps out of the building before hearing "Get down! Get down!" Members of a police commando team swarmed behind us, from around the building and from rooftops, with guns and rifles pointed at us. I had a pistol to the back of my head. Instantly I dropped down, Steve hit the ground, and as fast as they came, they took Steve and left me there. Steve was in prison on the federal charge for a month before he was bailed out by his mother, Shirley Ann, on a surety bond. When we got to the apartment in Creekwood, Steve and I decided to take out insurance policies: I made Daddy the beneficiary of mine and he made his mother his.

* * *

A short time later, Steve was called back to the office of his attorney, Mr. Lusk, in nearby Anderson, for what the lawyer called evidence collecting. After a few minutes of waiting, Mr. Lusk walked into the room with a recorder in his hand.

"Steve, the prosecutor's office has sent me over this recording," he began. "They say they can hear you selling drugs to some lady."

"What lady?" Steve asked. Lusk began to play the tape.

"I need an eight ball," we could hear a woman say, referring to a slab of crack worth one hundred dollars. The female voice sounded familiar, but I couldn't place it immediately. If I was the slightest bit unsure, I knew exactly who it was the moment I heard my favorite little cousin Montez say, "Mama, I'm hungry," in the background. The woman's voice replied, "Take your narrow ass up there to either one of them doors. You know somebody up there cooking."

My heart stopped. I slowly turned to Steve. "I know who that lady is," I said.

"Who is it, Brina?"

That female voice on the tape was no one other than Aunt Louise. "Those doors" she referred to were likely mine or Missy's, where our family knew they could always find a meal.

"It's Aunt Louise," was all I could say. This woman, my mama's only sister, had cooperated with the police and had worn a wire to help incriminate Steve.

When we got outside Lusk's office, Steve shook his head in disbelief as I begged him not to kill her. "Damn, Brina, your auntie set me up," I remember him saying. "How she gonna be the one that save my life and then turn around and try to take my life?"

It was true: more than a year earlier, my aunt did indeed save Steve's life. At the time, our relationship was new and we were still learning about each other, which meant we would argue a lot about things the other did. I, for one, was getting annoyed with Steve staying up all night and coming in and out of the house. After one heated argument, he jumped in his Mustang and left. That was unusual, because normally he'd just go to another room and return to bed later. After forty minutes of no Steve, I got in my car to look for him. There he was in the parking lot of Hardee's Restaurant with a police officer. I still don't know why he was pulled over, but Steve seemed jittery, was walking back and forth, and having trouble speaking.

From a distance, I could see Steve chewing on something plastic and spitting out blood. The more he spit, the more the officer asked him questions. Then, it hit me: Steve was trying to chew and swallow the crack he had in the car and was likely overdosing. The officer left, probably to get some backup, so I jumped out of my car, grabbed a container of Clorox bleach from my trunk, and poured it on the ground everywhere Steve spit. I then dashed into Steve's car. "We gotta leave now, Steve. They're coming back."

We sped to my aunt Louise's double-wide. I knew she would know what to do with Steve. By now, he was really acting crazy; he was in full-blown panic mode and stripping down to his underwear because he was feeling hot. Aunt Louise forced Steve to drink milk, which would help coat his stomach, as she tried to figure out how much crack he had swallowed. The milk didn't seem to work at all, so I rushed him to the hospital in Seneca. By then, Steve was acting even more erratic, and I was afraid they'd discover he was overdosing on crack, so we fled home before the doctor could even see him. I soon discovered Steve had swallowed an entire ounce of crack, and the only thing that likely saved his life was the milk Aunt Louise forced him to drink.

Back outside the lawyer's office in Anderson, I continued to beg Steve to not harm Aunt Louise until he agreed not to.

But unbeknownst to me, Steve would convince Aunt Louise to leave South Carolina and stay with his mother, Shirley Ann, in Georgia until his case blew over. Aunt Louise would hide out in Shirley Ann's basement for two weeks, until she got nervous and called Poopie and Missy, who believed Steve and Shirley Ann had kidnapped their mother. Worse, they thought I was in on it. It was the dumbest thing for Steve to do, but I don't believe he had tried to kidnap my aunt, but rather panicked and thought if Louise was hidden out of the way in Georgia, then she wouldn't be a problem.

* * *

A few weeks later Steve and I went to see a Clemson University game—by then, my brother Hummie was a huge star on the field. Then we drove down to Georgia for a function Steve's mother wanted us to attend. At that moment in time, in November 1992, we had barely any money—I had to do my own hair for his mom's function—but we were happy because we felt free. He was facing a hundred years in prison, but at least we weren't on the run anymore. We got all dressed up and spent the night at a hotel.

Early that Sunday morning we started making our way back home. I remember it was drizzling. We stopped at a Dunkin' Donuts—Steve loved their donuts. It was like a moment where nothing mattered because we were finally back together, we had our baby DeAndre waiting for us back home, and the rest of our lives ahead of us—I was twenty-two, and he was twenty-five.

We got back on the road, and it was still drizzling. The donuts were in a bag at my feet. At one point Steve changed lanes. He asked me to get him a donut, and I bent down to reach for the bag, but suddenly there was a big pressure on me. He hadn't said anything, but he just hit me in the chest. He had lost control of the car. It hydroplaned, and then went up in the air, flipped three times, and crashed down on the guardrail on Steve's side. The top was smashed in, the front was folded up, and we were trapped. I started to hear a strange noise, and then something was hitting me in my chest and on my face.

It was his blood.

It was streaming all over me from his organs. I had a big knot on my head from hitting the dashboard, and I put my hand on his chest. He was still not saying anything. I was calling his name. Then I heard people cutting open the car.

At the hospital they put me in a neck brace and told me I had a concussion. I heard Steve screaming my name. To calm him, they wheeled me over to his room, three doors down. At the edge of the curtain by his bed, I was calling, "Steve, just give them Shirley Ann's number!" They were trying to get his mother's contact number, but he refused until he saw me.

The ER surgeon came over to me to tell me Steve would need emergency surgery. "He has a collapsed lung. Ma'am, we've got to take him now."

I turned to Steve and said, "I'll be right here when you get out."

After the doctors were done with me, I sat alone in the waiting room as his family rushed in. Soon twenty people were sitting around, and everybody came in asking me the same thing: *What happened?* I had to repeat the story over and over because at that point, all I knew was I reached down to get donuts and he hit me in the chest. I didn't know that the car flipped. I didn't know that it came down on the guardrail. I didn't know all this until later. All I knew was that something bad had happened and when I woke up from hitting my head, the blood from his organs was spraying on me.

Some of my family arrived, too—my brother Hummie and his wife came; my mother came, and so did my father and his new wife. Steve was in surgery for thirteen hours. His mother and I took turns going into see him: Steve was connected to so many machines but was responsive enough to scribble on a piece of paper if we put a pen in his hand. But every day his health declined just a little. We'd go back the next day and he'd be semiconscious or no longer blinking his eyes or trying to talk a little bit, or he'd sip water one day but then he couldn't do even that the next day.

After a few days my family had to go, but Shirley Ann promised to take care of me. "I'm going to make sure she's straight," she told my family, but it was a lie.

As Steve's condition worsened, his family needed to blame someone and concocted a story in their heads that I was the reason Steve was fighting for his life on that hospital bed. They assumed that we were arguing in the car. Truth is, as the Feds closed in, we *did* argue a lot. Things weren't perfect. We were going through hard times. We were broke, and, before then, Steve had been on the run. Here I am at twenty-two with three babies, trying to figure out life, but that day we were still glowing from a heated lovemaking session in the hotel the night before. Still, Steve's family assumed that we had to have been fighting, which caused him to be distracted and that was how he wrecked the car. I couldn't live with myself if I had known I had anything to do with this tragedy. The truth is the last days before the accident were good. Steve was no longer running, and we were happy to be together.

But Steve's family wasn't there with us, and so they had their own ideas. One day, Tamara, Steve's sister, along with another cousin, came to me at the hospital. "We got to hide you because my brother Anthony is coming here to kill you," Tamara said.

"What the fuck? Like, what's going on?" I was bewildered.

Now, mind you, I'm by myself. My family had all gone back home, and Steve's family won't even talk to me or feed me. I had to build up the nerve to ask a nice white family I was talking to for five dollars, so I could buy food.

We found a dark industrial closet in the hospital for me to hide in. Hours go by, and I don't know if Anthony is lurking the halls ready to kill me, because no one ever came back to get me. The worst fear that I ever had was opening that door and seeing the man coming toward me. Hours passed before I got my nerve up to return to the waiting room. Steve's family was sitting in the waiting area, eating like nothing ever happened. Anthony, Steve's younger brother, was nowhere in sight. If they were trying to get rid of me, it didn't work. I vowed I would not leave the hospital. However, everyone, including me, believed Anthony would have killed me if he had a chance.

* * *

This all happened in 1992, the year the movie *The Bodyguard* came out. I was in Steve's room when Whitney Houston appeared on television, belting out her hit song "I Will Always Love You." Steve pointed to the television and then to me. He was telling me he'd always love me, but was he also telling me something else? It was a moment I'd never forget, but it also had me worried that maybe this was the end.

The next morning after the closet incident is when his organs started swelling. Whatever the surgery was supposed to do, it didn't work. I began to accept the possibility that he wouldn't make it. There was one day that we all went into his room together because they knew his health was rapidly failing. The first thing we noticed was how his body had begun to bulge.

Shirley Ann pulled back the covers from his legs. His testicles had swelled as big as grapefruits. I reached out for his hand and could see it was twice the normal size.

I went into the hospital chapel, which was empty, and not even knowing how to pray, I just stood there and talked to God.

On the seventh night, we were all sitting around, preparing to go see him again the next morning. Me and Shirley Ann were the only ones in the waiting room that next day. It was her turn to go, and then I was going to go in around noon. Minutes after she walked toward his room, she returned. She had a blank look on her face. "Steve is gone."

I backed away and shook my head violently and tried to run into his room, but someone blocked me because I couldn't go back there until they cleaned him up. "There's no way!"

I cried and I cried. Shirley Ann didn't console me, and I didn't console her.

I called Frances, DeAndre's godmother, who was watching six-month-old DeAndre at the time. I asked her to put the phone up to his ear.

"Baby, your dad went up to heaven, and Daddy loved you very much, but he's gone," I whispered into the receiver.

I felt like the universe was playing an ugly trick on me. How was it the one man I loved, the man who deeply loved me, was dead at twenty-five?

Frances got back on the phone. "I had a feeling when you called me this morning, that this would be the call."

I called her every day to talk to Nuk, even though he was a baby, but I wanted him to hear my voice.

"What is he doing?" I asked.

"Just staring at the phone, trying to eat it."

"Just tell him I love him," I said.

Frances was and still is a huge part of DeAndre's life. "I'm so sorry," she said.

By the time I finished making my calls, someone from the hospital told me that I could go in and see Steve's body. I wasn't nervous. In fact, I didn't feel anything. Shirley walked out the room and said, "You can go on in."

He was lying there, but still swollen. I grabbed his hand and just sat down. I started talking to him, telling him that I was going to take care of DeAndre.

"I'm mad at you, Steve, for leaving me." I looked over at his still body. "Remember that last movie we watched?" I'm talking to him as if he can hear me because I felt like he could. "Remember that last movie we watched with Whitney Houston, you told me I will always love you. I will always love you, too.

"I know we got a baby so I'm gonna make sure he's okay. I'll make sure he's straight. You don't have to worry about Nuk. You don't have to worry about the baby, he's going to be okay."

I sat right there and held his hand. I think I touched his forehead. Although he was gone, he was still warm to the touch. Hummie and his wife came to get me. I made it to the car and dropped on the floor of the back seat, where I laid in a fetal position, crying the entire way home.

* * *

Back in Clemson, I was like a walking zombie. I was able to pick out a black-and-white dress for the funeral and bought Nuk an outfit, but I didn't have the energy for anything else. A bunch of my family members attended Steve's funeral, including cousins I didn't expect to attend. Mama was there, of course, as was Daddy and his new wife. Poopie and Missy were no-shows, and nobody came from my aunt Louise's side.

Frances, Nuk's godmother, held DeAndre the entire time because everybody was under the assumption that I was not in my right state of mind and would do something rash, harming myself or my baby. Truth be told, I was at my lowest point.

The day before the funeral, Shirley Ann asked me to stay at her house in Georgia, and I said yes. I slept in the bed that Steve and I always slept in. My family had decided I could go to Shirley Ann's, but the baby wasn't going to stay with me in that house. My mama, my daddy, and Frances were all in agreement that if I asked to have the baby, they would tell me no. They made every excuse in the world to keep me from having DeAndre while at Steve's mama's house.

Even when we were all at Shirley Ann's house getting ready for the funeral, and later getting into the cars, I didn't have my baby. I walked into the funeral with Steve's family. Now mind you, I'm terrified because of the incident at the hospital, where I was told Anthony was coming for me. I was also in despair because the love of my life was gone. I sat numb at the funeral, listening to people moan and cry all around me. I don't think I took my eyes off the casket at all; I just stared because I was in disbelief.

As traditional Black families do, the family closed the casket at some point, and I screamed and screamed. I don't remember what I said, but this shriek burst out of my throat without me even trying. I still see Steve laying there and it hurts to this day.

What I remember next is that we all went out to the cemetery, which was near the church, but out in the woods.

I looked around and stood among everyone thinking to myself, *He don't want to be here. Why did they put him in the woods? Why did they put him out here by himself in the woods and the dirt? You got his insurance money and you couldn't put a headstone on the man's grave?* To this day, they never gave Steve a headstone. My baby is still out there in the woods by himself.

* * *

After Steve's death, I might have had twenty dollars to my name. All of that running, all of them drugs, everything was gone. I didn't even have a phone, so I had to walk to a neighbor's house to use her phone to call Shirley Ann, because she promised in the hospital that she would help me with DeAndre. Here I am, trying to get her to live up to her promise when she would make excuses and blow me off.

I was the one who told Steve's money-loving mother at the hospital that Steve and I took out insurance policies after he had got out of the federal prison. And because Steve died in an accident, Shirley Ann was paid double, a hundred thousand dollars, while I, the mother of his child, was left penniless.

I kept calling, and finally she seemed to give in. "If you come down here, I'll give you a little something."

When I got the nerve to go see her, Angela, my best friend, who I met in Creekwood, drove me to Canton, Georgia. This was all during the period where I'm grieving, depressed over Steve, and still trying to figure out how I'm going to take care of these three kids. When we pulled up to her house, I noticed there were two new Cadillacs in the yard, one off-white and one black. We walked into her house and sat at the table. Shirley Ann noticed a ring on my finger, one Steve melted down from some gold he had and gave to me.

Shirley Ann stared at the ring. "Is that Steve's ring?"

I told her it wasn't, but she knew I was lying. She then told me that the only way that she would give me three hundred dollars is if I gave her the ring. I gave her the ring, and she gave me three hundred dollars—out of a hundred thousand. Angela and I barely had gas to get back home, so I took the money.

Angela was so mad and to this day calls Shirley Ann that "greedy bitch."

Ironically, the same insurance man who sold us the policy later told me he would have fought for me to have the money since I was Steve's common-law wife, but I was just so naïve, I didn't know that I should have investigated it.

When I understood Shirley Ann wasn't going help me out financially like I knew she promised, I gave up. I didn't go back to Georgia again.

I was now by myself, on my own.

CHAPTER 10

The Woman Who Just Does Not Care

Everything in our apartment in Creekwood was exactly how we'd left it, because we jetted out in a rush. There was Steve's favorite pair of pants on the floor, the box of S-curl on his side of the bathroom sink. I could even smell his scent, a manly smell that to this day I can never describe. Having to enter the apartment after Steve's death was just as horrible as it could get. Everything in it reminded me of him, even the silence. Steve had a severe case of insomnia; he'd walk through the house late into the night, grabbing something from the fridge or turning on the television. When he was alive, his footsteps in the night irritated me to no end, but now that he was gone, and I no longer heard them, I felt a void deep within.

* * *

I was experiencing my first bout with depression, but I didn't know that at the time. Angela would come to the house to sit by the bed with me.

"I want to get up, but I can't," I said to her. "Something's just weighing me down."

I was depressed and turning into someone I no longer recognized, a mother unable to take into consideration that her three children needed her. Not to mention that my youngest was only six months old and needed his mother more than ever. But I couldn't do anything for my baby, so he stayed with his godmother, Frances.

I was so absorbed by the hurt, the shock, and the pain of Steve not being there, I couldn't even get up to feed my other two babies. Most times, Kesha, who was four, and Boodia, who was three, were in the living room with Mama, but they would drift over to my bedroom door or into my room to ask for a cookie or something. I gave them just enough attention before shooing them away. At best, I'd lift my head from the pillow to say, "Go ask your grandma."

Then I'd return to my crying. I wanted to feel sorry for myself, and for the pain to go away. Although I was tired all the time, Kesha and Boodia were just as happy and lively as ever; in fact, the only time they were still was when they were watching my brother Hummie on television. By then, he was a huge star at Clemson. So the kids would stand in front of the TV, cheering Uncle Hummie. "Uncle Hummie on TV," they'd shout. "Yeah!"

Every few seconds they'd point to the television, because in their minds any football player running across the screen was Uncle Hummie.

* * *

After weeks of living in the bed I shared with Steve, one day Angela literally dragged me off the mattress and forced me into the tub.

I leaned back against the hard surface, a memory flashing before me of the two of us, me and Steve, three days before the accident. We were sitting in a movie theater sharing our popcorn, laughing and feeling free and in love. We were still facing the unknown, but it was like we had started all over again, from the beginning. It was late November 1992, and we were watching *The Bodyguard*. The film was a big deal that year, and we were just happy to be able to be in a theater together.

Angela's voice interrupted my memory. "Brina, I'm going to ask you again. What do you want me to bring you?"

"I want my CD player." I started playing Whitney Houston's song, "I Will Always Love You," and sang it at the top of my lungs. Then I'd cry. I couldn't believe I had three kids. I couldn't believe Steve was gone. I'd scream and scream; I didn't care that people were coming in and out of the apartment. I would get out the tub, turn off my music, and go back in the room and lay in the bed. I did this for months.

At first, Angela started washing me because I couldn't do it myself. Once Angela sat me down and said, "You have children to live for, you just going to give up? It don't work like that. Get your ass out of this bed. We are going in the living room."

Truth be told, Angela kept coming to the house and it got on my last nerves. I didn't want to eat; I didn't want to feel anything. All I wanted was to just lay there, and I wanted Steve to come back. Angela would bring food to the bedroom; she'd set my pillow up on the bed and prop me up, and we'd talk. After a few weeks, I got to where I would wash my own body and dress myself. Eventually I made my way to the living room, but that took months. My children were innocent, I told myself. They didn't know what was going on, and they were missing Steve, too. I knew that I had to get it together for these babies.

* * *

Alone, I wasn't making ends meet. I borrowed cash when I could. Some people heard about Steve's death and would come and give me some of the money that they owed him. There were two or three guys, I don't even know who they were, but they would come to the house and say, "Hey, Steve, he was a good man. You know, I owed him three hundred dollars. Here, I just want to give it to you."

That happened a few times, which helped get me through, but I was still dead broke.

Every time I walked over to the neighbor's house to use her phone, a young man named Julius, who I eventually befriended, was there. I didn't have any business getting into a relationship with him, but I was feeling defeated, desperate, and lonely.

I was now twenty-three, and Julius was nineteen. He was always around Creekwood, just hanging at my neighbor's apartment with his friends. Julius would drink liquor, play music, and smoke with a group of young men. If Steve was alive, I would never have looked Julius's way. In fact, Julius and his friends had always made advances when they caught me without Steve, but I never responded. However, now that I was in all this pain, Julius began to look different. I knew I could have picked any one of those boys, but I chose Julius simply because he was the only one without a girlfriend.

Down South, when someone is challenged in the looks area, we say they have a good heart. Julius had popped eyes and a large nose; he wasn't short or tall, and he dipped snuff and drank eight balls, which is nothing but malt liquor. He smoked weed, and I mean a lot of weed. He didn't have a job when we first got together, but he was a good booty call. He'd come and go, which was perfect, because I didn't want no man in the house with my kids and certainly didn't want his clothes in my closet.

*   *   *

Nearly six months went by, and we were still playing this game. While I didn't love Julius, I liked him way more than I thought I would. But there would come a day, as it did with damn near every man I knew except for Steve, when I nearly killed him. It started with me and my cousin Missy getting our hair done. I returned home and noticed Julius had left that morning and took his clothes with him. We had started telling each other our whereabouts, but this day that wasn't the case. By now, I knew that Julius's baby mama had moved into Creekwood, and so I'd warned him not to be messing around with her. Meanwhile, he was angry with me that day because somebody told him I was messing around with somebody else, which wasn't true. I walked down the street and asked neighbors if they had seen him. I investigated a little further, and sure enough, I observed him all hugged up with the ex-girlfriend. I rushed back to my apartment and marched into the kitchen, where I scrambled through the drawer until I found a long kitchen knife. I slid it in the back pocket of my jeans and bolted out the door. Within a quick minute I confronted Julius. "What are you doing?"

He stared right through me. "I got my shit from the apartment."

"Oh, so you just got your shit and left. So you're not coming back?"

He shook his head. "No."

"He didn't stutter," the woman said.

"Listen, bitch, I'm not talking to you. Stay out of this. It has nothing to do with you."

Then Julius said, "I moved in with her."

I was calm but seething. "Oh, you did? Okay."

I looked at him and her. In my mind, I thought, *You about to get fucked up.* That's when he called me a "hoe."

"I got your hoe . . . bitch," I said, pulling out my knife and chasing him up a hill. I was a former track star, so he wasn't going to outrun me.

His baby mama screamed, "Leave him alone!"

I turned my head toward her. "You stay right there, bitch. You going to be next!"

I caught Julius and, in what was a blind, unthinking rage, stabbed him in the back. He screamed and dropped to the ground, face-first. And I didn't just stab him—I stuck the knife in him until it couldn't go anymore. When I pulled it out, I could feel his flesh slide over the blade. For a moment, I watched him scream and squirm. The police would say later that had it been eight centimeters to the left, it would have punctured his heart.

What had I done? What had become of me that I nearly killed this man?

Poor Julius didn't deserve any of that. He was a good guy. He was crazy about DeAndre, stepping in as a father figure to the baby. He probably had every right to take his stuff that day. I didn't only treat him badly, which I certainly did, but I had turned into someone desperate, someone who no longer thought rationally about her circumstances or her future. It's a blur to me now, but I'm sure this rage, which had everything to do with Julius wanting to leave me, was complicated by all the pain that had been done to me over ten years, everything that no one person should have to face—the rape, the beatings, the killing of my brother, my mother's drug use, and, of course, Steve's death.

Minutes after I stabbed him, I went looking for the baby mama, but she was gone. After what would later happen to me, I can't help but think back to this moment in time: I know what rage feels like, I know what it feels like to be at a place where you just don't care if you go to prison or not. I stabbed this man, and I was looking around for his woman, like a murderer, a killer. What I had become was the woman who just did not care anymore. I knew how to lie, manipulate, steal, and deceive. And I was damn sure going to get them, whoever *they* were, before *they* got me. All my mistakes erupt from the rage inside of me, the rage I had for everyone around me. And low self-esteem. Low self-esteem will put you in a place where you might consider yourself nonjudgmental. But sometimes you need to judge. I never developed that kind of radar. It was like if you show me any type of emotion or compassion, and, God forbid, you say you love me, you got me. So it didn't matter what you did, or where you come from, or how you treated me. Because you say you love me, you got me for life. I had befriended Julius, but then stabbed him when I found out he was cheating with another girl in the projects.

So after I stabbed Julius, I returned to my apartment, to the same home I shared with Steve, laid the knife down on my nightstand, and sat there.

My mother burst into my bedroom. "What happened?"

I said calmly, "I stabbed Julius."

She went into cleanup mode. "Give me the knife."

I shook my head. "No, Mama."

A few minutes later, I heard her talking to the police at the door. "She's not here. I don't know what you're talking about."

I picked up the knife and strolled down the hall to give it to the police. I turned around and put my hands behind my back. They arrested me for assault and battery with intent to kill, the same crime my own attacker would be charged with years later—and they locked me up in jail for the night. I no longer gave a damn.

Julius was collateral damage, as they say. By now the rage was eating me up from the inside, and I must have felt the need to turn all this anger, all this frustration, against someone else—preferably a man. I couldn't bear to be alone with so much pain.

It so happened that there was an insurance policy on the car Steve was driving, which entitled me to five thousand dollars after the accident. My lawyer took the whole darn check to defend me. But he gave me a piece of advice: he begged me to try to befriend Julius and to get him up in front of the court to decline to press charges—and that he didn't give a hoot how I did it. So I went back to the projects, even though I had been evicted after my arrest and was trespassing while looking for Julius. I kept sneaking in at night trying to find him. One night I rolled up on him as he was outside hanging with his boys. I asked if he could get in the car and talk. Of course, he said no.

"Don't you miss the kids?" I asked. "I love you."

Mentioning the kids must have tugged at his heart, because he got into the car. I told him about the insurance money and promised to buy him a pair of Timberlands and a leather jacket, if he'd just move in with me to show we're back together. I had no money, but somehow I got the Timberlands, and my aunt Louise boosted a leather jacket. I had a triple-wide trailer in the trailer park in Clemson all set up close by, which is where I was living and where Julius would also come back to live.

I was facing twenty years in jail, which was my wake-up call. When you know you might lose your children and your freedom, everything in your body comes alive. I wanted to work. I wanted to keep Julius with me, so he'd vouch for me, and I never asked him another question about that girl. I didn't give a shit. I simply wanted to live and keep my freedom.

As we awaited the trial, I treated him like a king. I was getting money here or there, and when there was extra, I'd get him what he wanted: eight balls, cigarettes, weed. I would even drop him off at his friend's house sometimes, so he could hang out with his homeboy, and I'd pick him up. I cooked for him. Then we started working together at Dayco, an automotive plant in Easley. Julius would give me his whole check. That's why I said, to this day, I have nothing bad to say about him, because he was crazy about my kids, and he would contribute to our household. All he wanted was forty dollars, just enough money to get a bag of weed, some cigarettes, and some beer. After six months, we moved to an apartment in the nearby town of Central.

Months later, Julius showed up in court and told the judge that he loved me, that he didn't want anything bad to happen to me and would not testify. The court dropped the charges. That same night I packed up all his stuff, while I concocted a story that I needed time, and I think he should move in with his parents for just a week.

"I tell you what, if you just go there, give me a week or two," I said. "Then, I'll be coming to get you."

I never went back and got that man, and thankfully, he let me be.

CHAPTER 11

Terry "Hummie" Allen Smith

In 1994, two years after Steve's death, things were finally starting to look up. I had sort of swindled myself out of a twenty-year prison sentence. Maybe *swindled* isn't exactly what it was with Julius. The way I had attacked him was awful, but I was still very much a captive of my own rage and anger, a product of my childhood experiences and the many disappointments in my still-young life. I did what I had to do to stay out of jail and keep my children. And so, I focused my energy on three things: creating a happy life for the kids, keeping my good job at Dayco, and helping my brother Hummie finish his last year at Clemson and preparing him for the NFL draft.

My home life was relatively stable by now—I was doing well at work— and so I fixed my attention very much on Hummie. A year earlier, in 1993, he had caught the winning touchdown at the Peach Bowl—a famous play that became a historic moment in Clemson football. Despite the glory and local fame surrounding him, Hummie was my younger brother and I wanted to make sure he knew I was there for him, too. I rarely missed a Clemson game—even if I had to sit alone among eighty-five thousand other Clemson Tiger fans in Death Valley.

I'd scream at the top of my lungs once Hummie emerged out of the bus and rushed down the hill onto the football field. Sometimes, though, I'd look down onto the field at my brother and I wouldn't see Hummie the star wide receiver, but instead I'd see Hummie as a little boy picking up trash after a Clemson game with Dilly, and that's when I'd imagine what would it feel like if grown-up Dilly was sitting next to me cheering our brother on.

Hummie didn't have Dilly, but he did find a brother at Clemson.

Rodney Blunt was Hummie's roommate and would become his best friend. They were both small-town boys (Rodney was from Pensacola, Florida) and highly recruited Clemson football players; Rodney was a running back and Hummie was a receiver. But my brother could have played football for any college of his choosing because he was that dern good.

Hummie and Rodney clicked immediately, and they did everything together. When they each got their first Pell grant, they went on a country-boy shopping spree, buying snakeskin boots and their first wallets. Eventually, on the field, both gained over 2,000 yards by their senior year. And they even got married and had kids at about the same time.

* * *

From the first day of Clemson practice, everyone knew Hummie was going to be a star wide receiver. Still, the fact that he could have gone anywhere yet decided to stay home at Clemson turned him into an instant hometown hero. Quiet, respectful, and a gentleman, my brother was the kind of boy who always said, "Yes, ma'am" and "No, ma'am." He never got into fights at Clemson, and no one had a bad thing to say about him. Rodney may have been the self-proclaimed "crazy one," but Hummie, according to Rodney, "was the serious one. Hummie didn't even start drinking until his junior year."

Rodney also said something I'd never forget: "I've never seen anybody that beat their body down on the field like Hummie and then have a smile on his face."

* * *

People flocked around Hummie like he was a celebrity, especially at Daniel High School, where he and Rodney frequented the games to see the high school boys play. Sometimes Mama would be there with some guy. But when Hummie spotted her switching around or leaving with a man, his whole demeanor would change. He'd stop cheering or cutting up with Rodney and become quiet and focused on the game.

Of course, Mama was just being Mama. She had a big butt and was still young and beautiful. I believed Hummie understood all that about her, her faults and all, but he never said a bad word about her. And although he loved her, he'd let me go on and on, complaining about the drugs and her most recent antics, but he'd never join in; he'd just listen.

Truth be told, Hummie was protective of me, too. For example, soon after he entered Clemson, he made a rule that I could not date any of his football teammates. "Man, don't mess with none of my team," he said. "Don't mess with nobody on campus."

At the time, I thought it was a reasonable request. "Cool," I said. "I have two children now. I don't have time for that."

Despite my promise, I started sneaking around with Clemson's quarterback. At the time I was nineteen and estranged from my ex-husband, Mark, and I just wanted to have fun. How would he find out anyway? Well, one day me and the quarterback were going up to his dorm room, walking up a back stairwell, when I looked up to see Hummie coming down the same stairs. If I could have melted and disappeared right then and there, I would have. I didn't know what to say or what to do when he looked at me and asked what was I doing.

"Oh hey," I said, trying to not let my embarrassment betray me.

I could see the disappointment in his eyes, and I regretted my actions for many years: I had not fully learned yet that breaking promises to family meant keeping secrets from them. And keeping secrets, as I would painfully learn, is what tears a family apart.

The thing is, Hummie loved family and football—those were the loves of his life, and in a way maybe both would come to disappoint him. Rodney said one other thing that haunts me. "Your father was there for Hummie but not for everyone, and Hummie felt responsible for that. Hummie put a lot of weight on his own shoulders."

It would not be a stretch for me to say Hummie had tens of thousands of fans while in college, but his two biggest fans lived in my household. Nothing was more exciting for Kesha, who was six during Hummie's last year at Clemson in 1994, and Boodia, who was five, than to get ready to see Hummie in Death Valley. Saturday mornings were loud, with the two of them jumping up and down and making a ruckus on the couch, singing, "We gonna see Uncle Hummie!" After breakfast, I'd lay out their Clemson outfits, including an orange-and-white cheerleading skirt for Kesha, which she hated but I loved, and a tiny orange jersey for Boodia, with the number 24, Hummie's number.

The excitement still washes over me when I think about entering Death Valley. The cheers, the people, the energy. Back then, we always had good seats, but the children liked to sit on my lap so they could see their uncle when he'd touch the rock—Howard's Rock—and rush down the Hill.

After the game, there was a designated place where fans, family, and the media waited for the team to exit the locker room. As the players emerged dressed in their business suits, everyone standing around always broke into cheers and applause. I'd have to hold my little ones back while Hummie greeted his fans and talked to the media. Finally, he'd get to us, lifting the kids high up in his strong arms.

* * *

By 1994, the same year Hummie graduated from Clemson, I was excelling as a lead supervisor at Dayco. I devoted myself to raising Kesha, Boodia, and little Nuk. I loved being their mama, determined as I was to be anything other than how my mother was to me. I was proud that I could provide for my kids outside of the drug life, without having to fear the police all the time. Over the years, I'd run around with the kids, getting them into Little League and every other sport we could find. Kesha loved track, and Boodia and Nuk took to basketball and football.

I was determined to stay close to my brother Hummie, but again he was a distant sort of person, and he was also having problems of his own. As you might recall, because of a knee injury, Hummie hadn't been selected in the NFL draft, but he was signed as a free agent by the Indianapolis Colts. One weekend in 1994, he came home to Clemson to visit. As usual, the first thing he'd do was go hang with our cousins Poopie and Squeenchie—all three had finished college on athletic scholarships. Even after that day in the car when Dilly was killed, or maybe because of that, the three of them remained close. Throughout high school, they kept their football numbers: Hummie was number 1, Poopie was number 2, and Squeenchie was 3. Although Squeenchie grew to be six feet and secured a scholarship to play football at Newberry College, the adults in the family always said he was born weighing three pounds with a hole in his heart. We were never sure if it was true or just a family tale.

However, on the day Hummie came to visit, the three of them were running up and down the court at Edwards Middle School, playing a game of pickup basketball, when one of them scored. As they started to race up the court, Poopie and Hummie realized Squeenchie had dropped to the ground. They ran back to his side to see what was wrong with him, but he wasn't responsive. And while being rushed to the hospital, he was pronounced dead, suffering, according to relatives, from a sudden cardiac arrest.

Hummie had watched his baby brother die eleven years earlier and now his favorite cousin, who was in the car with him when Dilly was killed, fell dead himself at age twenty-four.

Squeenchie's sudden death did something mentally to Hummie, because when he went back to Indianapolis he didn't show up for a few practices and basically quit. Although the Colts eventually took him back, the injury from his Clemson days was still plaguing one knee. He reinjured it, and the Colts cut him completely in 1996.

Daddy rented a U-Haul and drove the entire family—Hummie; Debra, Hummie's wife; his baby daughter, Daejha; and his young son, Terrance, to Orangeburg, South Carolina, where Hummie's wife was from. They only stayed there very briefly before Debra decided she preferred to move to Atlanta to be near her sister. My brother needed to find some work, though football was the only job he knew. He went through two jobs, but neither of them stuck. For a while, he worked at a telemarketing company making about thirty-five thousand dollars a year, which was a blow after making hundreds of thousands in the NFL.

Over the span of a decade, Hummie went from high school hero to superstar standout in Clemson, to now living in Atlanta trying to figure out how to make ends meet.

* * *

I can't really say what's going on behind someone else's closed doors, but I did know that Hummie argued a lot with his wife, who insisted on them getting counseling—something that a lot of Black men, especially then, just wouldn't do. And so Hummie was all on his own trying to figure out why everything was starting to go so wrong.

My brother came home from work one day to a pitch-black, empty apartment: Debra had taken the children and the furniture, which only sent him into a deep depression. His job wasn't working out and neither was his marriage; now he couldn't see his kids. He was separating from his wife and could barely take care of himself financially. Worst of all, his dream of playing in the NFL had faded away. Daddy would talk to him, I would talk to him, Rodney and Poopie would also try to talk to him, but nothing seemed to work.

One day, he must have been outside of Debra's apartment a little too long when he was arrested for trespassing and thrown in jail. He rang me all night: "Call Debra and see if she'll drop the charges."

I finally talked to her, but my phone kept beeping—Hummie was on the other line.

"Girl, it's him. What do you want me to tell him?" I asked her.

And she'd say, "I'm not gonna drop the charges."

"Just think about it," I'd say.

The moment I hung up, Hummie called me again. "What'd she say?"

This was a man who had never even jaywalked and did everything by the book. I'm the rebellious one. Tell me to go left, I go right. Tell me to stand up, I'm going to sit down. But this was all out of character for Hummie.

After he signed himself out of jail the next day, I started to wire him fifty dollars periodically because that was all I had. Hummie continued to talk to Debra, trying to rebuild his family and see his kids, which she allowed him to do.

He called me one day very excited. "Debra is going to let me take her out for her birthday. I need another fifty dollars, sis. You got it?"

I could hear the hope in his voice. "I'm on my way to Western Union to send it to you."

The next morning, he called even more excited, explaining they had sex and he believed he was about to get his family back.

For a moment, I let myself get happy, too, because my brother needed a break.

But the next day when he went by Debra's home, she told him that what happened between them the night before was a moment of passion, but their situation hadn't changed.

He seemed particularly low when he called that day; it was like all the air had been sucked out of his soul. "Hey sis, I went to go see the kids, but Debra stopped me at the door and reminded me I was on no trespass and that I needed to call her if I wanted to stop by."

From that day on, I decided I needed to check on him, so we began talking nearly every day. One evening, he called, sounding like a completely different person.

"Just calling to see what you're doing," he said.

"Same old thing, you know, just getting off work. Man, these kids getting on my damn nerves."

He normally would have laughed at that but instead was silent for a long time. Finally, he said, "Brina, I'm tired."

I rushed through the apartment picking up the children's toys as I held the phone to my ear. "I know what you mean . . ."

"No," he interrupted me. "I'm going through some things."

Wait, was he giving up? It sure sounded like it, but I knew that was not the type of person he was. I listened as he talked about his problems with Debra and not being able to see his kids. After giving money to Debra, he had no money for himself. "Life is messed up. I'm kind of down and out right now."

"I'll Western Union you fifty dollars, like I did the week before. Hope that can just get you through."

"Oh okay," he said. "I just gotta go. I have work tomorrow."

"Me, too," I said. "Them white people ain't playing. I have to clock in at seven."

"I love you," he said before hanging up.

I never really understood how depressed or down he was, but maybe I should have grasped how hard it was for him to be away from his family.

Hummie didn't marry to divorce. It was the same reason I didn't give up Mark, even when he was tormenting me. We were country like that—we married to stay married. Still, how was I to really know how depressed he was? Hummie might discuss his frustrations, but he wasn't going to verbalize his deep pain; then again, he was no different from anyone else in the family. That was the way our kin had been for generations, hiding the pain, not speaking about the unspeakable.

* * *

By the summer of 1997, Hummie had no money coming in. He was waiting on some check from the NFL, but that hadn't arrived, either. Hummie was no longer living with his family and had moved to a distant cousin's one-room apartment.

On July 4, 1997, Debra finally allowed him to bring the kids to Clemson. I remember that day starting out like it was just good times: I recall my children ripping through the apartment and bouncing off the beds with Hummie's kids. His son, Terrance, who was four, looked so much like Hummie that it was almost scary. Daejha, his two-year-old daughter, had a headful of fine copper-colored hair. We'd gaze at Daejha's pigtails, which Hummie always dolled up with barrettes, twists, and colorful bows, and we'd say, "Oh Daejha! Who did your hair?"

"I did it!" Hummie said proudly.

Despite being the attentive and loving father, he was not himself. He was staring off; he was just not there.

Shortly after that, I traveled to Atlanta with my kids for a track meet. Daddy drove down, too, but I was a coach and remained on the bus, which was packed with children and parents. I called Hummie, who came to see the kids perform, and then he drove to the hotel where we were all staying. While Daddy babysat the children, I got Hummie to drive me around the city to find a tattoo parlor, figuring we might be able to talk in private, but all he insisted on during the entire drive was to ask me to call Debra.

"She'll listen to you," he said.

I told him I would talk to her, but honestly, I just wanted to enjoy our time together. When I finally got settled inside the tattoo studio, I gazed outside the large window. There was Hummie sitting on the hood of the car, making a call. I assumed he was calling Debra.

Once I was done, he dropped me off at the hotel.

That was the last time I'd ever see Hummie.

*   *   *

Over the course of the next several days, we all carried on different conversations with Hummie, who by now was clearly stressed and depressed. Daddy got him to agree to return home in two days because Poopie, who was now a coach at Clemson, was trying to get Hummie a job at the university. A day after Daddy talked to him, I also had a short conversation with Hummie, begging him to come back home.

But he said sternly, "Brina, I'm not leaving my kids!"

At the time, I didn't understand the depth of what he meant, but all I wanted was for him to come home to Clemson and get himself together. Later I realized what he really was saying was that he'd rather die than leave his kids. In my mind, I was thinking, *I understand you don't want to leave them, but you can always go back and see your kids. So, you know, just come home.* But that's not how Hummie, in his depressed state, was seeing things.

Rodney also talked to Hummie that same day. "Hummie was unraveling," he told me later. "That last day we talked, and he couldn't put the pieces together. He saw no way out."

Rodney also had a plan for Hummie: he had invited him to come to Florida and stay with his family for a while, which Hummie agreed to. In Rodney's mind, the plan was set.

I knew nothing at the time about Rodney and Hummie's conversation, but I planned to continue to send Hummie fifty dollars every week, and Daddy was waiting for Hummie to come home like he promised. But my brother, despite whatever arrangements he'd made with Rodney, and who always did what Daddy told him to do, had made a plan for himself this time.

And no one was going to stop him.

* * *

What I do know is around noon the next day, on July 17, 1997, Hummie got into his maroon Toyota Camry and put on a CD, "Ready to Die," by Notorious B.I.G. His Oakley shades were on the dashboard as he drove to Debra's house. He arrived with an object in his hand that might have helped him pry open the door, which he eventually kicked in. Debra was in the bathroom with Daejha and Terrance, who was in the tub. Hummie grabbed Debra and they all ended in the living room. Debra's nephew, who was staying there at the time, called the police. Three officers showed up—they entered the house, setting off an intense standoff.

One officer asked Hummie, who now had a knife in his hand and was gripping Debra, if there's someone he wanted to talk to, someone that he wanted to call. And he says Grandma Zona. I can only think that she was somebody he idolized and who represented that one happy time in our lives. Debra later told me nobody moved a muscle right after that, but the police report said Hummie flinched. Two of the cops opened fire, first hitting him in the hands and then fatally striking his heart. His wife was hit by a bullet to her arm, and the baby, two-year-old Daejha, who was likely held by her mom, was grazed twice by bullets.

Depression and mental illness of course played a part in Hummie's choices that day. But I can't help but wonder whether he went there with the intent to hurt his family. He could have killed Debra before the cops arrived, but he didn't. Or did he go there knowing the police would be called, and that they weren't going to let this Black man get out of there alive? We all had a solution for him, but I believe Hummie chose his own way out.

* * *

That day Daddy got an abrupt call from Debra's father. "Hummie got shot. Y'all need to come check on him." And then he hung up. To this day, Daddy has not gotten over the almost inhumane nature of that phone call.

We all met up at Mama's two-bedroom apartment in Clemson when we heard the news that Hummie was in the hospital and had been hurt. Before we entered the apartment, I grabbed my friend Angela's arm. "Hummie's dead," I said. "I just know it."

Angela poked me. "Don't say that! Why would you say that?"

I squeezed her hand. "I just feel it."

Mama and Daddy hadn't spoken in years, but Daddy drove over from Easley with his wife at the time. Poopie arrived with his wife, Shirley. And Poopie's parents, Aunt Louise and Uncle Larry, showed up, as did Uncle Louis and Nuk's godmother, Frances.

At one point, Poopie and I sat on the sidewalk in front of Mama's door for few minutes asking each other when was the last time we heard from Hummie. Poopie and Hummie always bonded, maybe because they were both in the car with Dilly, but their strong bond started long before that. Poopie had become a distinguished college coach who exuded strength and power, but that day on the curb he had tears in his eyes. Hummie and Poopie were the last boys alive who were in the car with Dilly. I could tell Poopie was afraid for Hummie, and although he never said it, I am sure he was thinking, *I don't want to be the last one left.*

Inside the apartment, nobody was saying much because nobody knew anything. If the phone rang, everyone was like, "Who was that?"

Finally, my mother and father, along with my stepmother, decided to head to Atlanta because every time they called the hospital, they got no answers. They hadn't been gone thirty minutes before they walked back through the door. I was sitting in the living room wondering why did they return? When I looked up, I could see in Daddy's and Mama's faces all I needed to know. They were trying to be as calm as possible for me, but their eyes betrayed the pain in their hearts. Shortly after leaving the apartment to head south, Daddy had received a call on his cell phone from a doctor at a hospital in Atlanta.

Seconds after Daddy returned to Mama's apartment, he called out my name. "Brina."

I said almost defiantly, "What?"

"He's gone," Daddy said.

"What you mean he's gone?"

Mama screamed. They had been holding everything together to walk back through the door to tell me, but now Mama couldn't hold nothing back. Everybody in the apartment was in their own space, trying to make sense of it. Mama just fell to her knees, while Daddy held on to his wife and squeezed her tight. I grabbed Mama's vases and threw them against the wall. "No, no!" I said. "Hummie, you told me you would never leave me!"

I don't remember going over to hug Mama, but I do remember everybody kneeling there on the floor with her, and a few people grabbed me because I kept throwing stuff.

I'll never forget how Daddy raised his fists in the air and said, "Goddamn it. They killed my boy."

Everything seemed to go silent after that. We didn't know who to call. We did not know where to go, and we didn't know what to do.

This was the darkest time for all of us.

When Daddy embraced me, it was like the world had stopped, like life had stopped. Dilly was Mama's love and Hummie was Daddy's baby and Daddy was my heart. Daddy called me the next day to tell me he was driving down to Atlanta with his best friend, Gilbert. While in Atlanta, Daddy got the police and the coroner's reports. Daddy and his friend went to my uncle Reggie's house, who directed him to where Hummie was staying, with a distant cousin. Like a detective, Daddy began putting all the pieces together. When Daddy walked in the apartment, he realized the man, a cousin we hardly knew, had shut Hummie's door to preserve the room, knowing a family member would soon come by. He told Daddy, "You're the first person that's been in here since Terry [Hummie] left the other day."

Inside the room, Daddy could feel Hummie's presence. He looked around, picking up his jacket, and noticed Hummie had made up his bed. He turned toward the dresser, on which Hummie had lined the four championship rings he had earned as a Clemson Tiger. Sitting right next to the last ring was a handheld tape recorder.

Daddy picked up the rings and later told me he had a strong sense that Hummie knew he was coming. He packed Hummie's shoes, and at some point, he listened to the tape recorder. I'm assuming he listened to it when he got back home because I know Daddy wouldn't want to play it around anybody. Before leaving Atlanta, he sat inside Hummie's beautiful maroon Camry, which he'd eventually drive back to South Carolina. The moment he revved up the car, "Ready to Die," by Notorious B.I.G. was queued and began playing. It features the famous line: "I'm ready to die, and nobody can save me."

* * *

Back in Clemson, I decided to live with Mama for a while because me and the children were moving in a few weeks. I was dating a man named Richard at the time, who'd become Shanterria's, my fourth child's, father. He lived in nearby Seneca, so he stayed there some nights, but most nights he was at Mama's with me. During this time, I don't remember sleeping much because people were coming in and out of the apartment. In fact, people were swarming to Mama's apartment, the same apartment Hummie and his wife once lived in before she did. A few days before the funeral, Daddy arrived and said to me, "Brina, come here for a minute."

I followed him up the stairs, when he shoved a tape recorder in my hand. His exact words were "Take this. I don't want to see this goddamn thing ever again in my life."

I looked down at the tape recorder and then back at Daddy and said, "What?"

He pointed at the recorder. "It's all there." He turned around, slipped downstairs, out the door, and left. I had no idea what he meant. I put the recorder in my purse and decided to wait to listen after everyone had left the apartment. Mama's apartment was a small two-bedroom, but her home was packed with Hummie's teammates from Clemson and Daniel High School. His middle school, high school, and college coaches and teachers also came by. Cars were lined up in the parking lot. Finally, after mostly everyone was gone, I closed myself in Mama's bedroom, where I had been sleeping. Mama always preferred to sleep on the couch, and the kids were asleep in the second bedroom. On the tape, Hummie starts talking about his wife, Debra, and their tumultuous relationship. He suggested her family never thought he was good enough for her, and he believed he could not make her happy. Hummie went on to speak more in depth about their marriage and how the relationship was a source of deep pain for him. At one point, I could tell he turned over the tape, so I did the same thing. On that other side of the recording, he starts telling people goodbye, but he's not saying that explicitly.

The first person he mentions is our father. "Pops, you know I love you. I'm always going to love you. Be strong. I'll see you again. Don't worry about me . . ."

Then he said, "Mama, I've never seen somebody not get over a death like you never got over Dilly's death. I hope this don't set you back too much."

I sat on the bed, stunned. "Brina, take care of Kesha, Boodia, and De-Andre. Sis, I'll see you again. Man, you know I love you."

He said goodbye to one of his friends, Fredrick Morgan, who we called Bootman, and then told Poopie, "Poopie, man, you been there since Day One. I love you . . ."

The last person he addressed was Rodney. "Yo," he said, "I'll meet you at the Crossroads. I'm going out with a blast."

* * *

Daejha, Hummie's two-year-old daughter, was in the hospital from the shooting, while Debra was also admitted for stab and bullet wounds. For that reason, Debra did not attend Hummie's funeral, but even if she hadn't been injured and had showed up, half of my family would have wanted answers from her. It took Daddy many years to even say her name without wanting to say he was going to kill her. That's just not something I'd ever say or even feel, even though I still have some resentment for how she handled things, but I don't wish anyone dead. Even when my uncle Ottie killed Dilly I eventually got over the vengeful feeling of wanting him gone, too. And after what I went through with Steve, I know what it feels like for an entire family to believe you caused someone's death.

Hummie had two kids, my blood, and if everybody chooses hatred, then, hell, how are we ever going to get to know his children? I instilled that kind of thinking into my kids, that when it comes to issues of the heart, plant your feet on solid ground. In our household, we didn't say Hummie's death was Debra's fault because the truth is, since he's gone, we will never know.

* * *

For the second time in my life, I was asked to prepare my brother's funeral. I called his teammates to request them to be pallbearers and asked his female classmates to be flower girls. I had to go to the funeral home to pick out the casket. Neither Mama nor Daddy had the emotional ability to do it. I also had to go back and view Hummie's body to make sure he looked right. My mom and daddy did nothing—it was the same way with Dilly. They just couldn't do it. They didn't see Dilly until the day of the funeral.

Unlike in Dilly's case, I didn't have to go shopping for Hummie's outfit. Because the Clemson football players wore suits before games, Hummie had several fine suits he left in the closets between Mama's and Daddy's homes.

* * *

Hummie's funeral was at Easley Baptist Union Church, the same family church that my grandma Zona used to take me and my brothers to on Sundays when we were children. It's no megachurch, but it had a sizable congregation. Reverend Cruell, who was the senior pastor when we were little, presided over my brother's eulogy. The church was packed with former Clemson players and former high school teammates. One person after another stood at the podium praising my dead brother for his otherworldly athletic skills, recalling his nickname "Touchdown Terry" and listing the many records he broke. Tommy West, the head football coach at Clemson, told the story of Hummie catching the winning ball during the Peach Bowl.

But all the beautiful words went over my head, because all I could think about was my brother, who never made any mistakes, never did anything wrong, was the poster child for doing good, but here he was in a casket because three police officers shot him to death. Back then, there was no Ben Crump to rally support. So these sorts of things happened without families getting closure, let alone a straight story from the police about what actually went down. There was no organized Black Lives Matter movement, and very few crusading lawyers or national media reports brought attention to cases where a Black man was gunned down. If anything, Hummie's death was written off as a domestic dispute. Daddy got a lawyer to try to get justice for Hummie and answers for us, but it was the saddest day in the world when he later called me to say the money had run out and he had to give up.

* * *

At the funeral, I looked over at Mama and felt instantly guilty. There were two people in the church that day who knew more about Hummie's last thoughts than anyone else and had heard his last coherent words, and those two people were me and my daddy.

I wasn't sure what to do with the recording. Do I tell Mama I had it? I knew when my daddy said he never wants to see that damn thing again, he meant that. It was so confusing—what to do with this information? I just felt like I needed to go inside my head.

I looked over at the casket and then up in the air, hoping God would provide me a sign. I turned and gazed at all the young faces in the church, my brother's friends and former classmates and teammates. They all were so sad and confused. My heart began to palpitate. I was sitting in the pew stressing about the tape recording, ruminating over my brother's death, and all the while I could hear Mama crying to my left and see Daddy sitting with his wife, but me, I had retreated deep inside my head.

I was so confused to the point that I was sitting up, shaking. I started to hyperventilate. I was one of the only people in the entire world who knew about the tape. It was a huge burden—for one thing, I was not going to dishonor my father, but I also wasn't going to unfairly hurt Mama, who had tried to kill herself at least three times by now.

We'd bury him not knowing why he really died, other than he was shot by police, but there were other questions I didn't have answers for.

There wasn't a lot of weeping at the funeral because everybody was in shock. The ceremony was quick, but I wasn't there when they put Hummie in the grave. I was hyperventilating in church so badly that Richard picked me up and carried me off to the hospital.

I regret not just keeping it together, but I really couldn't help it. I felt like my chest was caving in. Still, I regret it because I didn't get to see him to the end, nor did Mama. Someone got Mama and asked if she wanted to see Hummie's burial or go to the hospital to check on Sabrina. "Of course, I want to go to the hospital to be with the child I got alive," she said.

To this day, I believe my best friend, Angela, is the reason I'm alive. I was losing so much oxygen that the doctors said, "She's having a panic attack, and she's going to die if she can't catch her breath." Angela was brought into the emergency room: "Bitch, you better fucking breathe, bitch!" she shouted. She literally scared the life back into me, and then I took a deep breath.

* * *

In the end, after the funeral, I shared the audio with everyone Hummie mentioned. I made an older child executive decision, and so me and Mama went up to her bedroom and listened to the tape. I told her to sit on the bed, and I sat beside her. As she began to hear her son's voice, she started patting her left leg the whole time the tape played. She never cried, but she also never said a word. I played one side and then the other. I didn't push my opinion on her. I didn't say, well, Mama, I think he went there to kill them. Or, Mama, I think he wanted to die. I did not say anything. I allowed my mama to come to whatever conclusion she needed to come to in order to give herself peace.

Afterward, I told her that "whatever you do, just don't ask me where I put the tape."

I called Poopie and later Rodney, who was still in town, and asked them each to come to Mama's house. "Hummie left you something," I told each of them solemnly.

When Rodney arrived and entered Mama's bedroom, he refused to listen to the tape recording, so I opted to just tell him what had been said.

After I finished, he said, "You can't tell me that my dawg is talking about he's 'going out with a blast.' I know that ain't him. He wasn't in his right state of mind."

As years passed, me and Rodney reconnected through phone calls and visits. One of us would always start crying. Soon we'd become best friends—if he was in my hometown, he'd come to visit, and if I was in his neck of the woods, I'll stop by to visit his family. Like kin, we both realized that something wasn't right about Hummie's story.

Rodney said the three letters first: "CTE."

"What happened in Atlanta," Rodney said, "that wasn't the guy I went to school with. He was the sane one. I was the fire plug. Hummie, this dude was the All-American guy. He wasn't no knucklehead, which is why everybody was totally shocked about what went down."

And that's what got us thinking so much about Hummie's unusual actions the summer of 1997. Rodney couldn't help but wonder whether Hummie had experienced multiple concussions, or chronic traumatic encephalopathy—CTE. "Things were not as safe back then as they are today," he said.

He said back when they were in college, Clemson had the number one defense in the nation, which meant Rodney and Hummie, who were both on offense, practiced with them daily. That also meant practice was brutal. "If you're lucky enough to play for a big college football team like Clemson, or the NFL, the last thing any player wants to do is let a coach see you've been hurt."

After the brutal practices, Hummie would go back to the dorm, eat dinner, and sit in a chair. The next morning, Rodney, still in bed, would peek over at Hummie, who'd be sitting in that same chair, snapping his body back together.

Rodney said Hummie didn't move from that chair "until the next day when we'd go to practice, because he was beat up so bad the night before. But when we got to practice you couldn't tell. I used to tell people all the time that 'this dude is built something different.'"

Hummie never missed games or practice, which meant drilling against very tough men happened often. "This was not powder-puff football," Rodney said. "Plus, think of everything he did in high school and Little League. That's a lot of contact. And we didn't have requirements that they have now to protect athletes. Nobody was talking about concussions."

This was nothing Rodney was guessing about. "I've seen him take some brutal shots and give some brutal shots," he said. "I played with a broken nose and crossed eyes. I used to talk to Hummie about what happens when you take a bad shot and you see double, so which ball do you catch? Do you catch the one in the middle or outside? We've had those conversations because it happened to me, and I am sure it happened to him."

The more me and Rodney talked, the more I started to realize that some of Hummie's unusual actions may be connected to all the hitting to the head. If he had CTE, he was not able to function at a normal capacity. I remember right after Hummie's death, Rodney said Hummie was unraveling, that my brother just couldn't find answers to his problems. I thought to myself, imagine being depressed, going through a divorce, having no money to take care of your children or yourself, and having CTE. Nothing makes sense. There's no solution to nothing. At no point is anything solvable.

Whether Hummie had CTE or not, he was still my brother, and I'd always love him, but I wanted to at least try to figure out what was happening to him. I began studying CTE and everything about it reminded me of Hummie, not the Hummie we knew, but the Hummie my brother had become.

Something we all see as a solvable issue, like dividing time with the children after a divorce, somehow overwhelmed him. If he had CTE, I suspect he literally couldn't see past what was going on in that moment—he wouldn't have had the mental capacity to compartmentalize a solution or resolution. For example, we all knew Hummie could probably see his kids, but he didn't think he could. Rodney said everything to Hummie was just a "buildup," and he was exactly right.

I'm convinced, in my brother's mind, he thought he was never going

142 · SABRINA GREENLEE

to see his kids again. He thought he had lost them like he lost Dilly, like he lost Squeenchie, and if I am to be honest, like he lost Mama, who wasn't there 100 percent. And he probably could have thought he lost me because I was focused on my three children.

Who's to say that he wasn't suffering from CTE? I've thought about exhuming his body because you can't determine CTE until the person is dead. I wanted to check his brain, but I wouldn't, I couldn't, do that to Mama and Daddy while they were still alive.

And so Hummie's truths remained buried, along with so many other family secrets that overwhelmed us in those days during our tragic lives.

CHAPTER 12

The Last Child

Three days after burying Hummie, I started feeling nauseous—by now I knew this feeling very well. I took a pregnancy test and then called Richard into the bathroom to show him the positive result. I will never forget that smirk on his face, but I didn't think anything was funny about me being pregnant with his child, especially with what was already hanging over me. Three weeks prior, Richard had sat me down, saying he had something to tell me. I took a deep breath, waiting for the other shoe to drop. "What is it?"

He lowered his bald head. "I made the biggest mistake of my life."

I narrowed my eyes. "What happened?"

He said three months earlier he'd had a one-night stand and got a twenty-three-year-old woman pregnant. I was pissed off, but I eventually was willing to work it out because I would do anything to create a stable life for my children. I didn't love him, but Richard was a nice guy, older, and had a good job, so I figured it was worth me coming to terms with what he had done. Now, barely a month later, I had to come to terms with the fact that I was also pregnant with his child. We started arguing in the bathroom. I thought to myself, *I know a child is a blessing, but I don't want to have a child by you.*

Mama must have heard us shouting because she started walking through her apartment, crying, "This ain't nothing but God. He took Hummie from us, but now Brina is pregnant, and we have another baby on the way."

This was only a few days after the funeral, so downstairs was still packed with visitors consoling us. Hearing Mama so happy about my pregnancy, I figured, shit, I have no choice now but to have the baby. In truth, an abortion never crossed my mind, but I was upset that I slipped up and got pregnant by a man who had another baby on the way.

* * *

When we had first met, I imagined I had found stability and peace in Richard. No one would have known from the outside looking in that Richard offered none of those things. He was about six foot three, with a slender build, one of those men who favored a clean-shaven head. He was eight or nine years my senior, with a good job at Englehart, a manufacturing company. He was from New York City and had a strong New York accent, though he moved down South with his parents and siblings many years before. He also had this New York City swag, and I liked that. He'd tell me about how he and his boys would run the streets and how he'd ride the subways; his stories fascinated me. I was like, "You did what?"

As much as I liked his stories, though, our relationship was toxic from the start because we were both so vulnerable. Hummie had just been killed, and Richard's nephew and best friend Dwayne had recently been murdered. I knew Dwayne from my days of going to house parties with Angela. Later in the year, even though I was already six months pregnant with my last child, Shanterria, I dutifully attended Dwayne's three-day murder trial with Richard. Ironically, Hummie's other roommate at Clemson (not Rodney) was one of two people on trial for killing Dwayne. It was strange seeing a man I knew on trial for killing another man I knew, but I was there for Richard; my deepest sympathy was with him because I too had just lost a loved one in a violent way. And like all the men in my life, I bonded with him through a tragedy. I only wanted a broken person like me: a man with his shit together would have bored me, but a bad boy with a dark past not only intrigued the hell out of me, but I could relate to him, too. No, I didn't love Richard, but I fell in love with who he was in that moment—a man in deep pain. Back then, men like this fit me like a glove.

* * *

After I discovered I was pregnant, things moved fast, probably too fast. I stayed with Richard for several reasons. For one thing, he was willing to put in the work to make me love him. In fact, once he told me just that: "I know you don't love me, but I'm gonna make you love me." No one had ever said that to me. We started going to Abel Church, my family church, where we both sang in the choir. We moved in together, trying to make things work, but Richard was still struggling with Dwayne's death and the pregnant twenty-three-year-old was calling the house asking for Pampers, even though she hadn't given birth yet. And although my own mental and financial stability were in check, I was still worried about my parents, who were anything but stable.

My strong, honorable father was barely making it. He always dabbled in alcohol, but after Hummie's death, he started calling me in the middle of the night, sounding sloppy, pissy drunk. "Brina," he'd say, "I don't want to be on this Earth without my son."

He'd be so drunk that I could barely understand him, and worst of all, he wouldn't let me get a word in.

He'd say, "I don't think you know how hard it is to live without Hummie."

I never said it to him, but in my mind I was screaming: *I'm still here!* Even as an adult, I felt like the little girl people forgot about.

He'd keep going on. "I should just blow my fucking brains out."

After these calls, he'd not pick up when I called back. I'd sit up in my bed, alert and scared, but couldn't understand why me, his last child, wasn't enough for him to live for.

"Daddy, just let us come over," I'd beg him, but he wouldn't listen or want that.

Other times he'd call and say, "This is the night your daddy is going to die."

He'd also express his desire to kill Hummie's wife, Debra. "If I saw her walking down the street right now, I'd blow her brains out." It was the hurt and alcohol talking, but I believe his pain contributed to the breakup of his second marriage.

* * *

I was stressed over the other baby-mama drama the entire pregnancy, but it was the easiest pregnancy I ever had because we were financially stable. I worked the entire time I was pregnant with Shani, up until I took leave. I got up in the morning with my big belly and headed to my job. Outside of that responsibility, I was trying to cope with Hummie's death and Richard and his other situation, but I didn't take my problems to work. All they knew was I had a boyfriend and life was good.

My coworkers at Dayco threw me a baby shower, and every day they fussed over me. Someone would say, "Oh, you look so pretty." Somebody else would say, "You are glowing."

It was my only pregnancy in which I was around a lot of people, where they could say those kind things. My other pregnancies, in retrospect, were relatively dark and horrible. Steve was on the run living a very fast life when I was pregnant with DeAndre, which meant I was alone without my man.

But the pregnancy with Shani, my last child, felt privileged and planned. In fact, it was the only one not paid for by the government! Richard and I had insurance, so we split the cost of the pregnancy down the middle. I bought so many clothes before Shani was born because I had the money to buy her outfits.

With this pregnancy I also had help. Richard was there to make sure that the kids had everything they needed. My water broke at home, not in a grocery store or an elevator like with my other children. When it was time to head to the hospital, everything went as planned and without any drama. Shanterria was born April 14, 1998, exactly nine months after Hummie's death. She weighed eight pounds, my smallest baby. She was so pretty and calm, with Richard's full lips. I used to say, "My baby got soup coolers"—lips so plump you could cool off a bowl of soup quick.

Shani was the sun after the darkness, a true blessing because now that we didn't have Hummie, we had this beautiful child we could love on.

In 1999, a year after Shani was born, Richard's sister mentioned a mortgage program that could help us buy a house. I took the information and set it aside. I eventually called the program, and Richard and

Me at three months old,
my mama's little doll baby.

Mama always made sure we took family photos every year.
From left to right: Mama, me, Hummie, and Dilly.

My youngest brother, Dilly,
at age eleven, a year before he died

Me at age thirteen. I loved running
track, being a cheerleader, and
attending pep rallies at school.
(Go Panthers!)

Hummie rubbing
Howard's Rock before
running down the hill
at Death Valley

Me and Steve in 1991. We had been dating for about a year and a half.

Me in Jamaica in 2001. I loved being in the Caribbean sunshine and experiencing Jamaican culture.

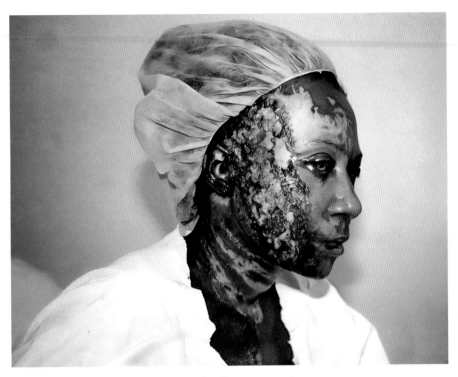

A month after the attack

Three months after
the attack

Me and my babies in 2003, keeping our tradition of family photos going. *From left to right:* Marcus, me, Shanterria, Kesha, and DeAndre.

An unbreakable bond: DeAndre hands me the football after each touchdown he scores.

Me and my best friends always remain solid through the good and the bad.
From left to right: Destiny, Tiffany, Lauren, me, Angela, and Veronica.

Me and Daddy
at the ESPYs.
It was our first
time attending
the event.

Onstage at a speaking engagement in Washington, D.C.

Christmas, 2015. My kids all grown up.
From left to right: Marcus, Kesha, me, DeAndre, and Shanterria.

Me today, feeling bold and bodacious!

[*Courtesy of Sean Coleman*]

I both completed a tedious application process, but Richard's credit wasn't good enough. The organization called my job at Dayco, but the company revealed a pattern of me calling in sick or missing days at work.

They were not lying. I was always trying to manipulate the system, not realizing the system was watching me and I was only hurting myself. I was working the first shift, which meant I had to get to work by 7:00 a.m., but that still wasn't an excuse for all those missed workdays. The mortgage company informed us that I couldn't miss a day for another three months if I wanted to get a house loan. While I was stressed out at work and continually worried about my parents, I was nevertheless determined to purchase a home for us, someplace me and the kids could finally call our own. Everyone at work tried to help me. One older woman, her name was Ms. Jean Turman, called me in the mornings to make sure I was up and out the door. Coworkers even waited outside of Dayco so I could jump out the car and race to clock in while they parked my car. By the grace of God, I wasn't late or absent in those three months.

During that period, I learned a major lesson about the power of consistency. Those bad habits I picked up would always come back to haunt me, because I thought I was getting over. Like most people, I felt I was entitled to steal a day here and there from work instead of balancing my life, so that I wouldn't have to jeopardize my future. After all, once you've avoided something for so long, you think you can't do it. But as soon as I became committed, I realized I could get to work on time and not miss days. During that period of consistency, I became lead supervisor and secured a $75,000 loan for my house. After the loan was approved, Richard and I had our eyes on three different homes, but I picked a cute canary-colored house with a long driveway at 115 Hilltop Road. I signed for my home at age twenty-eight. I picked the home simply because it was big enough to hold a huge "grandfather table," a shiny cherry oak dining table and glass hutch I spotted at Rooms to Go. Richard and I picked out $3,500 worth of furniture, including the dining table, the matching hutch, and a living room suite. I was fixated on a big table because I imagined all my kids sitting around it—something I was determined to achieve. I filled the matching hutch with my collection of Black angels. When I turned the lights on in the hutch, they were the most beautiful thing, and when I opened the glass door of the hutch, I imagined the angels fluttering around the house, which was always filled with gospel music—Yolanda Adams and CeCe Winans were my favorites.

In my mind, I had made it, not dreaming that this house would bring a lot of sadness along with a lot of great times, too.

* * *

My new home was within walking distance of Mama, who by now was using crack more than ever. She'd crash into the house every day and wreak havoc. Although, at the time, she made our life pure hell, in hindsight I'm not sure she would have survived if she didn't have us to talk to or see every day.

Unlike Daddy, who was melancholy, Mama displayed her pain in a sinister way, turning all her hurt and anger toward me—her last surviving child. She was lonely and sad, which left her bitter. She made it her mission to come to 115 Hilltop Road, which we called "One Fifteen," to turn the children against me, telling them stories and lies about my past.

"Your mother was a hoe back in the day," or "Your mama smoke crack back in the day" were common refrains—even though Mama knew that while I sold drugs, I never used them.

Truth be told, my biggest challenge may not have been the rape I endured when I was a girl or my brothers' deaths, but confronting and undoing what Mama tried to put in my children's heads. Her troublemaking would always start a terrible fight between us, but after I ran Mama out of the house, she'd come right back the same day to start more problems.

"Oh Lord, here comes Grandma," one of the children would say, knowing the two of us would start arguing—again.

"Mama, my children love me," I'd say. "Just because you don't, doesn't mean they shouldn't."

"They lying," Mama would say about the kids.

Sometimes I'd feel great sympathy for Mama, but other times I just couldn't take it. "Get the fuck out my house," I'd yell to her routinely after a fight. Eventually, she'd leave the house again, slamming my door behind her. And the next day, she'd return like nothing ever happened.

I'd tell her to stop telling my children about what I did and who I did it with, but Mama was ruthless and wouldn't stop. You best believe she was going to tell two or three stories about me, and you can bet your bottom dollar that barely even one of them was true.

*   *   *

After nearly three years being with Richard, I figured we might as well make it official. I put a dress on layaway at David's Bridal and was picking my bridesmaids, but things began to change, and I felt that Richard started to despise me. Yes, he made sure the bills were paid, came to the kids' events, and bought them school clothes and presents on their birthdays. But in the privacy of our home, Richard's true self came out.

Words were Richard's weapons, and his verbal abuse would cut me down to size. If I looked his way, he'd say, "Stop fucking looking at me."

And if I said, "Hey, what are we gonna eat tonight? Something simple?" he would say, "I don't know, you figure the shit out. I don't care what we eat." His harshness and constant criticism became a way of life that I accepted. Because Richard was a master manipulator, he knew that all he had to do to keep me captive was threaten to leave. Then no matter what he'd said or done, I'd be the one apologizing and doing whatever I had to do to get back into his good graces, scared that if he left, I might not be able to handle the bills to keep me and the kids in the house.

He never said anything demeaning about my hair or my weight, but his comments were rude, and he never stopped snapping at me. He once told me he was trying so hard to show me that he could be faithful after he cheated, but I was keeping him away from his family and his baby in Seneca.

*   *   *

It all started when I heard a rumor that Richard tried to talk a young woman into our bed while I was at work. Apparently, she bragged about it enough that Angela found out, and that's when all hell broke loose.

"Bitch, you better go whoop her ass or I'm coming to whoop her ass for you," Angela said.

I was listening to her on my cell phone, heading home from work when coincidentally I saw the woman; she lived down the street and was standing by her car. I pulled over, got out the car, and asked her about the rumor. To her credit, she confirmed everything.

I looked toward my home to see Richard observing us as she and I talked. I pulled the car into our yard and confronted him, but he jumped in his car and peeled off like a coward.

* * *

Still hanging on to my need for stability, and still stuck in my ways with men, I took him back days later. And predictably, Richard became even more verbally abusive. I would have left him a long time ago if I had not gotten pregnant. All I could think about was I got four children and will have no help if he's gone.

One day, I kept calling Angela, telling her that Richard was cussing me out and being mean. I picked the wrong day, because Angela had had enough of me. "I'm tired of you calling me," she said. "If you don't leave that motherfucker, I'm coming down and packing his shit because I'm tired of you calling me and crying."

"I can't!" I said.

"Brina, you can do it, you can make it without him."

"Angela, I can't do this on my own."

"Don't call me tomorrow unless you tell me that Richard got his shit and gone!"

And she hung up.

The fact that I was not going to be able to talk to my best friend scared me more than losing Richard. One day, Richard went to see his other child in Seneca and didn't come back for two or three days. He claimed he was at his mom's house, but I didn't believe him, and I no longer cared. I packed his up his clothes, and he disappeared from our lives for good.

I was the last surviving child of my parents because of horrible happenstance, but Shani being my last child was my choice. I got my tubes tied and promised myself that never will another father of my children walk out of their lives again.

CHAPTER 13

Caramel

After Richard left in 1999, when I was twenty-nine, I obtained the mortgage myself, signed a purchase agreement, and I settled permanently with the kids into "115." I was still working at Dayco. I loved my job and we—me and the kids—were good. In my mind, I had made it.

Not too long after, a guy from work named Jamie walked up to me out of the blue and told me I should really be working in a strip club. "You have a stripper's body," he insisted. I had no idea what he meant by that. I was at the tail end of my twenties, with four young children, but slim with small breasts and a big butt like Mama. I remember a guy I know saying once, "Man, you're like Benjamin Button. Every time you have a baby your body don't get worse, it gets better!"

Maybe my tight body had something to do with me having all my children naturally. I spit out four kids, and still to this day, I don't have one stretch mark on my stomach. It had been years since I ran track in high school, but I remained a good dancer and naturally inclined to create dance steps like I did as a cheerleader. So, although Jamie's comments that I should be a stripper came out of the blue, dancing in front of people wasn't unfamiliar to me. Dancing with no clothes on? Well, that was something I could never dream about doing, but I admit I was intrigued to see if I had the nerve to try.

So I met Jamie on a Saturday before noon in Easley, and he drove me to a club called Lady Godiva's in Greenville.

I had no idea what to expect; it was the first time I had ever put my foot in a place like this. The bar was dark with hot neon lights flashing. The front doors of Godiva's opened into an entrance where customers would stop at the desk to pay admission. A dancer greeted the men there, and once on the floor, I saw a female bartender at a long, dark, wooden bar that stretched to the wall. It was situated across from what was obviously the main stage. The club, I'd quickly learn, was constantly in motion, starting as early as lunchtime. There was always someone hustling something: men hustling clothes, girls trying to hustle men out of their money, and someone trying to hustle the dancers out of their draws. To the left of the bar was a common area with chairs and tables. That's where there was bound to be a girl or two giving a ten-dollar table dance, or some other dancer sitting in a man's lap. Groups of men, as well as others sitting alone, would watch the dancer onstage, while others came in just for the cheap watered-down drinks and food. Every Saturday featured a buffet packed with fried chicken and French fries. Everybody came to get that fried chicken, but I wouldn't try it at first because the cooks came in there looking like any which way. Eventually, though, I would be starving after dancing, and I soon realized it was the best chicken and ranch dressing I've ever had.

* * *

That first day Jamie led me up to the bar, the bartender handed me an employment application. Before long, Merle, the house mom, walked up to me. "You want to start today?"

I wasn't prepared for that.

"You need somebody else to cosign the application," she added. So the bartender, who I had just met, put her name down as a referral.

Meanwhile, a tall white girl wearing white boots strolled past. Her name was Red, and we made eye contact before she backed up and looked me up and down.

"What's up?" she said. "You want to go to the back and try on these boots? What size do you wear? We might wear the same size."

"Oh, hello," I said, surprised. "How you doing? I'm a size ten."

I followed her to the dressing room and tried on the boots, which stretched all the way up to my thighs. "Basically, when you get up there, be free and do what you normally do," Red instructed me. Do what I normally do? I was thinking, *This ain't normal, and I don't know what I'm doing.*

I believe Red saw me standing there a little lost and decided to help me out. The boots had platform heels, which were not only sexy but made them easy to stand up in. But the outfit wasn't complete yet—in no time, Jamie drove me to a tiny shop called Pandora's Box, a little 10 x 20–foot hole in the wall, where you could get sex toys and the perfect outfit for a stripper—mine was a pair of tiny white booty shorts and a matching tube top that looked like a small band around my breasts.

I never dreamed I could take my clothes off in front of strange people, but part of me wanted to see if I could. Plus, I was not going to have Jamie tell the guys at work I chickened out. It was a dare kind of thing for me. After we returned to Godiva's and I got dressed, I was sent out to the DJ booth. The DJ, whose name was Kevin, swiped off his headphones. "What's your name?"

I had just bought two boxes of Girl Scout cookies for the kids. "My name is going to be Caramel Delight."

He shook his head. "Nah, that's not going to work. We going to call you Caramel; we gotta take the 'delight' off."

He announced that Caramel was coming to the stage—I didn't even realize it was me he was talking about. He nodded at me. "You! I'm introducing you, Caramel!"

Oh shit, I thought to myself.

I climbed up onto the T-shaped stage as the drumbeats from what would be my first song—Mystikal's "Shake It Fast"—started up. I had no idea what I was doing and just started dancing as if I was with Angela at Carl's Place back in the day. There was nothing sexy about it: in fact, I held on to the pole for dear life. My moves were the furthest thing from sensual or exotic. As Mystikal's rough voice gave way to Pharrell's high-pitched croon, I kept dancing but also talking to the men, like I was a patron in a club. But of course, here, I was up on the stage for everyone to gawk at.

Kevin's next song was Nelly's "E.I.," and I started dancing like my life depended on it. No one had told me I was supposed to move around! I'm sure it was just a horrible sight, but eventually I strutted up and down the stage, not noticing that men were tossing money my way. Nobody even told me I was supposed to stop to collect their money, and I didn't have a garter belt to keep it all in. Eventually, it all started making sense, and I began picking up a whole lot of money. And this was how Caramel was born.

*   *   *

Despite being green that first day, I made $350—a hard *week's* work at Dayco. This was totally unexpected, and the idea of supplementing my income with such easy work got me hooked. And once I decided I was in, I went *all in*—like I do with everything else. Yes, I'd come back to the club to dance, but I didn't want to just come back and be a regular girl. No, competitiveness is in my DNA; I came from a family of great athletes, people who supplemented their God-given talents and their genetically agile bodies with hard work and practice to be better than everyone else.

Not only did I see the potential for a huge boost in income, and not only had I made up my mind to be the best stripper at Godiva's—I decided I was gonna be the greatest—*ever*. That night I went home and studied the film *Player's Club*, starring Lisa Raye, who played the main stripper in the movie. I watched it at least six or seven times and repeated her moves in my mind, the way she walked onstage unconcerned, swirling, rocking her whole body and licking her fingers all at once. I was determined to go back to Godiva's and perform a dance scene just like the one in the film, which I eventually did. After getting my costume, it was time to change my look. Back then, I usually wore a bob haircut, but a customer on that first day at Godiva's took a look at my hair and said, "You're either the po-po or a schoolteacher."

Now, the last thing I wanted was for someone to think I was the police, so I went home and put in a weave that hung down my back. I had also bought seven-inch stilettos from a store in Greenville called George's Bootery. I waited until no one was home one day and pranced up and down the hall. My heels were spilling out the shoes, and I nearly fell several times. At one point, I stood in the hall, defeated. *I can't do this. I just can't walk in heels. How do these girls do it?* I thought to myself.

But I kept at it, though it wasn't easy. Yet, after a couple of hours, I was able to sashay in those heels. I returned to Godiva's looking like a different person—no makeup but simple lip gloss and, instead of a bob, a long weave and stilettos.

The next item on my to-do list was to call Daddy to tell him what I was doing. I wasn't ashamed of stripping, but I didn't want Daddy hearing about it from someone else, either. He only asked me to promise two things: first, never do a Super Bowl party or bachelor party outside the club, because usually when girls do that, they get naked and have sex. And second, never have sex with those men inside the club.

I kept those promises.

*　*　*

One of my good friends put something in my head that I never forgot: treat stripping like a business. He suggested I create a persona, the "girlfriend" fantasy that men dream of. First, he said I had to imagine and then believe people would come to Godiva's and spend money because I was their fantasy. But he cautioned that if I slept with any of these strangers, then the fantasy would vanish. With that in mind, I began to forge a persona that men lusted for but would never actually get. That same friend told me to keep my nails and hair done and change my outfits regularly to keep the men curious. I took heed, going to Korean salons for weekly manicures and making sure my fourteen-inch weave was never out of place. While my outfit was sexy, the choice to wear no makeup gave me a natural vibe: I could be your best friend, the around-the-way girl, or your lover. I was friendly and approachable but still a mystery.

I put my heart and soul into conjuring Caramel; Godiva's became my university, and the other dancers, unbeknownst to them, were my instructors. I looked around, and everything I saw I rolled up into Caramel. I never emulated one person, but I took a little from this one, and a little from that one, and then made my own thing. And that's how Caramel became my work of art.

But creating her did not come easy. I walked into Godiva's at age twenty-nine, a mother of four, but I had never known how to be a seductress. Growing up in the country, you had sex with a person a couple of times, which meant you automatically were "going together."

Mark never asked me for my hand in marriage or to be exclusive, but that was the way it was. It's just what I saw everybody else do. Nobody taught me how to own my sexuality, or how to express it in subtle ways. However, Godiva's helped me discover my powerful sensuousness. I'd not only study how the dancers would sit down and talk to men, but I also focused on the way they touched them on the shoulder or how a squeeze on the knee could get a man to do anything. I watched closely how the women slung their hair back, how they cut their eyes, and how, when they laughed, they'd touch the man's knee right then and there. By now, I wanted to imitate these dancers not for money—because I knew that would come—but because they were teaching me how to walk, how to talk, how to sway, and how to *be*. Eventually, Caramel was like a phoenix: she rose, and once she was unleashed, she was on fire and there was no stopping her. She was my artistic creation, and she was badass. She could sit and talk to a person, and within five minutes they would do anything that she wanted.

*　*　*

Godiva's marked the first time I really found myself—the attention and the adrenaline were intoxicating, but so was the improvement in my self-esteem. I had so many men lined up for private dances, I could never get to everybody. Then, by the time I finished three dances, I was being called back onstage. As time went on, I became what they called a feature, which meant everybody came to see Caramel. I would strut from the back to my signature song, a rap song called "Still Fly" by Big Tymers. The moment the song started and the DJ called my name, I knew it was showtime. Everyone would pull their chair up to the stage. Caramel was the star. Every time I got up there, the other dancers did not want to follow behind me.

I wasn't a pole dancer climbing to the ceiling, but I was thin and had a big booty, and I learned how to make it clap. I knew how to make it shake. We were required to take off our shirts during the second songs, so I did that. I had the smallest little titties, but the men were there to see my booty jiggle.

Truth be told, my dancing technique helped make me become famous at Godiva's. I'd clap my booty then put my legs together and make my butt pop up and down. To this day women ask me to teach them how to do it, but the secret really is genetics. I had Mama's big loose butt—and the looser the butt, the better chance you had to make it clap. Tight behinds can't clap!

* * *

This was the first time in my life I was getting this much attention, not only from men, but from ladies, too.

My fellow dancers loved me because I was a hustler. All of us girls had a dance quota of ten dances a night. If you made the quota, you didn't have to pay a thirty-dollar tip to the house, that we called a "tip out." The private dances were in small rooms with a couch in the back. Getting a dance with us girls would cost thirty dollars a pop, with ten bucks going to the house. When a dancer goes into a private room, she dances to one song, but if the client wants two songs, it's sixty dollars; if the client wants three songs, then it's ninety dollars, four songs cost one hundred and twenty dollars, and so on.

I always met my quota, and I often danced in the champagne room, which was only a slightly bigger room than the private rooms and with a slightly bigger couch, but it cost $150 (I got to keep $100) to enter. Before heading to the champagne room, we were handed two cups and a cheap bottle of Pinot or white Zinfandel, which likely cost the club $10. The champagne room was upstairs, away from everyone. It was usually where the girls had sex. Although I never had sex in the champagne room or anywhere else in Godiva's, I couldn't go up there to just dance and then sit on the couch. I had to work smart and especially use my wits and manipulation to make it worth it for these men, and so I did—the money was good, and I didn't compromise my promise to Daddy, so while it could be monotonous, it wasn't too bad.

Three months after I started dancing at Godiva's, I got a wake-up call. One morning as I came home from the club at 6:00 a.m., I had fallen asleep at the wheel. My car spun around three times in the middle of the road and ended up on the other side of the street, facing the wrong way. It was terrifying. When I finally pulled into my yard and saw all the kids were already up to go to school, I realized that was it for me: I had to either stop stripping or working at the Dayco plant; I couldn't keep doing both.

I earned in a couple of hours at Godiva's what I made at Dayco in a week—I was often making a thousand dollars a night.

Leaving Dayco to strip full-time was an easy choice.

* * *

Whether the man was white, Black, or Mexican, he came into Godiva's knowing what he wanted. If he wanted someone to perform oral sex or just wanted chicken wings and a beer, somebody was always selling. It was simply a matter of negotiating a price.

Of course, some—but not all—of the dancers had sex with the men in the private rooms—and I suppose everyone had their own definitions of what sex was. If I'm to be honest, I didn't mind for men to just do their thing—by themselves. After all, whatever excited them, they did what they needed to do, and who was I to judge? Still, once their hands started moving toward their crotch, I moved out of the way. Some guys remained on the phone while you danced, and others would snort powder. Some would just sit there and stare at you while others jacked off. There were men who came in there with fetishes—some just wanted to play with your toes for forty minutes.

Then there were other people who wanted to create a fantasy on bachelor night by having sex with two or three women. Every man had his own thing that got him excited. Some wanted two of us girls in the private room, so we'd dance on each other. Ironically, most of the girls at Godiva's were gay, which didn't bother me. Some of the women wanted to "turn Caramel out." Those were the dancers I never joined in the private room. But all of us stayed away from men we called "the Regulars." They came every day in big groups, loading up on chicken wings and beer, but they wouldn't pay for a dance. We stayed away from them because usually it was a whole table full of them wasting your time. They had their beer and wine and chicken while looking around at everybody but wouldn't spend a dime on us girls.

The songs in the private room went on for about three to four minutes, but men always wanted another song because they wanted to sit and closely look at me, like they were memorizing me, while I danced. Others just wanted me to sit on their lap while they told me about their day.

Finally, I'd say, "Listen, let's just get a champagne room if you really want to keep talking." And a man would agree. If he was a talker, I'd coax him into getting three champagne rooms—that's three hundred dollars straight into my pocket.

I had a little routine. I'd dance in the beginning for two songs. Then I'd play like I'm tired. "My feet hurt. You really don't want me to dance five songs, do you?" Then I'd touch his shoulder and say, "Listen, how about if we just take your jacket off? I sit beside you; we just talk, I've been here all night, I'm tired."

The men always agreed. I had the gift of gab, and I was intent on getting the money, but I was for damn sure not going to dance to all those songs. The men never got upset; they were in the room with Caramel, and they did not want to piss her off.

Soon, a whole year went by, and the club stopped taking fees from me because I was bringing in so many people. I was constantly being called to dance on Friday nights because everyone was there to see Caramel. The most money I made onstage in one night was about $3,500. Kevin, the DJ (who also doubled as the club's bouncer), would scoop up my earnings from the floor with a bucket and lock the money in the DJ booth. After I pranced off the stage, I'd be hot and sweaty, but men would still be begging for a table dance and conversation. Eventually I'd go upstairs and get my money. The stage was my bank.

* * *

Because I didn't wear makeup, I didn't need to spend hours like other women getting ready for the night. I was in and out of the dressing room because I wanted to focus on making money. But I couldn't count the number of times I walked in on girls in the dressing room doing drugs or having oral sex with each other. I never judged them for the drugs; who am I to say what they needed to do to get them through the night? Instead, I'd laugh and joke with the girls; that was about all I had time for, especially on Fridays. There were only a few strip clubs in the region, so on Fridays, dancers came from all over the Southeast—from Charlotte, Atlanta, and Augusta.

One night as I dressed, a new dancer burst in. Brown Sugar was a short, mocha-skinned woman who was also drop-dead gorgeous. Her beauty was legendary, as were her tricks. She could put a lollipop in her privates and push it and in out, as if she had been sucking the lollipop right there.

She was the top dancer at Shakers, a strip club that had recently closed in nearby Spartanburg, and she had heard I was the top dog at Godiva.

"You must be the one everybody's talking about," she said. She looked me up and down as I got undressed. "So you really do have a big ass."

I didn't respond.

"Turn around," she demanded, as I stood naked, wiping the sweat off my body. "Ha! You got an ass, that's for sure. But a little coochie."

"Whatever, bitch," I said.

Brown Sugar placed her hands on her hip. "They say, I got"—she winked slyly—"the big coochie."

The room roared with laughter, but I only rolled my eyes. Still, I wasn't mad at Brown Sugar, who I grew to respect for her talent and the care she took in mentoring young strippers. Nonetheless, my time was spent outside the dressing room, either onstage or in a private room. While my style was sensual, I liked to come out on a fast song. Kevin knew how to get the crowd stirred up on a Friday night. When it was my time to go onstage, I was usually in the dressing room, wiping off sweat, or in the private room dancing for a customer, but when I heard my name called, I quickly got it together.

As a dancer, if you were late making your way to the stage, you were fined, but I never was. I would strut through the crowd walking by the bar. As my signature song started, the crowd parted like the Red Sea. I'd pass by Kevin, who had become a great friend and had shown me the ropes, along with pointing out which men spent money, which ones only wanted to eat wings, and which ones were drug dealers. When I needed a break, he'd lock the door to the DJ booth so I could just sit and rest on a stool beside him.

As I made my way through the room, men pulled their chairs to the edge of the stage. When I finally stepped onstage, I turned my back to the audience as I swayed to the music and checked myself in a giant mirror on the wall. I'd turn, making my way to the leg of the stage, where the customers were waiting. I'd walk around the pole a few times, lifting my legs and finally placing my back on the pole before sliding down. I would open my legs at the first man who was sitting there, staring, and looking in his eyes. I always wanted to make contact, letting him know my attention was fully on him. I was in the moment, dancing just for the man I had my eye on. Because there was so many men waiting, it was a challenge to get to them all, but I'd do it, changing things up just a bit for each man, sometimes sliding my booty in one man's face, shaking it and throwing my legs up. Other times I'd hold on to the pole and bring my legs down like I was doing a split in the air and then go to the next customer and do it all again, adding a little twist—of course.

* * *

Of all the dancers, one of them became a close friend. The first time I saw Destiny, she was sitting at the bar by herself smoking a cigarette. She was dressed simply and sporting a ponytail, looking like a plain Jane, even though she was a beautiful girl. Tall and thin, Destiny was light-skinned with freckles, the product of a very dark-skinned mother and a very white daddy.

"What's wrong with you?" I asked.

She blew out a stream of smoke. "Ain't nothing wrong." She didn't sound convincing.

"Something must be wrong. You're too pretty to be sitting here by yourself. And you're not going to make no money with that ponytail."

She didn't respond, so I wasn't sure how she took my suggestion. I

rarely talked to new girls, but I was drawn to her. I knew she was looking for a way to make some cash and wanted to help her, to explain to
her how it's done. Later that night she pulled her chair to the stage and
threaded a bill in my garter belt as I danced. This was common among
us dancers; it was our way of saying, "I see you and I appreciate you." One
thing we didn't do is throw money at another dancer, which was a sign
of disrespect since men did that to us all the time. Her gesture let me
know she was not offended by my earlier comment about her ponytail.

We talked again the next day, and then I called her that weekend to
see if she wanted to hang out with me and my kids.

It was a scorching South Carolina day, and she was in her apartment
alone. "I'm with the kids at the mall," I said. "I'm coming to get you." I
walked in her apartment, which felt like a furnace. Her boyfriend had
shut off the electricity, leaving her there to fry.

"Get your shit," I said. "You're coming with me."

She stared at me. "Where we going?"

She stayed with me at 115 for three days, and we've been best friends
ever since.

Although I was ten years older, we were a lot alike. For one thing, we
were both athletic and knew how to use our bodies in a way that made
us stand out. Destiny, who at Godiva's was known as Strawberry, had a
long torso and long legs and could put both her legs behind her head;
that was her signature move. Her thing was to throw her legs up in the
air and make them shake. While sitting in a chair, she'd put one leg behind her head and then take her other leg and fold her body to make
herself look like a pretzel on stage. Nobody else could touch that.

The two of us could make a man's day. During a bachelor party, Strawberry and Caramel would put on a show. We'd place the groom in a chair,
and I would sit in his lap, while Strawberry would do a flip, resulting in
her head in my lap; then she'd toss her legs in the air, so that her behind
would be in the groom's face. Though we never practiced, everything we
did was sensual, and everything came together seamlessly.

I spent all my youth raising babies, but Destiny was young, sponta-
neous, and liked to party, which might be why I loved being around her
so much. I was finally having fun and feeling free, but not free enough to

do drugs. Back in the early 2000s, Ecstasy was almost like candy, which is why I guess they called it Skittles. Occasionally, Destiny would have a "bad roll" of Ecstasy, which gave her headaches and made her nauseous. I never understood why someone would try a drug again after they had a bad experience, but my girl would do it again. If she had another bad roll, I was going to make sure she got home okay and that no one took advantage of her. There are many rules in the stripper world, and one is that older strippers would take the younger strippers under their wings. I didn't need to teach Destiny how to dance, but I did give her life tips. The day she chased a girl around Godiva's with a knife, I grabbed her by the throat and threatened her to stop: "This is not the day you're going to jail."

I was also the one who encouraged her to get a weave and start looking at dancing as a business rather than a job, which she ultimately mastered.

Eventually me and Destiny would laugh about all of what went on in Godiva's, but a lot of what happened to some of the younger girls was not funny at all and hurts my soul to this day. I've always been conscious of what I drink, what I put in my body, because given my family history, I'm a blink away from being addicted myself. If it was that easy for my mama, it'll be that easy for me. I'm terrified of getting addicted to anything. I've always had that fear in my head, and I thank God for that because it kept me alive and kept me from ever putting drugs in my body. I've been around so much dope in my life it's ridiculous, but I've also never been persuaded to try it.

Time after time, I'd see people numbing their pain with drugs at Godiva's, but despite my hardships in life, it never crossed my mind to do that. Now, of course, I numbed myself with a lot of Hennessy—and even men—but never drugs.

And yet, I've seen girls at the strip club, not even eighteen years old, snorting up cocaine. I remember one young white girl who came to dance at Godiva's. She started off innocent and fun loving, but her boyfriend died in a car accident, which turned her into a person who'd let men run through her. I walked in the dressing room one day and witnessed a guy shooting her arm with heroin.

"Why would you be in here and letting these dudes run through you?" I asked her. She seemed lost in life and would let all kinds of men have sex with her. "You're a cute white girl," I'd reason with her. "You don't need to do this."

I don't know what ever happened to her because I never saw her again after that night, but I pray she listened to me.

*   *   *

While dancing brought a lot of pain for some girls, it brought me independence. I didn't have to stay with a man I shouldn't have been with just to pay my bills or to ensure my children had a stable life. Dancing at Godiva's allowed me to buy Mama a brand-new, smooth-riding burgundy Chevy Malibu, and I purchased myself a pearl-white Lexus right off the lot—though I only drove my blue Honda to work. I also had a Ford Expedition on 22s, which were blinged-out rims. Back then, I was living two lives. On Wednesday, Thursday, Friday, and Saturday, I was Caramel. Sunday through Tuesday, I was the soccer mom. I attended all my kids' games and missed nothing. Whatever they needed for the team, if it was my time, I made sure that I did it over and beyond. If Kesha said, "Mama, it's your turn for snacks," I was the type of mom who would go set up a whole table and arrange rows of subs and chips and soft drinks for the team.

On the days I worked at Godiva's, Mama watched the kids, but really, she had to watch only Shanterria, who was still a toddler. DeAndre was in middle school and spent a lot of time with his godparents on the weekends, and Marcus and Kesha were preteens.

Still, I'd give Mama a hundred dollars on Friday, and I'd give each child twenty dollars a day to go to school, because now I finally had it like that. I kept my money in a safe under the bed, but sometimes I'd lay out the cash on the bed and show Kesha, who was about thirteen or fourteen, how to count it. I'd say "Kesha, face all the hundred-dollar bills the same way, and let's put them in stacks of five." And then we would create rows of five until we covered the entire mattress. The first time I did it, we counted eighteen thousand dollars, but the amount would continue to grow.

* * *

The children embraced our modern-ranch home, which brought us so much happiness during this time. They personalized their rooms with Clemson Tigers posters. There was laughter, and fun, and a lot of time sitting around that big grandfather table, just like I had hoped for and imagined.

When the kids weren't playing basketball right outside the house, everybody was active in recreational sports, and they were all excelling. Kesha was one of the best point guards in South Carolina—the girl could handle a basketball like nobody's business. None of my children ever played middle school ball but went straight to high school varsity because they were always just that good. They were all the captains of their teams. DeAndre and Marcus played football and won championships left and right.

One day I was headed to work at Godiva's with my little stripper clothes on, when I passed by Kesha's bedroom. Back then our big computer screens had screen savers that would jump from one photograph to the other. I noticed she only had posters of girls on her walls, and her screen saver was filled with women from the Clemson basketball team.

I backed up and stood at her door. "Kesha, are you gay?"

She was about to lie but I imagine something in her told her to just say yes.

I nodded. "Well, you know I'm not gonna love you any less. I got to go. Bye."

And that was it.

She later told me she was in her room holding her breath waiting for my response to her being gay. She had seen her friends get put out of their homes and disowned, especially her teammates. She was afraid I'd do the same, but when I told her I'd love her no matter what, she felt free to be herself, a young, gay adult.

* * *

While all this was going on, I was having a thing with a man I met at Godiva's. Barry worked at the giant Bi-Lo warehouse in Greenville.

Good-looking, with low-cropped, wavy hair, he was tall and lanky, with swagger. Every Wednesday, he'd come to Godiva's right before I got off work and take me to his home, where we always had sex. That was what our relationship was about and not much more.

A low-key single dad raising his son, Barry was different from most of the men in my life. Every single time I'd spend the night, he'd have my towel and washcloths ready. He never judged me; in fact he was fascinated about the whole stripper lifestyle and asked a lot of questions about it.

Barry was a once-a-week-kind-of-hangout guy, until he wasn't. He would stick around at Godiva's until I got off, and I'd follow him to his house nearby. I knew we'd never be anything more than sex partners, but secretly I longed to be in a relationship with him. I loved the idea of being with him because he was so easy; he listened to me and was very compassionate. It was a good friendship. Both of our birthdays were in April, and sex was great during our Wednesday-night hookups. But I never said anything to him about wanting more, because I didn't think he'd accept my lifestyle other than being cool with our hookups. I guess, as a stripper, and even though I was a popular and successful one, I was still feeling insecure deep down.

One rainy Friday I was driving to work, thinking I'd finally have a slow night at Godiva's, when my phone rang. It was Barry. I was excited that he called me right before I headed into work. He would sometimes come in, stand around, and leave, but he never called before work. His voice was quiet.

"I'm going back to my girlfriend."

"Damn," I said. "Girlfriend? I didn't know you had a girlfriend." I laughed, trying to mask my surprise. "I've been coming over to your house for over a year now, and she was never around."

"Well, she was," he said. "She just lives in Spartanburg."

At that moment my heart dropped, and I tried not to let him hear my voice trembling. I still remember how calm his voice was. I thought, *How dare you call me and tell me this bullshit!* Me and Barry never solidified our relationship, but it was our thing, and it worked for me. But he really didn't know me and had never seen the other side of me—the craziness.

I knew I couldn't scream or shout at him. "Okay," I said politely.

"So I will see you around."

"Yes," I said, hiding my fury. "Sure."

I pulled my blue Honda Accord over at the nearest exit, parked at a gas station, and just sat there. I was pissed off, and I had a million questions for him, but we didn't have the type of relationship where I could ask a lot of questions.

Deep down I wanted more of him, but believed I wasn't good enough. It hadn't occurred to me until then that in many ways nothing had changed. Yes, I was desired by dozens, sometimes more than a hundred men, on a Friday night, and I was making great money and supporting my family on my own. But inside I was still the girl abused by Reverend Lottie, mistreated by Mark, and dumped and used by a string of men I thought I had loved. I sat there in my sorrow and cried for twenty minutes until I pulled myself together, but I was visibly upset when I drove into the Godiva's parking lot. I sat alone in the car for another ten minutes, gathering my thoughts and emotions.

By the time I hit the front door of Godiva's, I was all the way back together. I saw Barry only once again at the club—he was not there for me but with his friends. I tried my best not to look his way. Once again, another man that I liked and thought could possibly be my boyfriend was gone.

CHAPTER 14

The Lying Game

As upsetting as it was, the fact that Barry abruptly ended our Wednesday-night hookups didn't amount to much after all, because my life was about to take a very exciting turn.

One night after dancing, Destiny and I went to an after-party, where I met a famous rapper who had just performed in Greenville: JT Money. I was familiar with his music because my sons listened to him, and I also knew he pioneered the rap game in Miami. As I left his after-party that night, JT grabbed my hand and said, "You're the most beautiful woman in the room, which is why I thought you were here for me."

Within minutes, he was inviting me to come with his entourage to Atlanta.

His ego and presumptions about me made me laugh. "I can't," I said, faking a sad look. "My son's birthday is tomorrow."

We exchanged numbers, and he called me the next day. "No one ever turned me down like that," he said. "Let me fly you to Miami." It was an enticing proposition.

Most of my childhood and young adulthood were spent raising children—Dilly, Hummie, and later, my own. I'd never really spent any time out of Clemson, much less in the presence of a celebrity. So flying to meet a rapper was something I could never have imagined would happen to me, but I was up for the challenge, though nervous about going by myself.

But from the moment I touched down in Miami, JT made sure I had the time of my life. We strolled up and down the strip on South Beach, where he took me shopping; he even picked up trinkets for me to take home to my mom and friends. I bought shoes for nearly everybody I knew and stuffed my suitcase full!

That trip to Miami would be the first of many; JT also came for a quick visit to Clemson, where he took photographs with DeAndre and Marcus.

During another trip to see him, JT took me to his studio, where I got to meet his friends—the rappers Trina and Trick Daddy. I also met his mother, father, and siblings. The great Isaac Hayes even visited the studio that day. Whether we were backstage at a concert or a party, girls were always coming in and out, but I was never intimidated because JT always made sure that I was good. His staff paid me the attention I needed, and if he had to leave, they were certain I got to where I needed to be.

Meanwhile, Destiny hooked up with another successful rapper. Here we were, two small-town girls hanging with big-time celebrities. We were living that life—a feeling I hadn't truly had ever since Steve. It was no big thing for the rappers to fly us to Miami for a weekend visit. Destiny was who I called my "road dog"; she loved nothing more than to be on a road trip with me, behind the wheel of my new burgundy Expedition. I'd sit back and listen to her music selections booming in the CD player as we took random road trips together or drove, usually to Atlanta or Miami, to hang with our famous flings.

The limousines, the concerts, the celebrities, and the sex with JT made me feel like a star. JT brought out another side of life—one of glamour, excitement, and wealth. Destiny and I were basking in the light of celebrity, and I couldn't ask for more, right? I had a glow and high about me that I never thought I could achieve.

Like always, though, I was missing something. But what?

I think it was that this new normal was abnormal to me; chaos was all I knew. And somewhere, deep down in some dark, psychological place, being treated well and showered with affection felt foreign.

Though we remained friends, things with JT soon fizzled out—as these things do with celebrities—but I was fine with that because while the relationship was fun, it was also never deep.

* * *

At the peak of my dancing career, I befriended a gentleman named Harry, who became my sugar daddy. He always entered the club wearing a three-piece suit and smelling like Old Spice. He'd buy one glass of wine at the bar and spend time with me in a private room talking about his wife, whom he was divorcing. Harry was fifty-five and was coming to the club for companionship, but he didn't come across as creepy or lonely. Instead, he was full of life and a great conversationalist.

He'd spend hundreds of dollars in the champagne room with me, where he'd drink white Zin while I listened patiently as he talked about his divorce. We did this for months, but we never had sex, even though it was tempting at times only because he cared for me so deeply; he would ask about my children and hand me a thousand dollars instead of the three hundred he owed for his time in the private room. Often, he dropped into the club to make sure I was safe.

Once, when I complained about bills I owed, he met me at a Ruby Tuesday and straight-up handed me three thousand dollars. Harry never asked for sex, but instead would say, "I don't want you to do something strange for a little change." Back then, I was in full manipulation mode, and so it was easy to play along with Harry. Once he took me to Jamaica—that was the only time he wanted to have sex, but I was able to get myself out of that by saying I was on my period. Still, we had a great time, visiting the dunes and ganja shops and attending a reggae concert.

* * *

Those times with JT and Harry were periods when I wasn't longing for a man to love—at least that is what I told myself. After so much trauma, I was living my best life, with a feeling that something better was around the corner. I had no idea what that something was, but I knew I was starting to get a little tired of Godiva's.

I was dancing for almost two years before a drop-dead handsome man came into the club. He had gorgeous hair: you can pull a piece and it'll snap back into a curl. He also had a wide face and something special about his eyes—they were dark and set deep. He'd come into the club and just stare. He wouldn't speak to me, and so I tried to pay him very little attention.

One day when I got up to dance, strutting to the stage and finessing my way through the crowd, he grabbed my arm. I looked back but never halted my stride. He pulled his chair up, but I didn't see any money. I guess in his mind he thought he was all that, which honestly intrigued me. We made eye contact while I was dancing, but he remained in his seat with a smirk on his face. I always know when a man wants Caramel because they start to tip me, but this man never did. He would simply look but wouldn't speak.

After drying off and changing my outfit, I flew back out onto the floor when the man stopped me cold. "What's your name?"

I laughed and shook my head. "You know my name."

His smile was intoxicating. "You're not gonna tell me your real name?"

"No," I said. "Why is it important?"

A couple of weeks later I was out at a Mexican restaurant and club called La Isla, and this same man came up and introduced himself to me. His name was Antonne. And he told me that he'd be going home with me that night.

I smiled and rolled my eyes. "Whatever," I said, shaking my head.

Antonne flirted all night but never offered to buy me a drink. If that didn't tell me he was broke or cheap, the fake gold necklace that had turned slightly green and had smeared on his beige sweater should have. But what really should have given me pause was that Antonne didn't have a car. He was from Greenville, and it seemed every Black man growing up in Greenville was industrious enough to always have two things—a nice car and either a job or a side hustle, which could range from cleaning vans and cars on the weekend to wiping down the insides of corporate buildings at night. But Antonne, I'd learn, had none of those things.

"I'm riding with you," he declared.

I flashed him a side-eye and then blushed. "No, you're not."

"I am riding with you," he repeated himself.

When I got ready to leave, he followed me out. "Where *we* going?" he asked.

"We are going to my homegirl's house." He was gorgeous and seemed harmless enough, so I let him get in the car with me and my friends, where he jumped in the back seat like the freeloader I'd later learn him to be.

While at my friend's apartment, he persuaded me to take him home to my place—the man did know how to talk. We didn't leave the house for three days, which is when I first realized he was still living with his mom. Meanwhile, the whole time he's telling me we're going to be together and that he wanted to take care of me.

I knew, of course, that he barely had two nickels to rub together. And I had my doubts about shacking up with a guy who hadn't left his mama's home. But he seemed so devoted to me, like a puppy would be, and I was all about that. After Richard, and the fling with the rapper JT, I was thinking I was ready for a boyfriend who was devoted, who put me first, who chased me, who I could manipulate and control—rather than the other way around.

Man, would I be wrong.

* * *

Despite warning signs that Antonne wasn't the sweet and loving person he pretended to be, my relationship with him developed quickly: I thought I finally had a man who worshipped me, not the other way around. I came to trust him enough to let him be around my kids—the first man I'd allowed into their lives since Richard.

Of course, with Antonne there were plenty of red flags. He was a liar and a narcissist who loved to play games, but I was too caught up in the lying game myself—this fantasy of who I was when I was dancing, my overconfidence about playing men for their money, and the special attention Antonne paid to me—to notice the danger signs. In my head, I was Caramel, the manipulator of men. I thought I could control Antonne like I could control Harry and the others who came to Godiva's, but I would learn that I had met my match. Antonne was never one of those men: he was the real master manipulator, whose power and control sprung from an environment of confusion.

How did I get here so fast? A few months earlier, I was all smiles, being showered with gifts and awakened with coffee and bagels while a celebrity rapper laid next to me. I had been living the life, but now I was once again feeling empty and inadequate.

Antonne brought the lies, the cheating, the manipulation I had not experienced in a long time, but dysfunction was all I really knew. He would lie, and so I would lie. It's said that abused people are prone to returning to the environments that traumatized them as children because it's what feels familiar. Unfortunately, this was also true for me: I was once again in self-sabotage mode. How I got to this place with a man I had just met, it's still hard to understand.

Before Antonne, I was riding a wave of attention, and I was happy—or was I? Truth be told, I knew Caramel was a fantasy, and once the men ran out of money, they knew it, too—before long, they were home with their wives, and I was home in a bed by myself. At least with Antonne I wasn't alone; confused, yes, but not alone. So instead of getting rid of a pathological liar and game player, I devoted my energy to trying to understand or even match his game and his next moves.

Everything about him felt tilted—like I was always climbing uphill; something didn't feel right. He'd want me to pick him up, and he'd give me some address, but he wouldn't be there when I'd arrive. And then he'd give me another address, and he was again nowhere to be found—like it was a game. At one point I was so done with it that I threw a plate of food at him, hitting the back of his head. He just looked at the food on the floor. "Baby," he asked, "who's gonna clean this shit up?" Nothing I could do would run him off.

To prove he loved me, he got a tattoo with my name across his chest in the biggest, boldest black letters you can imagine. And I was thinking maybe he really does love me—it hadn't occurred to me yet that this guy was actually psycho.

One day while I was taking a shower, he burst into the bathroom and jumped in under the water with me. Then, when his phone rang, he said, "Baby, get that. It's probably my sister." I got out of the shower to get it, but it wasn't his sister—instead, it was this female. I later discovered that her name was Savannah. She was asking for him, but of course, me being petty me, I told her he was in the shower. So then I hung up, but the phone kept ringing.

What was up with this Savannah?

* * *

I started seeing something else about Antonne. He wasn't just a liar who always tried to confuse me, but I soon realized I was dealing with someone darker than I ever thought, a controlling manipulator, someone I'd learn I could not out master. But I did not heed the signs that I was playing a very dangerous game with a jealous and resentful man.

There was one time he started arguing with me while we were out with the kids at a restaurant. He stormed out, saying he was going to get some air. When our meal was done, we exited the restaurant to find Antonne leaning again my SUV, smoking a cigarette. I went around to the passenger side of the car and discovered a new, long key scratch from the front of my truck to the back. The man obviously keyed the vehicle, but of course he denied everything.

Antonne always had a smile on his face, but his actions proved he was seething inside. One night, he had my burgundy SUV while I was working in the strip club. After my shift, when I walked to the truck that night, the first thing I noticed was one of its windows had been busted out. He lied, telling me some kids threw a rock at the vehicle.

Antonne's actions were subtle and sinister, designed to throw me off. I always liked to collect decorative plates when I traveled, and I kept them all on my fireplace mantel. Every time Antonne showed up, though, another plate would disappear. He did things like that over and over. For instance, I opened my photo album one day and found six of my pictures were torn in half and replaced in the album.

Antonne was not a normal person—he was a handsome maniac I should have kept clear of. Despite my success as a stripper, I still saw myself as not quite enough without a man, and once again I found myself lying to everyone by making excuses for the very inadequate man in my life.

" " "

Weekends with Antonne were the roughest, because he really didn't want to be at my house. It was more that he was obsessed with fear about me being with another man while he was away. So instead of going home, he'd hang out at my house just so he could torment me. One night I heard him talking to another girl on his phone. "Baby, Baby, I need you to come get me."

I walked in on him. "I know you ain't telling another bitch to come pick you up from my house."

"I need to be out of this house," he said.

I shook my head. "I'll tell you what. I'll do you one better. I'll take your ass home."

It was midnight, and I wasn't about to leave the children alone. So I packed everybody up in the SUV. "Hey, get up," I told them. "I'm taking Antonne home."

As we drove up Hilltop, me and Antonne started arguing again. During all the fussing, he flinched at me, like he was about to hit me.

I slammed on my brakes. "Get the fuck out my car, you got to get out now!" I screamed. "Call them and tell them to come get you, or you got to walk!"

He jumped out the passenger seat but rushed around on the driver's side. I could see him coming, so I got out of the car because I felt vulnerable sitting down. The kids also tumbled out the car onto the street. DeAndre—who at just ten had hidden a kitchen knife on his person to take with him on our ride—told me later he planned to stab Antonne in his chest if he flinched again or hit me. To this day, I thank God he didn't do that. He was fed up with anybody hurting me, but as a boy, he was no match for a grown-ass man.

* * *

After just three months of dating Antonne, I was completely stressed out. He was exhausting to even be around because if he wasn't on his phone telling lies, he started coming to the club. He wouldn't ever leave me be. He would stand out in the hallway by the dressing room or walk up to me while I was dancing or at the bar to beg until I gave him a hundred dollars.

One of the girls approached me to say, "Girl, he ain't shit. You need to leave him alone."

Antonne embarrassed me because even though he was handsome, he always looked a little dirty, a little unkempt, with his pants running three sizes too big. Poor fashion sense aside, being with Antonne was like taking care of another child.

Looking back, I'd say he was intent on driving me crazy.

*　*　*

By spring 2002, I needed a break and decided to go to Daytona with Destiny and a few other girls for BET's Spring Bling, which was a big televised school break special that attracted students from across the country. Nikki, one of my friends I met through the rapper JT Money, had connections to some of the artists there. Destiny and I picked up Nikki in Atlanta, and several other friends of Nikki's in different parts of Florida. I was feeling young and free in the car with these girls. I felt good.

But there was one black cloud over the whole situation. The entire way to Daytona, Antonne called me more than a hundred times. I didn't want to shut my phone off because I knew that if I did, he'd just fill up my voicemail. Plus, I needed my mama and children to be able to get in touch with me in an emergency. But Antonne was jealous and frantic that I was going to Daytona without him, and he was determined to walk a cruel path to make my trip miserable.

The girls in the car laughed at the calls but also sounded a little worried for me. "Oh my God, that's your boyfriend again?" one would ask.

I'd call him when we'd pull up for gas, thinking that that would stop him. And he'd say, "I hear niggas around you. I know you with somebody! If you were going to fuck somebody, tell me. TELL ME. TELL ME!!"

One of the girls in the car, her name was Tammy, said, "Girl, a nigga like that, you can't trust him. He might do anything to you when you get back home. You need to leave him alone."

"I will," I assured them as we pulled into Daytona. Truth be told, I wasn't nervous at all, just ready to have a good time.

* * *

We stayed at the Adams Mark hotel, which is where you'd see the celebrities, football players, cool and famous people everywhere. And once we got to the hotel, I shut off my phone for a while and felt free and happy.

Although I was thirty-one and many of the girls in Daytona were college students, my body after four kids was at its best. Everywhere I went that week, people were gawking at me and telling me I was cute or beautiful. Stripping was not hard work for me, but most people don't realize we're working out all the time. My muscles were tight, which meant my clothes looked perfect on me. That week, I squeezed my size-10 booty into a size-5 pair of white shorts. I also wore a red knit halter top with no bra and high platform sandals. Everywhere I went, people kept calling me Beyoncé because my long microbraids that hung down my back were made of three different colors.

* * *

The hotel divided the building into two parts: the regular people who came to see the concerts stayed on one side, and the celebrities had the entire other side. In fact, we couldn't get on the celebrity side of the hotel unless we were invited. Fortunately, Destiny befriended someone who gave her two passes, which allowed us to move among everyone in the industry and also go backstage during the shows.

We hung out with some of the top rap stars of the day, including the Cash Money crew, Juvenile, Mannie Fresh, and Trina and her crew. We met Lil Wayne when he was really young and Lil Jon before he got big on *The Apprentice*. Singers Jaheim and Ginuwine all tried to holler at me, but I ended up talking to Big Tigger, who created BET's top show, *Rap City: The Basement*. I had walked into a hot Black male Chocolate

Factory—meanwhile, the whole time Antonne was blowing my phone up and screaming at me.

What I didn't tell any of the girls was that he wasn't just pissed, he was threatening to kill me. I blew it all off as hot air and hung out with Big Tigger, who was fun and polite. And soon enough the two of us would be involved in an "entanglement."

By the end of the weekend, we all packed into my SUV to head home. On the road, I received a phone call from Tigger's secretary. "Hi, Sabrina," she said. "Tigger wants your address. He wants to send you some flowers, and he wants to make sure you had a good trip home."

Getting flowers from a celebrity made all my other worries disappear.

* * *

I did not expect that I'd return home to find Antonne sweet as pie, cooking red cabbage and stuffed chicken for me and "Baby this," "Baby that." In my presence he could be very cuddly, kissing my arm or even my leg, and he'd be so into me, but it was confusing because when he wasn't with me, he definitely was not to be trusted.

It was his method of operation to get very angry and hold a grudge but not always show it. But the weekend was great, and now he was acting so nice that I had let my guard down, forgetting that Antonne's Dr.-Jekyll-and-Mr.-Hyde personality could surely, eventually, come back and cut me like a double-edged sword.

One day he got mad at me for something, revealing the sweetness was all a ploy. "The only reason I fucked you was to see if you had sex with another nigga in Florida, and you did, bitch."

"What?"

"Your coochie wasn't the same, hoe."

I finally figured out that Antonne was both jealous of my success and also obsessed with keeping me away from other men. As it turns out, he was playing a long, long game. In just three months' time, Antonne gained access to my home, my children, my cars, my friends—my entire life. And I knew I had let him turn me upside down into a whole different person, as I was constantly struggling to keep up with him and his lies and trying to figure out what was what.

Still, I never let anyone know that I wasn't myself because, in my mind, I got a man. As desperate as that seems now, I had a man.

Unfortunately, I wouldn't have imagined in a hundred years what horror was still to come.

CHAPTER 15

The Attack

Antonne was devious enough to always look like he had something going on, but nothing was actually going on. He would talk about getting a job here, or he'd be doing this there. And whatever it was, it sort of made sense but in a confusing way—he was a master at keeping me off-balance.

Over that summer of 2002, he had decided to enroll at ITT Technical Institute, located about twenty-five minutes away in Greenville. I didn't know what he was studying, or why he thought it was a good idea, but he was there. After a bad argument one Friday, he woke up next to me on the morning of July 20, acting all loving and speaking in a soothing way, and he said, "Baby, I need the car, I got to go to school." I had just gotten to bed after dancing all night. I mumbled for him to take the car—the older, blue Honda. And so, I laid there after he left—this was maybe at 9:00 a.m.—until I woke up a couple hours later.

I did my little morning routine—I checked on the kids: Shanterria was in Kesha's room watching cartoons. I took a shower, thought about what to eat, and before long I noticed that my keys to the Lexus were gone. When I realized he took my brand-new, pearl-white Lexus, the car I called my fifth child, the car I had just purchased, I got pissed off, real quick. The first thing in my mind: *I know this nigga better not have taken my keys.* I called him; there was no answer. I sat down at the side of my bed—furious. I thought he should know better than to take my car. I called him again, but still no answer. I then got a call from my cousin Missy.

"What you doing today?" she asked.

"Oh nothing, this nigga just done took my car."

"Antonne?"

I told her he used it to get to class at ITT Tech.

"Girl," she sighed, "you know I go to ITT, too. We ain't got no school today." The campus was empty that day; no classes were being held.

"You lying."

"Brina, meet me in Greenville. Let's have lunch."

"Let me go get my damn car, and I'll call you went I get to Greenville."

There was no way I was going to lunch with my cousin, because now I was furious with Antonne about lying about having school and for taking my car. I didn't have any plans to go into the city that day, but it looked like I had to go and fetch my damn car in Greenville. I called Antonne again—still no answer. When I got dressed and bolted toward the door, Shani started crying. She was four, and she was my baby. That was one of my last memories of any of my children for a long time. I remember her walking outside the screen door crying for me. I made her go back in the house, and she stood at the screen door as I pulled out the driveway upset. My baby needed me, but there I was running behind foolishness and a man. While I was in the car, Missy called several times. "What he say?"

I was halfway to Greenville in my Honda when I got that other call—this time it's Antonne. "Wait . . . this him now," I said to Missy, switching lines.

"Where you at?" I demanded.

"Baby, baby, meet me at my mom's house."

His mother was living in Travelers Rest, a town another fifteen minutes north from Greenville. This was out of my way, and I was tired of him by now. I was tired of this man's shit. "Why would you take my car?" I asked him over the phone.

But he didn't answer the simple question. "Just meet me at my mom's. I'm going to explain everything."

I was confused and pissed. He was playing the typical "Antonne game," by not being where he said he was going to be or being vague at where he was. The whole time I was cussing him out. "You knew not to take my fucking car. I'm done."

"Baby! Baby," he'd pleaded.

The truth? Although I had been "done" with Antonne a hundred times, this time, I really *was* done. I caught him in a lie and could prove it. I knew I didn't deserve how he was treating me, and I was tired of all he had put me through. At that moment, I didn't want him around me or my children anymore. Going to Greenville to get my car myself, and being rid of him, was my way of getting some control over my life. I also wanted to prove a point, that I finally caught him in a lie. That was important to me. The person I was back then had a sick and twisted constitution: if I was going to end the relationship, I needed to be the good guy. His lie had given me ammunition to end this charade with me on top. He played his Antonne game well, but I had finally beat him at it. But here's the tragic thing about all this. Finally, I was done with this man, but it nearly cost me my life.

* * *

It took me thirty minutes to get to Greenville, but it felt like seconds because the whole time I was on the phone switching between talking with my cousin Missy and with Antonne. The closer I got to Greenville, the more red I saw. *Why in the hell did I have to go out of my way to get my own car?* Who could help me with all this? I needed another driver to take the Honda back once I found the Lexus. I was thinking of asking Missy to help when Antonne called me again.

"Baby, I'm not at my mom's house. I'm at another house, at another place."

I was driving faster now. "Tell me the address."

"Baby, I don't know it." But then he gave me some vague directions to find a gas station and convenience store, then to go down that road and turn this way or that.

I kind of knew the vicinity, and I was close. "Okay, I'll be there in a minute."

So I proceeded to head to where I thought he wanted me to go. This plan was easier for me—at least I didn't have to go all the way to Travelers Rest. Meanwhile, my blood was boiling; I was going to raise hell about my car. Then I planned to go meet Missy, not really thinking how in the heck I was going to drive two cars. But, like always with Antonne, he knew how to distort my state of mind. Once again, I was playing his game. How many times had this man told me to go to a place only to find he wasn't there? This was just another day with Antonne, me looking for him at some house where he may or may not be.

Of course, he wasn't at the gas station where he said he'd be. So I just happen to turn on a side street, where I came to a stop sign. I had no idea where I was or where I was supposed to go or what he was up to. I could turn left or right; my gut told me to turn right. To this day, I have no idea why. Up the block, I saw a new white Lexus parked outside a brick duplex apartment building. I pulled behind it and got out to make sure that it was mine. *It's my car all right.* But why wasn't it where Antonne said it'd be? Where was Antonne?

As I walked around the car, making sure there was no damage, I heard a voice coming out of the apartment building.

"Baby, baby, what are you doing here?" Antonne asked.

"What do you mean, what am I doing here?"

"Baby, I told you to pull up down the street."

I had my hands on my hips now. "What difference does it make?"

We were standing out there in the street, arguing, when he turned and grabbed my wrist. "Baby, baby, it's not what you think. She says she's pregnant, and that's the only reason I came here."

I stared at him, probably with my mouth open. I was never even thinking a woman was involved. "She who?"

By now he was squeezing my wrist really tight. His back was facing the apartment building at first, but he was now trying to spin me around, turning me away from the building. I was trying to pull myself free from his hold on my wrist. Again, we started cussing back and forth.

"You ain't nothing but a damn liar!" I said. "You was never at ITT Tech! Why'd you take my car?"

Right then someone behind me called my name: "Sabrina!"

I didn't recognize this angry high-pitched female voice. I tried to turn around, but Antonne's holding both my arms. So I pulled my right hand real hard from his grip until I was able to jerk away; he's still squeezing my left arm. I turned the right side of my body to face the building, and as I did, I caught a glimpse of a woman, who was presumably the person who just called me by my name. Suddenly I felt a warm sensation on my face. With all the tussling, my back was to the door, and I turned only the right side of my body to the female voice. If I had been facing the door like Antonne was, I would have seen her coming.

I first thought, *Why was she pouring water on me?*

But it wasn't water. My face began to tingle, burned to the touch, and soon skin started to come off in my hand. Strangely I felt little pain. If someone had thrown a brick at my head, now *that* would hurt, but my body was going into shock and everything was starting to shut down. My mind began racing, as I tried to process all that was happening around me. I hit the ground, fell to my knees as more skin started sliding off my body—down my back, my neck, and my face. There was blood everywhere. I knew it was mine, but I couldn't understand what was happening. Finally, I fell flat on my back. I looked up at the sun, but it was as if someone had drawn a curtain over my eyes.

I blinked and blinked, but all I could see was darkness.

* * *

That day was July 20, 2002, a Saturday, at noon. The sun was bright, and it was hot. It was a beautiful day. I could hear muted voices that seemed to be around me. And for some reason things were moving very slowly. The curtain over my eyes had come down, and everything was now all white. As it descended, my breathing felt shallow. I wasn't scared. I was more trying to figure out what was going on with my body; what's happening? When I felt my skin in my hands, I started panicking and panting for breath. I was trying to get up, but I couldn't. It's as if a ton of bricks had buried me. Vaguely, I heard Antonne shouting, "Savannah! Why'd you do that?" He kept hollering and shouting, but after a while I couldn't hear him anymore. I'm focused on getting air; I could not breathe. I managed to lift a hand to touch my skin, but it felt like raw muscle.

I knew I must be dying.

In that moment, I thought this is what it must have been like when my brothers, Dilly and Hummie, took their last breaths—this is what it was like when they died.

I, too, was really dying, but I never stopped trying to breathe or get up.

I don't know how long I laid there, but eventually somebody—it was Antonne—scooped me up off the ground to put me in the white Lexus. I held on to the car door, struggling to stand up, desperately gasping for breath. He pushed me into the passenger seat and drove for what felt like forever but was actually just two minutes away to the gas station, the same one I had passed on my way there. He sped into the parking lot, bumping and jostling the car. He parked and dragged me out of the car. There was nobody but an attendant behind the cash register. I couldn't see her, of course, because I was totally blind. She started screaming.

"Oh shit! What do I do? What should I do?!" she yelled.

She went and shut the door. "Should I call 911?" she asked.

I assume Antonne must have said yes. Or maybe I did. The two of them dragged me over to a water fountain near the cashier counter. I held myself up against the fountain as the attendant splashed water in my eyes and face. I was screaming: "I'm blind! I can't breathe!"

I slid down the water fountain onto my knees—I couldn't hold myself up any longer. I still don't understand what exactly happened, but I was certain these were my last moments on this Earth. The attendant was still screaming; she was panicking, too. But I didn't hear Antonne anymore. He left, abandoning me on the floor of a gas station to die.

Suddenly I sensed other people crashing in—this must be the EMS, I thought. Someone lifted me onto a stretcher. They asked for my mama's name.

* * *

Close to a month later I woke up from a medically induced coma. I was in a burn center in Augusta, Georgia, where I had been taken by a medevac helicopter. Seventeen percent of my body had been burned. I was told later that my heart had stopped beating at the hospital in Greenville the EMS brought me to. And that it stopped again on the helicopter flight to Augusta.

At first, I didn't realize I was blind. I remember the TV was on. I remember thinking my nurse must be Black, because I was on so much morphine, and so many other drugs, that when I woke up in the hospital, I thought I could see—in my mind. I remember asking the nurse to get in the bed with me to watch TV. I asked her what shows were on, wondering if they could put on this show or that. Yet I also knew I wasn't myself and that something bad had happened.

But I couldn't figure it out—nobody just out and told me right there that I was blind. I couldn't remember meeting Antonne that day; I didn't realize someone had tried to kill me. I just wanted to know when the next meal was going to be served.

Then I heard my best friend, Angela, hovering over me; she was holding my hand and praying. I was angry at her, saying, "I can't believe you did not come to see me. Like, how could you not have come see me?" I yelled at her. "You supposed to be my friend, and you didn't come and see me."

Her voice was soft. "Brina, I was here yesterday."

I was in a state of confusion—the pain hadn't set in yet. Boodia's birthday was around this time, August 1, and in one of my dreams in the hospital, I saw white people holding me captive, chained to the floor. I was begging and pleading with them to just please let me go so that I could get to my son for his birthday. I was in a prison, whether I was awake or asleep.

Gradually I began to regain a sense of myself, at least to the extent that my mind was becoming more aware of the gravity of my situation. I realized that Mama had been at the hospital with me, in Augusta, almost the entire time. And so had Daddy. He'd been at the hospital in Greenville, too, where Antonne, who hadn't been charged with anything, was free to come and go. Depends on who you asked, Daddy had nearly killed Antonne in a hospital hallway after the man insisted my Lexus was his. I don't believe that story is even close to being true. My cousins say Antonne did come to the hospital, and they ran him off. If you ask ten different people, they will tell you ten different stories about how they saw him first, swung at him, and was the first to punch him. All of this had to be told to me later because I was in a coma, fighting for my life.

The news from the doctors was grim. One of the physicians, an ophthalmologist, in a heated conversation with Daddy, had told him that the only medical solution left was to sew my eyelids shut to keep my eyes from disintegrating, but both Daddy and Mama refused to accept what this doctor was saying.

Shortly after, a hospital attendant was by my side, telling me about a young "miracle doctor" he knew—Dr. Bala Ambati—who might be able to help.

* * *

After one month in the hospital, I was brought home to Mama's apartment in a wheelchair, swollen and wrapped in gauze where I had skin grafted onto my face, neck, and chest. I was told my pupils were totally white, and my eye sockets were covered in thick ointment. My attacker, Savannah Grant, the other woman Antonne had been seeing, had been arrested for assault and battery with intent to kill. She had attacked me with a concoction of Red Devil lye, Clorox bleach, and boiling water that she'd mixed up just for me—that almost instantly begins to burn at a temperature of 400 degrees.

Meanwhile Antonne squirmed away from facing justice—he wasn't charged.

* * *

The gauze on my face sometimes turned a bit red from the blood, which scared Shani. In my head, I still looked like me, but reality set in when Shani screamed, "That's a monster!" I might as well have been, because the old me was gone. That my daughter was scared of me was hurtful.

I told everyone, "I can't take it and she can't take it, give her a week, give her some days."

She stayed over at her godmother's while everybody started trying to figure out ways to get Shani to come over to me. I think it was Mama who came up with the idea of putting toilet paper and ketchup on everyone's faces, in order to look like me. It took about three weeks, and finally

Shani came over. She put her hand on my leg. I was still as a person could be because I didn't want to scare her. She said, "Mama?"

I said, "Yes, baby. This your mama." She looked at me, then she looked back at the others like, "Are y'all sure?"

Tears were rolling down my face, and finally she sat up on my lap. It took some hours for her to really come to me. The more I talked, the more she realized it was me, and then she wouldn't stay away, she wanted to spend the night. It was just the best feeling to get my baby back. I tell her this all the time: "She ain't left me ever since."

CHAPTER 16

The Room

A week after Shani returned to stay with me, I asked Angela, who was now living in Columbia, South Carolina, to take me to visit my home at 115.

"Are you ready for this?" she asked.

Was I? It was hard to say what I could be ready for, but I knew I had to get out from Mama's. "Yeah, I'm ready," I said, half lying.

As soon as she opened the door, the familiar smell of my home hit me and nearly brought me to my knees. I was overwhelmed with emotion. While everything seemed the same, everything also seemed very different. I knew the couch was to the left and felt around for it. Carefully, I inched toward it until I made contact. I dropped to my knees in despair. "I can't see my things, the things I worked so hard for!" I screamed and cried. "I can't see my shit! Angela. You hear me, I can't see anything in my house!" I screamed for twenty minutes.

After a while Angela grabbed my arm. "Okay, now you pull your shit together. You have one cry session a day, you have to suck it up," she said. It was just like Angela to give me her signature tough love, whether it was what I needed or didn't at the time.

Angela walked me around the whole house patiently, and I felt every surface; touch would be the closest thing to seeing now. I sat at the big cherrywood table I wanted so badly for my family but now couldn't see. I ran my fingers up and down the dining chairs as I recalled their beige, plush cushions and their circular backs. I held my hands out in front of me as I walked down the main hall, trying to reacquaint myself with my house's layout without the benefit of sight: I knew that the first room was Kesha's. Shani shared the room with her. The room next to it was for the boys.

When I entered my own bedroom, which was only a few feet away from the boys' room, it felt especially dark and scary. I began to sob again. "What did I do to deserve this? Why is God punishing me? God couldn't allow this to happen to me!" I asked no one in particular.

A week later, I moved back to 115 for good, although, to be more precise, I really moved into the four walls of my bedroom. Once my beautiful sanctuary, this room became my hellhole, my prison, a bunker I seldom left for three long years.

*   *   *

Within the confines of my bedroom, I attempted to maintain control over the space as much as possible. I added a lock on the door, which allowed me to permit someone—or no one—into the room to see me. There was never a second thought of me venturing into the living or dining rooms when people visited; they had to come to me. Whomever cooked that day would have to bring me my plate and set it on my nightstand. On top of the nightstand were fifty bottles of medication I took for pain and other ailments, and stacks and stacks of Ensure against the wall—doctors had urged me to drink this stuff at least three times a day to help restore my nutrients.

There were so many thoughts I had while stuck in that bedroom during those early days after my attack: confusion, sadness, hurt, and anger. How had this happened? Why me? My world had been reduced to the voices in my own head, and at times a dark energy would come over me. For a while after the attack, I didn't have a television in the room because my heart couldn't take knowing the world was moving on without me while I just laid there, day after day, screaming in my head for someone to help me figure out how in the hell did I get in this situation.

Some days, I believed I would end my life in that room. Occasionally, I'd have fleeting dreams—passing thoughts, really—of possibly, maybe, becoming a mother, active and attentive to my children again.

*   *   *

Little Shani, who was only four years old at the time, was, in a way, the first light I could see, or at least offered the first glimmer of hope that I might rise someday out of my self-pity. About ten weeks after I was released from the hospital, she came into my bedroom, saying she was hungry. I had been lying in bed, same as always, feeling empty, and had no energy to help my child. I started hollering, "Mama! Mama! Where's everybody?" but nobody was there to help; Mama probably had stepped out to her apartment, which was only a block away. Up until now, I was always escorted to and from my bedroom: I hadn't been anywhere on my own, not to my living room or even down the hall. But with Shani standing there asking for me to help her, I knew something had to be done. I coaxed her to come in the bed with me, hoping I could stall her out. After a while she said, "But Mommy, I'm hungry." It was then I realized I had no choice but to face what I had been avoiding for almost three months. I knew I'd need Shani's help. "Listen," I started, trying not to let the fear show in my voice. "You have to lead me to the door, out the room, and then lead me down the hall. Can you do that for Mama?" I said to her.

Shani's tiny fingers gripped around mine, and I fought back tears as I stood. She gingerly led me out of the room with one hand, my other touching the walls as I passed. As we walked, I spoke to myself: *Right across my room is the boys' room, and to the right is the bathroom. Once I reach the living room, take a direct right into the kitchen.* After a few dozen careful steps, Shani and I finally arrived at the fridge. I opened it and turned to her: "Tell me what you see."

Shuffling my body to the other end of the kitchen, I felt my way around the counter for some bread, and to the cabinets for a plate. I now had bread, and turkey meat from the fridge. I reached around for a butter knife and headed back to the fridge to feel around for a jar of mayonnaise. Terrified, I dipped the knife into the mayo, then reached again for a slice of bread. I took the turkey meat, counting it slice by slice, and placed it on the bread. Took another slice and placed it on top.

I placed the sandwich on the plate and set it down on the big cherry oak table and carefully lowered myself into a chair. I could hear Shani set herself down and begin to eat. I turned my head so she wouldn't see my tears. She had no idea how much it took for her mama to come out of the room, but I knew I had to do it for my little girl. Shani started humming a song, and as she munched on her lunch I knew she was happy and unaware of the hell I was in. The whole time, I waited desperately for someone to walk in the door to relieve me, so I'd have an excuse to return to the room and crawl back in my bed, but nobody returned. As Shani hummed with delight, I sat staring in her direction, but unable to see. Despite the fear of being out of the room, I thought to myself: *I just came up out of my room, by myself, and I just fixed my baby a sandwich.* Shani never knew it but her small request was the first ray of hope in my darkness.

* * *

If you asked my kids, they'd tell you their grandma, my mama, cooked every day. And while that was true, I've also never heard of anyone who could cook a whole meal in fifteen minutes.

Mama meant well, but the undercooked chicken she'd make during her time in the kitchen wasn't always edible to me or the kids. Mind you, Mama was ordinarily an excellent cook, but in those days, she was in full crack mode and wanted nothing more than to get out into the streets and get high. It got so bad that DeAndre and Marcus began to eat at a Mexican restaurant not far from the house. I was none the wiser: I believed we were all suffering together as we ate Mama's poor cooking, but it was years later when I found out the restaurant's owner was providing them free meals. In the early months after my attack, Mama and I were not getting along at all, hard as it was to believe. In fact, she was making my life even more of a living hell by stealing things to support her drug habit. She'd bring her large pocketbook to the house and come in and swipe our toilet paper, dish detergent, and all sorts of other things. Little did I know household items were the least of what she was taking from me.

Every month, Poopie's wife, Shirley, along with my cousin Missy, would help me by going through my bills. They'd come over and spread the bills in front of them on the dining room table and ask me, "Hey, what you want to pay this month? You want to pay this or pay that?" It was always a tough pick between the mortgage or other bills, but deciding between my kids eating and a credit card was a no-brainer. I told them that only the essentials mattered—keeping my house, my cars, and putting food on the table. That was it.

Shirley and Missy were both super organized and determined to find resources to help me survive. One month, they discovered I had signed an insurance policy that covered the $780 a month car note for the Lexus for the remainder of the contract. I didn't even realize I had done it. I might only have a twelfth-grade education, but I go with what sounds right to me. I didn't even know I had signed the policy, but truth be told, this small blessing was nothing but God.

During this period, my children and I were driven around in a brand-new Lexus until I sold it six years later. That car, which I wouldn't have been able to keep without the insurance, ended up being my ride for all the trips back and forth to Augusta for my eye operations, and I would use it to bribe friends to take the kids to their practices.

Missy and Shirley looked under every rock to help me find other ways to pay my bills, including a victim's advocacy program that paid for all my dozens of prescriptions. Between all the help, supporting my household became possible.

I did have one more trick under my sleeve, though. Under my bed was twenty-four thousand dollars of my stripper earnings, stashed in a safe. Although I knew it wouldn't last a lifetime, it would continue to help me make ends meet for a while.

During one of their visits, I asked Shirley to retrieve the safe—they were over at the house again to help me process some new bills—but when Shirley returned to the dining room a few minutes later, I could hear her and Missy whispering.

I said, "What is it?" Why y'all not getting the safe?"

"The safe's not there, Brina," Shirley said.

"What do you mean 'the safe's not there'?"

"It's just . . . not there."

The room went quiet; I think we all knew what had happened. It had to have been Mama.

Mama had to have come in my room one night, went under my bed, and grabbed the safe, literally right out from under me. She must have retrieved it while I was asleep because I seldom left the room, and often slept heavily because of my medications. I never heard her do it.

I was enraged. Mama was in the laundry nook, folding clothes. "Mama," I screamed. "Where the *fuck* is my safe?"

I heard her step into the kitchen. "Hold on, Brina, hold on," she said defiantly as she slipped past me and out the front door to her apartment. A few minutes later, I heard the door open again and footsteps heading toward and then past me. Missy and Shirley were sitting with me in the kitchen in silence. I could tell they were thinking it was about to go down.

Finally, one of them said, "Your Mama just walked by us with your safe in a brown sack, and she went in your room."

I snapped my neck around. "She did what?"

I shot up, feeling my way to my bedroom. "Mama, what are you doing?" I said as I walked into the bedroom. "You got my safe?"

I could hear Mama moving around. "Brina, I don't want to argue with you. I don't want to hear that shit today."

She left in a big huff, slamming my front door behind her.

With Mama out of the house, Shirley and Missy found that only fifteen thousand dollars was left: Mama had used nearly ten thousand dollars to buy crack. I was furious, but I had to make a choice because I didn't have anybody else to come over to feed my kids. I not only had lost my sight, but now most of my money was gone, too. I didn't know how the money left was going to last us. But I didn't know what else to do, so, as devastated as I was, I still let Mama into my home every day.

With me and Mama at each other's throats, we filled the house with toxic energy. I was still fuming about the money. Mama claimed some other friends of mine probably took the safe, but she was the one who walked in the door with the safe right under her arm. She insisted on her innocence and blamed everyone else for the missing money. It would take Mama twenty years to halfway admit that she had taken the cash.

About two weeks after this incident—after literally robbing me—

Mama stepped through my bedroom door. "You want to eat or not? The food is ready!" she said coldly.

I was crying about my state of life and still upset about allowing someone who stole money out from under me into my house. I was fed up with Mama and her negative energy.

"Get the fuck on," I said in her direction. "I don't want you here no way."

She snapped back with a vengeance. "You blind bitch," I heard her say. She marched off, leaving me stunned.

Blind bitch? My own mother called me a blind bitch. What kind of hell is this? A crazy woman nearly kills me and takes my sight? I'm not even physically healed before my own mother robs me of my hard-earned money and curses me? What did I do to deserve such pain? How the fuck am I expected to survive? I leapt out of the bed and made my way down the hall to the living room, where I could sense Mama was.

I needed her to say something to figure out where in the room she was. "Get the fuck out my house," I said, coaxing her.

"That's why you by yourself and alone," she said. That was enough for me to know exactly where she was standing. I picked up my entire coffee table and hurled it toward her. It was as if I was confronting the Devil himself. I was so angry, I could have killed her that day. I had no idea if I hit her, but she fled the house, (again) slamming the door. I stood in the living room, seething and screaming, surrounded by jagged glass and sharp splinters of wood. I didn't even try to clean it up; I knew I couldn't. I walked back calmly down the hall, crawled in bed, and cried. I was so lost. I wanted to die. God had abandoned me for sure.

* * *

There are some things I wouldn't do to a dog that people I love have done to me.

Months after leaving the hospital, two of my friends guided me into my bank to withdraw some cash. I had five thousand dollars of my stripper money in an account and planned to take a thousand out for various expenses I knew would be coming.

I asked for Julia, the bank manager. I loved Julia—she was a former high school classmate of mine. Although she was white, Julia and I had a lot in common. In high school, we were both considered the popular, pretty girls. She always treated me kindly and watched out for me when I came into the bank, sometimes deleting late fees I had accumulated.

So it took all the courage I could gather to walk in that bank, where I knew I'd bump into so many people I knew, including Julia. The right side of my face was burned, red and raw. My leg was still in pain. Although I could walk without help, I still needed assistance from my friends because I couldn't see a thing.

I could feel the tension in the air as soon as I made my way through the bank lobby.

My friends whispered that everybody was looking at me, but I learned not for the reasons I thought. I figured they were staring at me because of my face and because no one had seen me since the attack, but that could not have been further from the truth.

I could feel a frantic, nervous energy in the air as I made my way through the bank lobby. "What's going on," I whispered to Julia.

"Oh my God," she stuttered. "We thought you died." Died? I knew people had heard about the attack—it was reported in the local paper—but reports of my death were obviously exaggerated.

Julia led us into her office, where she explained.

While I was in a coma, Mama had gone to the bank and announced that I had passed away from my injuries from the attack. She explained that she needed the money in my account to bury me and to support my children. Julia recalled that upon hearing that news, everyone at the bank was distraught and crying that day.

I could feel Julia's distress. "The bank gave your mom all your money," she said finally.

I was angry, but I was also trying my best to hide my humiliation. This, of course, was one of Mama's ways to show me that she hated me. I figured she was trying to break me and would do everything she could to do so.

I returned home and, as usual, went straight to bed. My friends stayed with me the rest of the night, all of us trying to make sense of what happened, but at the end of the day there was nothing I could do about it. That money, like much of my money in the safe, and life as I knew it to be, was gone.

* * *

As bad as Mama could be to me, so many men in my life were worse. I had been violated by men from the time I was a child until now in my early thirties and a mother, and fighting for my life after my attack. And so, I feel like God must have sent me a woman to help save me; He knew that I would have never completely trusted a man.

I met Pastor Ova McCauley through Sonya, a close friend who was also Shani's godmother and a member of Pastor Ova's church, New Life Ministries. Sonya would come over to pray with me, and soon she began to bring Pastor Ova along on her visits.

While only in her midforties, Ova seemed much older and wiser and was truly a woman of God. It took a while, but I began to let my guard down little by little and trust her, eventually confiding in her about what was going on with Mama and the many other things in my life.

Sometimes she'd come to the house by herself and settle in my room with me. Other times, she'd arrive with a group of women, all angels, who'd clean up and pray through the house. I never left the room, but she'd approach me, peek her head through the door, and whisper, "Hey, I just came to bless the room and lift your spirits."

Initially, I tried hard to run her off: I'd often yawn or pretend to fall asleep. My tiny bathroom was a few feet from my bed, and I would sit on the toilet for like twenty minutes while she was in the room, hoping that would wear her down so she could leave. But she never left.

Sometimes she would stay for thirty or forty minutes, and other times, she'd stay for hours. During most of these visits, she'd come with a young woman named Veronica, and the two would go through the house anointing the doors and handles with holy water. Then, after prayer, they would play songs by Yolanda Adams.

As I told Pastor Ova about my struggles, she'd say things like, "Lay hands on yourself and say, 'by Jesus stripes you are healed.'" I'd have a hard time doing as such; I was still angry and confused why God had allowed this to happen to me.

She'd share with me stories from the Bible that initially I didn't care to know. She'd refer to "Mary and Martha and their brother, Lazarus, who died, and Jesus brought him back to life." She'd give me Scriptures to read like, "The joy of the Lord is your strength" and then come back and ask, "Did you pray what I prayed?" And I'd be like, "Mmm-hmmm," but I was lying.

In time, those stories began to intrigue me, as did Pastor Ova herself. She had so much positivity that I began to imagine myself being like her. I was sick and tired of being me, exhausted from being depressed, and I knew I wanted something different and something bigger for myself.

I started to gravitate toward her light and then would ask her little questions here and there. This—me inching closer and closer to healing—went on for about three years.

She knew I was broken. I'd sit up in my bed and ramble, but Pastor Ova never made me feel like I wasn't making sense. The truth is, as I look back on it, I was filled with so much medication during that time that I likely *wasn't* making sense. But Pastor Ova began to plant seeds into my life. "Sabrina," she'd say one day, "God has revealed to me that you will be in front of millions." Or, "I see you speaking in front of women and helping them one day." She often liked to remind me that "God has a plan, and we just had to step in it."

Naturally, I was skeptical. *Yeah, whatever,* I'd think. *How can she see me in front of millions, when I can't see myself past this bedroom?*

At the end of her visits, she'd hold my hand and we'd pray. Before leaving and from the moment she left, there was peace. Half the things that she was saying, I didn't even know what she was talking about, but her words gave me comfort. I never had somebody make me feel that way.

I had always been funny about spiritual things. I've had my weak moments, but ultimately, I believe and trust God—but I don't believe that everybody who says they're a messenger of God truly is. You can't just tell me anything. I don't know, maybe I'm just stubborn. But I did listen to this Christian woman because I was certain she was a true believer. I knew that God was working through her. Years later now I can say that

I am a living testament of her blessing: the calmness that I have today, the peace that I have, is because of her. At the time, though, I possessed none of that. Pastor Ova saw me in my darkest, darkest hour. She saw me on the pills, off the pills, hair combed, hair not combed. She was there on the days I had crust in my eyes and didn't care to live, and she still would come and meet me where I was. That was important for me, because she never tried to force God upon me when all I needed was some prayer.

* * *

Shortly after Pastor Ova, another angel came into my life: Tiffany Garrison. A young friend of my cousin, Tiffany and I had never met but she heard about the attack and took it upon herself to see if I needed company. Like a whirlwind, she flew into my house one day with two of her sisters—not to be nosey or curious, but to say, "Hey, I'm here for you if you need anything." From the moment she walked into my bedroom with her sisters, I saw myself in her: she was sassy and a boss, just like me.

"I believe one day we will be best friends," I told Tiffany, and to this day she's one of my closest and dearest friends.

The three Garrison sisters had their friends come, and then their friends' friends even started coming around. They all had heard about Clemson's famous stripper who was surviving through a tough time, and so they were all curious about me. Soon, those girls eventually became my found family and saving grace.

Months after the attack, Tiffany and her large crew began taking me out to clubs. Angela didn't like them, but these girls made me feel whole again; they made me feel normal. Even though I was older than these women, I still wanted to hang with them. I was slowly feeling a desire to go outside; otherwise, I'd lie in my bed, drowning in sorrows. Soon, I began to run the streets at night with twelve very young, very high-spirited women.

The first time I agreed to go clubbing and drinking, I was sitting in my bedroom with the three Garrison sisters and four of their friends. We were listening to a song by Lil Jon and drinking vodka and Hennessy, just laughing and cutting up. I would tell them stories about my stripper days, which they all loved to hear.

Tiffany suddenly piped up with an idea. "We should get dressed and go out," she said in a way that told me she was serious.

I laughed. "Y'all do know I am blind, right," I said. But deep inside, I did wonder just whether it was possible to go out and do something I once loved again.

After a few more drinks, I allowed the girls to dress me, put some makeup on me, and style my hair before we all piled in my SUV. I was scared shitless that I'd see someone I knew, so we went to a small club in Clemson. When someone did walk up to me, the girls led me to a corner, and there we spent the night talking and laughing. Soon, I was brave enough to go to a larger club in Greenville, and that became our spot.

When I went out drinking with these twelve young women, I presented an alter ego. When I was with my best friend Destiny, we were bougie, traveling with celebrities and shopping for hours, but these young girls were wild and free. Twelve girls, my twelve angels, would lock arms and head to the middle of the dance floor. They'd make a circle around me, and we'd drunk-dance, touching and rubbing all up against each other and laughing our hearts out. We'd give each other friendly lap dances and hump playfully on each other. And the next weekend we'd do it all over again. The girls were loud and energetic—I would have been just like them at their age if I hadn't had so many children at an early age!

Maybe I befriended these girls as an emotional rope to hang on to—I could feel, at least for a night out, that life was normal.

The moment they protected me in the club that day, putting me in the corner so I wouldn't have to be confronted by curious people I used to know, I was sure I could trust all of them. Sometimes they'd pile in my room and want to learn stripper tips from me; I'd hear DeAndre laughing. I'd have them put their hands against the wall as if the police were frisking them, then get on their tiptoes and try to bounce their booties up and down. We'd laugh as I encouraged them to clap their asses.

I could hear my kids in the hall saying, "Lord, there they go again."

We called it "Shaking Ass Class 101," and I was the professor. Once the music started, we were bouncing our booties and taking shots of

Hennessy. It was the best time, but when the girls left, it was like the air was sucked right out of the room. I'd be alone again in my hellhole.

* * *

The girls and myself would come home to my house pissy drunk after a fun night out, falling all over each other laughing, and wake up the kids, who had to go to school the next day. Having never touched liquor until I was blinded, being reeling drunk wasn't something I was used to. But the girls coaxing me to go out—to hang with them and have a good time—that empowered me. Being able to go clubbing at night when no one could really see my face was an emotional outlet. I could dance and laugh all night and leave the pain on the club floor. The Garrison girls had offered me a lifeline.

These women were by my side as I began to emerge from my room and fight to somehow, against all odds, regain my eyesight. Some of these girls, Tiffany specifically, would take my car and drive me to Augusta, Georgia, for my operations, help me with errands, or just provide an understanding ear when I wanted to vent.

I remember one time during a drive to Augusta, I opened up to Tiffany about the rape by Reverend Lottie. I hadn't talked about this to anyone prior to that long drive to the hospital.

"Darn, Brina, that's fucked you had to go through that," she said. She'd also share with me about her own childhood and the men she dated.

I felt lucky to have two very different but equally impactful groups of women in my life during this unfathomable time: Pastor Ova and her church group, and Tiffany and her crew of girls who took me out to party so I could drink my Hennessy and be somebody other than a depressed blind woman who lived in her bedroom.

* * *

Eventually, I started babysitting the Garrison girls' toddlers and newborns. Mind you, I'm babysitting blind. Now that I think about it, I would never let no blind woman babysit my babies for hours, but they did it because they saw how I moved around, and they trusted me. Tiffany's older sister, Tara, was the first to call. "Brina, I don't have a babysitter for Amani. Can you please watch her for a few hours? She's little and she doesn't even turn or crawl yet."

I told her yes because Tara had done favors for me. I figured all I had to do was stick the bottle in the baby's mouth and cuddle her. Then Tiffany called, and Tiffany's other sister also called and asked me to babysit, too. I said yes to all the girls because I needed the babysitting money after my stripper money had dwindled, but I also liked the feeling of purpose I got from being with the children.

I fed the babies and changed their diapers. I'd keep the little babies in bed with me and cradle them to sleep. When I would have to open the doors for the toddlers or go into the kitchen to feed them, it gave me a sense of accomplishment. If I had to go down the hall, I made sure all the little ones were with me; we traveled as one unit. I needed to hear their voices, so sometimes we played the game Marco Polo. I'd say "Marco!" and they'd say "Polo." I even potty trained one child. At times, I'd have five or six babies in the house, smaller ones in the bed and bigger ones on a pallet beside the bed, children all watched by a blind woman! When the kids didn't come around and I had no one to care for, I began to feel empty and depressed.

Other days I'd have a dozen young women and their babies with me in the house. This was the beginning of my journey to letting these girls live with me. One girl after another started moving into 115 because they needed help with their children, and they needed a place to live.

The girls told me dramatic stories from their past because they knew I wouldn't judge them; and we had a lot in common, after all. So many of these girls reminded me of myself, because, like me, so many were young victims of rape and domestic violence. One woman, Tawnya, asked me to babysit her three-year-old daughter, Kira. I was already babysitting two other babies and was happy to take another. These girls had done so much for me, I wanted to make sure not to let them down.

While I couldn't see her, I began to notice something peculiar about Kira; something was off. Every time boys or men were around, the toddler acted nervous or frisky. About a year after I started babysitting Kira,

Tawnya came to the house one day and told me her boyfriend kicked her out. I invited her to live with us at 115 and began to see more of Kira.

"Is something wrong with her?" I asked carefully. I paused before I continued. "Has she been molested?"

Tawnya was quiet for a few seconds. "I can't prove it, but once I left her with a boyfriend and I always thought something happened."

That deeply bothered me to the point I lost sleep, worrying about how I could protect this child. I vowed to protect her and other children, who, like me, had been touched or molested and nobody helped. Kira stayed with me for about two years.

Every last one of these girls was ten to twelve years younger than me, and, exactly as Pastor Ova predicted, they began to seek counseling and mentoring from me. While many didn't ask for advice, I was nevertheless in a place to offer it because I had lived in their shoes and experienced many of the things they experienced. I shared with them what I knew, encouraged them, and never judged. I was able to help them with their children and their life, while they were supporting me by paying me to babysit and helping me to feel protected and needed. I didn't realize it then, but Pastor Ova's vision for me was coming to pass in its own small way, and my interactions with the girls served as the stepping-stones toward the work I now do with women across the country.

CHAPTER 17

Justice

A year into my self-isolation, the assault trial of Savannah, my attacker, was approaching. Antonne, of course, would be a key witness.

As hard as it might be for even myself today to believe, he and I had been sneaking around, talking on the phone months before the trial. I was weak and broken and somehow continued to entertain his calls, because I didn't think anyone else would want me. That's how traumatized I was; that's how badly I was lacking self-worth at the time.

During one of our phone conversations, Antonne asked to see me, and I said yes. So one night, he came to the house about 3:00 a.m. We had sex in the bedroom and fell asleep. I wasn't in my right mind, or he would have never been there. The whole dynamic was pure insanity, because there was nothing rational about my thinking at that time.

He conned me into believing that we were going to still be together. I went along with it, and while I wasn't in love with him anymore, I thought we were friends. The catastrophic act he was involved with a year prior nearly took my life, but at the end of the day, what I wanted from Antonne was an explanation: I wanted to know what he was thinking. Why did she do this to me? I wanted him to know how Savannah hurt me. I also yearned to find out the truth, to discover the missing piece of the puzzle: Did he have any clue why Savannah would try to kill me? Could he know? Was he not telling me something?

I planned to get him out of the house before Mama got there, but we overslept and were awakened by Mama moving around in the kitchen. When she knocked on my door and noticed it was locked, she began to bang hard—not because she was worried about me but because she figured I was up to something. How she knew it was Antonne in the room, I will never know.

Within an hour, Daddy and Uncle Louis were in my yard. I could hear my father, or maybe it was my uncle Louis, say, "Brina, you need to let this man alone. He already tried to kill you." I cussed Mama, hating her for not minding her business. "Here you go calling people to my house!" I screamed to her. "This my damn house!"

Inside the bedroom, Antonne sat on the bed, shaking his head. "Your mom is a trip. Your mom just starting shit."

I nodded. "Let's make sure the coast is clear, and then you can leave," I told him. But the coast was never clear, so at some point, I just told him to walk out. Antonne slinked away past the glares of my family and left the house.

"Just don't say nothing and keep walking," I yelled out toward his back.

It was clear: I was out of my mind.

* * *

Savannah's trial convened in Greenville around Mother's Day 2003. Of course, going into the trial, I had no idea how long it would last. I remember laying in the bed thinking, *This is it.* Savannah would finally have to face the consequences of what she did to me.

Several days before the trial, Antonne asked for my Honda because he said he didn't have a ride to the courthouse. I told him, "You can sneak out here and get my Honda. Don't come in. The key is going to be in it." I had somebody put the keys in the car. He did as told, and he didn't come in the house that day but got the Honda and left. I needed him to testify at the trial, so I spent a lot of time in the room plotting like hell to make sure that this man got to where I needed him to be.

I knew he might end up keeping my car for a whole week, but when he showed up to court, I thought, at least, *Okay, good. He's here.*

He walked in saying, "Oh baby, oh baby. How could she do this? I love you, baby."

I had finally come to my senses that this man was no friend of mine. I was disgusted by Antonne, as everyone in my family was, but the prosecutor had warned us that we had to be nice to him as he was a vital part of the trial. As she put it, "Only three people knew what happened that day." And so I allowed him to sit next to me in court, hold my hand, and tell me over and over how much he loved me. It was revolting, but I needed his testimony on the stand to get my attacker convicted.

*   *   *

On that first day in the courtroom, I didn't know what to expect; I didn't even know if Savannah, my assailant, had been in jail or not since the attack because nobody really told me anything. I had entered the courtroom with Mama, Daddy, and Tiffany and the rest of the girls, who made sure I had my outfits together. Missy, Aunt Louise, and Shirley were there, as were a host of cousins and my four kids. We packed the courtroom every single day and stayed quiet and focused.

Everything went so quickly, with the attorneys spending all their time picking the jury.

Though I couldn't see anything, I kept wondering, *Is she . . . Savannah looking at me? Is she not? Does she feel remorseful? How was this going to go? Was she going to get off the hook?*

I got some relief. The judge instructed the bailiffs to detain her throughout the trial, because he said she could be a flight risk. At least I had the satisfaction of knowing she was spending that night in jail.

*   *   *

To everyone, including me, my attacker was just this mystery. Who was this Savannah? How did she look? What was she like? It was unsettling knowing so little about her.

Some consolation for me was that the prosecutor was badass. A white woman in her forties, she hardly ever lost a case. When she spoke, she was very direct, and when she asked a question, you listened intently to how it would be answered. I was confident in her ability from Day One, and seeing how she conducted herself in court made me feel better at the end of the day.

During the first day of the trial, Kesha, my eldest, recalls leaving the courtroom to use the restroom. When she walked out of the stall to wash her hands, Savannah was standing there washing her hands at the sink. Kesha stopped and glared at her. She told me later, "Mama, all I could think of was choking her and beating her, but I could hear you say, 'Don't do it.' I just stared at her. All I could think about was that here was this person who tried to hurt my mama."

To this day, standing next to Savannah in the restroom is the only moment Kesha remembers about the trial.

* * *

On the second day, my doctors from the burn center, as well as my eye surgeon, Dr. Ambati, testified, appearing remotely on a big screen. The defense asked the doctors, Had I missed any appointments? They all said no. They asked what kind of patient I was. They had a weak case, attempting to establish my horrific injuries were not so severe.

On this day, the prosecutors introduced intense, gruesome photographs of me right after the attack. Before showing the photos of the burned side of my face, the attorneys warned my kids of their graphic nature. Looking back, the children weren't ready for it. They began to cry and someone escorted them out of the courtroom.

* * *

The second day of trial was also the day Antonne was to take the witness stand. There was always the chance that he wouldn't show up again. My family, the prosecutor, and I all held our collective breath until he walked into the courtroom.

Antonne took the stand and answered all the questions the prosecution and defense asked. When the prosecutor asked if he loved me, he testified, "I do love her. She's my boo."

He actually pretended to cry, too. I could hear someone behind me say, "I know that nigga ain't trying to cry."

He told the court everything that happened—how he had taken my car, had gone to visit Savannah, and had left her in the kitchen as he went downstairs to see me. "I never thought she would do what she did to Sabrina," I remember him saying. He must have turned to Savannah next. "I don't know how you could do this to her," I heard him say. He almost sounded believable. Yes, he was on my side, but I knew it was all only to save his own ass.

After testifying, Antonne sat next to me. A short time later in the courtroom, and to this day I do not know if it's true, he made a startling boast: "She had cut another girl some years prior, but I talked the girl out of pressing charges. You were not the first person that she hurt over me."

Antonne also confided to me, but never told the police, that Savannah had told him she was planning to kill me weeks before the attack, that she wanted to shoot me. He claimed he told her, "Why would you do that to her? Plus, that would be too messy." He also admitted that Savannah had learned from her grandmother how to mix a chemical concoction like the Mafia used back in the day to make their enemies suffer.

None of this came out in his testimony.

*   *   *

On the third day, the defense called only one witness—a bondsman Savannah had contacted when she was locked up. That was it.

It wasn't long afterward that the foreman announced the jury's decision. Daddy, who I was now sitting next to, holding hands, turned to all my supporters. "No matter what," he said, "we came here with dignity, and we are going to leave with dignity. Regardless of what happens, don't nobody shout anything."

The judge cleared his throat and began solemnly. "The City of Greenville owes you, Ms. Greenlee, an apology," the judge said. "In all my years, I've never seen such a heinous, disgusting disregard for another person's life."

Of course, I was baffled. I whispered, "An apology? What for?"

The judged continued, explaining that the prosecutor sufficiently proved that Savannah had acted with malice of forethought: her waiting for her concoction to boil suggested that she knew what she was doing and had acted deliberately. Something else I hadn't known. on the day of the attack, Savannah had called the police to report that *I* burglarized *her* home. During the trial, a policeman testified that he checked her home but found no sign of a robbery; in fact there was no sign I'd been near her door. They didn't make the connection that the woman dying in the gas station was attacked by the woman claiming she was burglarized! In fact, they didn't make the connection until hours later, when Savannah was arrested and charged with assault and battery with intent to kill.

The judge also shared that the police weren't informed that I had been in a coma for thirty days. Had they known this, Savannah would have been charged with attempted murder, but there was nothing they could do about that now.

Then the judge added, "Rest assured, I'm going to do everything in my power to give her the maximum time." And he did: a year after my attack, Savannah was convicted and sentenced to twenty years in a South Carolina penitentiary.

Savannah never apologized, but she had the chance to. When the judge asked if she had anything to say, Daddy told me she shook her head no.

Outside the courthouse, as we were about to leave to go celebrate, I could hear Antonne asking my friends who was going to ride back in my car with him. My father leaned into me, his disdain for Antonne evident. "Here he come over here, walking up here with a smirk on his face," he whispered to me. "But I'm about to cut this shit short."

Loudly, I could hear Daddy's booming voice. "Give me my daughter's keys right fucking now," he said to Antonne. Reluctantly, Antonne gave them up and we all went home.

*　*　*

I returned home to resume my life in the bedroom. It helped that I was given a bit of justice and that Savannah was in jail, but understanding that my blindness was a permanent part of my life now was a very slow process. There were days after the trial where I wanted to get up and some days I didn't.

I felt vindicated that the justice system didn't fail me—I don't know what would have happened to me emotionally and mentally if it had. Still, after the trial, there was no light bulb that switched on, instantly directing me how to start living my life. I had to work on it and still had a long, long way to go.

I could not get it out of my head that Antonne and Savannah might have together plotted the attack against me. After all, it was just a year earlier that Antonne himself was threatening to kill me because I went to Daytona with my girlfriends. What he had whispered to me in court about her premeditation boiled inside me. He was the one who repeatedly called me and led me to her building that day. Alone in my bedroom and left to my dark thoughts, a rage was ignited that I could not put out. Savannah being in prison was no longer enough.

One day soon after the trial, he asked to see me. I didn't trust him, of course, but a seed had been planted, and I was hungry to find out exactly what he knew.

We hung out at his mama's place that night. While I sat there unable to see him or my surroundings, my mind started spinning. *What am I doing? I shouldn't be here with him. I'm blind. Did he have something to do with me getting hurt?* I was having a panic attack. So many thoughts were racing through my mind, a million emotions shooting through my body—fear, pain, and mostly disgust. My subconscious was screaming: You almost lost your life because of this man. He is nothing but scum. You're stupid for even being here with him; he could be setting you up like he did before.

I had turned off my phone for twenty-four hours, so no one knew where to find me.

I was talking to myself: *You should be home with your children, but no, you're here with the man who got you into this hell.* The more I thought about it, the angrier I got. And that anger turned from madness to the point of murder.

"I want to go home," I demanded.

"Baby, I thought you was gonna stay a couple of days."

"I said, I want to go home now."

The very next day around noon, he borrowed a friend's truck. I was sitting on the passenger side waiting for him to drive me home, but he said he was hungry. Women at a local church cooked chicken on the weekends, and he wanted to go get a plate.

"Antonne, I want to go fucking home. Take me home!" I remember yelling.

By now I must have turned red from rage. Because I didn't trust him, two nights earlier I had slipped a knife in my purse. I had had enough: I pulled the knife out of my purse and started stabbing him—first in the shoulder and then in his chest. I was not trying to stab to kill, but to scare him. "You're fucking stabbing me!" he shouted, trying to slip away.

When he pulled over and jumped out of the truck, I sat back in the passenger seat with the knife in my hand, unable of course to run or go anywhere, or even to see him. But I heard him slip back into the driver's seat. I started to slash at him again.

He gunned the truck down the road as I continued to stab him. For a moment, I thought about opening the door and jumping out, but then I decided he was so not worth dying for. He could have called the police on me, but he instead called his brother's boyfriend, who came to drive me home. I led him to my house, but we said nearly nothing. I told him that since I'd been gone for two days, there was no telling who would be in my yard waiting for me (and the person driving me), so he should just drop me off by the mailbox. And that's what he did before speeding off.

I stumbled my way to the front door. "Hey, who in here?"

Shani and my mama were in the house. Shani came outside as I made my way to the screen door. She said, "Mama, what happened?"

"I don't know," I said.

Mama came to the door. "You got blood all over you. Brina, you need to tell us what happened."

They later told me my face was but a blank stare. I made my way down the hall and took off my bloody clothes and jumped in the shower. I was still in the shower when Mama and Shani came into the bathroom asking me again what happened.

I never told anyone.

* * *

Meanwhile, I resolved to clean my hands of Antonne, who still called me multiple times a day. He knew our relationship had come to an end, so he was no longer nice but instead threatening to kill me—not because I stabbed him, but because he believed I used him to testify in court. Each day, his threats got worse. He could be ruthless with his words. The devil came out of him in ways I could never explain. "Bitch, it don't matter, I had you in your best days. Bitch, you done, you scarred up and nobody going to want you but me."

One day, he threatened that he was on his way to my house. I called the police, who came to my house and began to listen in on the calls. He continued, crying, "I helped send Savannah to jail, and this is how you treat me? Now I don't have her in my life, and if I can't have you, I'm gonna finish the job and kill you!"

He did not even care that the police were listening. In fact, one of the detectives said on the call, "Antonne, tell us what you're going to do." That monster, knowing he was talking to the police, simply said, "I'm getting her."

There was no doubt in my mind that Antonne was intent on harming me.

Antonne was charged with multiple offenses, including stalking and harassment, violation of protective order, and unlawful use of the telephone, receiving a sentence of one year in jail and one year of probation. And because he was trying to come for me in my hometown, he ended up going to jail in Pickens County, where I am sure he encountered many people who knew and loved me.

Finally, Antonne was gone, but his threats still held me captive in my head.

CHAPTER 18

Blind Eyes Can't See

Despite the efforts of Pastor Ova and the Garrison girls, and I'm sure partly due to the new trauma with Antonne, I still rarely ventured outside the house in daylight. I didn't want anybody to see my face.

But on Memorial Day 2004, two years after the attack, I decided I would go out. It was a particularly nice day, and my friend Jamie, one of the Garrison girls' friends, had invited me to hang out with her at her mama's trailer. Me and Jamie were sitting on Miss Lucy's porch when a man named Wayne Anthony, who everyone called "Blunt," walked into my life.

I know exactly how he looked because I later asked everyone I knew. He had long dreads that seemed like they had been on his head ten years too long. He was light-skinned with the dark lips, what Black folks call "smoker's lips," and he had a broad forehead. I didn't know he was a dope dealer at the time, but I liked that nothing about me intimidated him.

Blunt was from Florida but arrived in South Carolina to play football for Clemson. When his football scholarship didn't work out, he remained in the area, rented an apartment, and started selling crack and weed.

Blunt did his business inside a trap house right across from Jamie's mama's trailer. Meanwhile, the group of dealers sat around chilling, playing PlayStation all day, drinking and smoking weed, while random groups of girls came to hang out and keep them company while the crack addicts knocked on the door every five minutes, looking for their fix.

Blunt later told me that he and his boys had been watching me on the porch, and when I bent over, all the boys placed a bet to see who'd go talk to me first. It was two years after the attack, and I couldn't see a thing, but it turned out that the first day I went out in broad daylight to just hang out would be the day I met the damn devil again.

That very night, Anthony Blunt came to my house. It was the first time I had been around a man since Antonne. We sat and talked all night. He was considerate and fun to hang with, and of course we had sex.

He gently touched my face with the back of his hand. "I know somebody that's been burned like you, so this doesn't bother me at all. I see the beauty still in you."

Everything about him was refreshing. Until the next day, when he handed me a wad of money and said he needed me to wire his mama this cash through Western Union.

As always with a man, I simply said "okay" and did what was asked of me, no questions asked.

He gave me her name, address, and telephone number. It was his way of saying "I like you." In my mind, though, I wondered: *What the hell? I'm blind, how the hell am I going to get to Western Union?* But I found someone to do it for me.

* * *

Blunt knew I was confined in that bedroom, but he didn't mind; better for me to admire him, he'd say. But he also had two sides to him. One day he would lift me up and convince me that I was still beautiful, then the next, he would tease me, reminding me how lucky I was to be with a man like him. He'd stand in front of the mirror butt naked. "Damn, I look like I need to be in *GQ* magazine," he'd say.

When he walked into the house, he never said hello to my family. Instead, he'd just come straight to the bedroom, folding his clothes before he got into the bed. After sex, my stomach would ache with the thought of him leaving.

In the morning he'd torture me all over: he'd leave and then he'd return in fifteen minutes. "I can't be away from you this long." And he'd get back into bed. Other days he'd leave and wouldn't return for three or four days at a time.

Still, it blew my mind that this man was willing to enter my world and wanted to sit in the bedroom—with me. Our relationship—and I mean "relationship," because I was always up under him, and he was always up under me, and we both wanted to be up under each other—moved fast. During those first weeks of meeting, Blunt told me he loved me, and I told him the same thing. After my attack, when I thought I'd never have a man after Antonne, I clung to Blunt when I shouldn't have.

One day I got a phone call from a friend who told me they had seen Blunt just drop off a girl at the nearby Edgewood projects who looked about nine months pregnant. So two months into our relationship, we got into our first argument.

"Did you just drop off a girl in Edgewood?" I asked.

"What nigger called you? Could not have been no bitch snitching on me."

"No, no, no. Do not deflect. Who was it?"

He said the girl's name, and he said he had gotten her pregnant.

But if Blunt was anything, he was gangsta: "I mean, so now that you got this information, what you want to do?" It was obvious he thought that I shouldn't be concerned with who else he was seeing, as long as he took care of me, too. I smirked. "As long as I'm taking care of you and your household, it shouldn't matter who I'm fucking."

Blunt could be Dr. Jekyll one minute and mean as Mr. Hyde the next. He took a puff of a cigarette and blew the smoke in my face. "Listen, you want me to leave, or you want me to stay? It's up to you."

And, of course, I cursed him even more and made a huge fuss, but he stayed. Only now do I realize how low my self-esteem had to be at that time. Two months later he told me he got *another* girl pregnant. This meant both girls were pregnant at the same time, but by then I didn't care—I was hooked and deeply in love with Blunt.

Blunt was my lifeline, the bridge between my isolation in my room and the outside world, and he knew it. He was also the closest thing to a father DeAndre ever had, though Blunt's paternal instincts made no sense. He once took Marcus, who was thirteen, and DeAndre, who was twelve, to a trap house, the same trap house he was working in when I first met him. A girl walked in, an actual friend of mine, and Blunt asked if they wanted him to pay her to have sex with them. They said no and told me as soon as they got home.

He also taught DeAndre, I'd learn later, how to cook crack just in case school didn't work out. I also learned that Blunt gave Marcus some weed to sell.

I was furious. "Why would you do that?"

"He asked me for money," he said. "No man should ever have to ask another man for money."

"That was your logic? Giving a child weed to sell, fool?"

Once, he took DeAndre to one of his baby mamas' homes, but that wasn't all. He actually told DeAndre to go sit in the back of my Lexus while he drove the woman to the bank. Afterward, he gestured for Nuk to get back into the front seat. "There are certain things men keep between us," he instructed him.

DeAndre rightfully understood that if or when he told me, it would cause a huge fight between me and Blunt, which is exactly why it took him three months to share what he knew.

*　　＊　　＊*

One day Blunt was laying in the bed when he turned to me and began the most insane conversation—but at the time no one could tell me it didn't make sense.

He cuddled close to me. "You got your tubes tied?"

I leaned into him. "I do."

He moved closer to me and touched my face. "We got to figure out a way to get your tubes untied. Tell you what, I'm gonna start giving you some dope to sell, and you put cash in the pot, and then I put some in the pot. And then we going to have enough to get your tubes untied, because I want you to have my baby."

I smiled and said, "Okay," just like I've done over and over.

And that's how blind-ass me started selling drugs again.

*　　＊　　＊*

Before I got started selling, Blunt asked if I knew people—he had no idea I used to sell with Steve in Creekwood. I told him not only did I have contacts, but I knew how to cook crack. First person I called was Aunt

Louise. "I got something for you," I said. She told some people, and they told people, and soon we were in business.

One day, Blunt left me some crack, some powder, and Xanax—the latter we called footballs—on top of a mirror. When he returned, he was shocked I hadn't touched it.

"You ain't mess with none?" he said incredulously. He then explained his intention: by leaving drugs around women, he said, he'd observed what they liked and eventually got them addicted.

"That's how I test my women," he said. "That's how I hook them."

Unfortunately—for him—I never did drugs.

That should have been the moment I left Anthony Blunt, but as with every man before him, I'd ignore all the warning signs.

* * *

At this point, I'd do nearly anything to make money to feed my kids, and so I started to prepare crack and sell drugs again, but only to older people in their fifties and sixties. Customers would ring the doorbell at 115, and there I was, blind, selling crack. I was good at cooking crack because Steve taught me well, and although I couldn't see, I kept cooking it myself. I was so desperate at this time that I even enlisted my kids to help, asking if a particular rock was a 10 or a 20 before I'd hand it over. I blindly dropped rocks on the floor, and secretly the kids would pick them up to put back in my stash without me knowing.

I slowly began to learn my house again. I'd make my way to the kitchen, trying to prepare meals from time to time as best as I could and occasionally sitting everyone down at the table to eat as a family. Occasionally, I'd even come out to cheer them at their school games, even though I was afraid of how people would look at me. I kept hearing all their rumors about the attack—and none of them were true. All the while, my family kept telling me, "You're still beautiful," which confused me and made me wonder what I really looked like.

As awful as it may sound, selling crack gave me a sense of purpose, along with a lot of money. Despite us sleeping together, me and Blunt were strictly business partners: I did not work for him but bought from him. He never gave me a discount on the product, or any extra. But if I got an ounce of crack from Blunt, I could make as much as two thousand dollars in one day. That meant I could give each of my children twenty dollars a day again, like I did when I was making money as Caramel. After years of struggle and self-pity, my survival instinct had kicked back in. No longer a walking zombie, I was finally feeling alive.

* * *

There were so many women and so many different times when I'd receive a call that Blunt was in my car with someone. He put me through pure hell, but in 2006, after nearly three years of him, he finally got busted selling crack cocaine and went to jail. After a week, I was almost weaned off Blunt, because I next found out all these girls were coming to see him in jail. I tried to hang in there that first year, but I was angry every time I visited; it felt like torture when I would just sit there across from him, cussing him out about things he did. I knew he was crazy about me, and I was crazy about him, but there was too much hurt between us. Finally, I cut him off and stopped visiting.

* * *

During all this time—the drama with Mama, praying with Pastor Ova, my nights out with the Garrison girls, the assault trial, my attack on Antonne, and the continued crack dealing with Blunt—I was also spending a lot of time with a genius named Dr. Bala Ambati, whose name came up soon after I emerged from the coma after the attack.

Two weeks after I was released from the hospital for the first time, I returned to Augusta to meet him. Mama and Daddy usually don't get along, and they darn sure would never be in the same car together, but I remember them going down there with me because this doctor was my glimmer of hope. He was—and still is—a famous physician. Among his many accomplishments, he's recorded in *The Guinness Book of World Records* for being the youngest physician ever licensed—at the age of seventeen—and his life is believed to be the inspiration for the fictional

young doctor on the popular 1980s television show, *Doogie Howser, M.D.*
Dr. Ambati will say he has no idea whether that's actually true or not.
When I met him, he was all of twenty-four years old. On the day we met,
the first question the young doctor asked me was simply, "Do you believe in God?" No doctor in my lifetime had ever asked me such a question. From that moment on, I knew this doctor was special.

But what I remember most about that moment was when he took
my hand. Dr. Ambati's hands were as soft as Charmin. His touch alone is
what gave me great hope.

"Before this is over," he said to me, "we're going to be best friends. But
first, an examination."

When he was done, Dr. Ambati again took my hand. "I have some
good news. Your retina is intact." He explained to me that the human eye
was like a camera. And my flash in the inside, he said, was working just
fine—given the severity of my attack, that alone was a miracle.

Over three and a half years, Dr. Ambati performed over forty surgeries
on my eyes, countless transplants as my eyes first accepted, and then
rejected, donor corneas. He never gave up on me, and he never pushed
or judged me. The first time he learned about the details of the attack,
the only thing he asked was whether I had a safe place to be. "Are you
safe? Are you okay?" He was probably the first person in my whole life to
ask that question.

* * *

"It was very sad, very tragic," Dr. Ambati said as he recalled when he
saw me for the first time. I had extensive facial and neck burns and was
hospitalized for several weeks. The corneas in both of my eyes were severely damaged and white. Dr. Ambati said if I had come to the hospital
a few years earlier, they would have told me that nothing could be done.
Luckily for me, technology had advanced in a way that gave someone
with injuries like mine a chance.

And that chance is what I grabbed on to for dear life.

Dr. Ambati was a realist, though. He told me after that first exam that
I was in a very bad situation. I could only see light, but I couldn't detect

any motion in front of me. He explained that there would be a long process ahead to treat both corneas and the lens in each eye, which had turned into cataracts.

Still, he had a plan, deciding to first attempt to stabilize the surfaces of my eyes and then rebuild what he called the "support system" of my eyes' surfaces.

I recall him explaining to my parents: "When you have a chemical burn, like what Sabrina experienced, the epithelium cells, the surface cells, are largely wiped out, and those need to be given a chance to regrow, so that the eye doesn't get infected. One of the main purposes of using the amniotic membrane is to help rebuild the surface."

Amniotic membrane? Having so many children, I knew that when a baby is born the amniotic membrane is the layer around the baby that's usually discarded after birth, but Dr. Ambati told us it had healing properties.

The first part of my regimen involved taking oral medication and eye drops and utilizing the amniotic membrane to provide a cover for the surface of my eyes to heal and stabilize. The plan was this: A few months after the amniotic membrane procedure I'd come back for a stem cell transplant. The doctors would take stem cell tissue from a donor eye and suture it into mine. Then, assuming that the stem cell transplant took, Dr. Ambati would perform a cornea transplant.

This would be a very long road, and I prayed everything would go as planned. I and my family were all committed to doing everything we could to hopefully restore my sight, even if partially. It was a team effort: Daddy would often take me to Augusta, and so would Blunt, along with many others, who pitched in to do everything from driving me to appointments to walking me down hospital corridors.

*   *   *

Eventually, the membrane was laid onto my eye and sewed securely with tiny stitches, about one third the width of a human hair. These stitches would dissolve within three to four weeks. The hope was that it would reduce the inflammation in my eyes and encourage some of my damaged tissue to regrow.

The surgeries were excruciatingly painful. However, I know God was covering me because I somehow never sat idly at home in pain: the pain was in my heart, but not in my eyes, when I was at 115. Dr. Ambati made it very clear we'd only be able to work on one eye at a time, which often meant the surgeries went on for months and months.

He then told me to pray—everything would have to work for us to continue on to the next phase to restore my sight.

He had a humble confidence in himself, so every time he spoke and every time he touched my hands and my shoulder, it gave me hope. And I did everything he told me to do, and together with Pastor Ova I prayed and prayed and prayed.

* * *

Before meeting Dr. Ambati, I had denounced God. I believed in Him but was angry. But this young, brilliant doctor, who believed in God, helped to renew my own faith.

He prayed before performing any surgery. "When I'm scrubbing, just to myself, before I get under way, I say a prayer," he once told me. "I look at what I do as it's not really me doing it. I'm doing the surgery of God. I'm just really an instrument. This isn't all about me. My parents, my training, my mentors, it's all by God's grace."

The only time I looked forward to anything in those days was to see Dr. Ambati, because he gave me hope that I might see my children again.

* * *

There was so much medication, a lot of eye drops, and a lot of visits. Some months I would head to Augusta every week. The amniotic membrane procedures took about a year to complete, and a limbal stem cell transplant followed, but one of those transplants had to be redone. Once the stem cells were taking, and the antirejection medicine was working, my body accepted the stem cells. A cornea transplant was next, along with removing the cataract and stitching a new lens—a donor lens from someone who had died—inside my eye. I did well with that for a while, but my body rejected the cornea transplant. It then rejected a second cornea transplant.

In fact, it was the cornea donor transplants that caused many highs and lows. I'd come home in 2005 and sit around for a week or two, and I'd start to see a glimpse of color, and at times I could even see motion. I'd never know how long any of this was going to last, but it devastated me each time it would vanish. It would get a little bit better, and then everything would go fuzzy and then dark. If one eye went dark, they had to try the other eye. We went back and forth in this stage of hope and defeat for about eighteen months. And when Dr. Ambati's colleague, a retina doctor, said, "I don't like the way the retina is looking," that could be three weeks I'd have to spend in the hospital in Georgia, which I couldn't bear to do because I knew the kids wanted me home.

After the cornea failures, Dr. Ambati explained what he thought was going on: the blood vessels in my eye were attacking the new cornea and ultimately causing its rejection: That didn't mean we would stop trying, but after being pushed into the light and then waking up into darkness, I was at a breaking point.

* * *

One day, I awoke in the middle of a surgery and touched my eyes and realized my eyeballs were gone. I literally put my hands inside my empty eye sockets, and I let out the most gut-wrenching scream. Suddenly there was a lot of movement and arguing in the room among the doctor and nurses, but before I could say another word, they put me back under. Despite all the progress, I knew in the end there was always a possibility the corneas wouldn't work. I was emotionally drained by things working and eventually failing. When I was able to see light and motion, 115 was a very happy place, but when I was pitched back into darkness, it was not. Some days, I'd walk around the house when nobody was looking and chase after glimpses of light or a red flash of my kid's shirt. Or I'd go in my kitchen and see the movement of stainless-steel objects. Or sit on the porch and see the motion of a car and sometimes its color, if the vehicle was bright enough. Then I'd wake up in the morning or the next week or month in nothing but darkness.

There were many nights I laid in bed and couldn't really *feel* my body: I was that numb, so empty, that I wasn't present in my own skin. The years of blindness were coming now, one after another. In my lowest moments, I wanted to die. On those nights I would wonder: how the hell did I get to a place where I didn't even want to live for my children? You can't get any lower in life than when your kids aren't even enough for you. The pain of the dozens of surgeries for the past two years was so excruciating, not only to my body, but to my mind. Everybody walked in and said, "Oh, Sabrina, you're so strong," and I'd be thinking, *How strong could I be? All I want to be is dead.*

* * *

At this point, one too many surgeries had failed. The last failure triggered something in me that I could not shake. Now, I had to wait for another surgery and in another eye, but for what? To see a glimpse and watch it fade away all over again? That pain was worse than the surgery itself. I was on a never-ending roller coaster of emotions and I was over it, ready for it all to end. All I could think about was how to end it. How does a blind woman commit suicide?

I concluded that if I could make it to the end of my driveway, and if I could count three mailboxes up, I would be at the end of the road. If I heard a car coming either way, then I could run out into the street, and that's how I'd end my life. I was so tired of always having to fight. I was so tired of the pain.

I waited one night for everyone to go to sleep. I got out of bed with no fear. I made it to the front door. I left the house, leaving the door wide open, fearful that I'd wake someone up if I closed it shut behind me. I reached the first neighbor's mailbox. Then I somehow got to the second mailbox. That's when I slowed up, because now I had to find this third one.

Meanwhile, something had woken up Nuk—he was about twelve or thirteen at the time. He came out of his room, and he checked on me—

I'm not in my bed. He checked my bathroom, he checked the kitchen, and then he saw the front door open. He walked out the door and noticed my silhouette stumbling down the street, trying to get to that third mailbox. He started following me. Of course, I didn't know he was behind me. I got to that third mailbox. I imagine it was then that he realized that something was very wrong—I'm walking blind on the street in the middle of the night wearing pajamas. Suddenly, I felt his hands over my shoulders. I turned around, and he grabbed my arm. We went back into the house together. He locked the door. I went to my bed. He went to his room, and for years we never spoke another word about that night.

I finally saw that it was my children who were the people in my life that I could fully trust. It was my children who pointed me toward what faith could possibly be; and I never knew what that faith was until I was thirty-one years old. I couldn't see it because it had been stomped on from the time Reverend Lottie violated me. And maybe I never would've come to grasp it if it wasn't for people like Pastor Ova, who came to the house to talk to me even when I didn't want to hear her and she knew I wasn't listening. But after Nuk turned me back home when I walked toward suicide, and I thought about leaving this world and my children in it without me, I called Pastor Ova and asked: "How do I pray for my children?"

"I've been waiting for this call," Pastor Ova said. "I'll be right over."

CHAPTER 19

Wake-up Calls

Thinking about getting out the bed every day when depression has a grip on you is one thing. Doing it is a whole other thing.

Even though I had emerged from my bedroom after all those years of wallowing in my tears after the attack and later, being locked up in there fighting with men, the room was still my comfort zone, the place I'd return to when depression hit. It also had become my office, where I'd make my calls and conjure up plans for the family, as well as a place where I had long talks with each of my children. And I believe that's why my kids always said, "Mama could move mountains from the bed."

By 2007, Dr. Ambati devised a new approach in his determined effort to help me regain sight. Previously, I had received two transplants that allowed me to see motion and some color in both eyes, but this time Dr. Ambati inserted two plastic corneas called KPros in my eyes. The hope was that these could eventually improve my eyesight tremendously.

Having sight again after blindness is nothing like the movies. There's no pulling off the bandages and having an "aha" moment. Instead, regaining the ability to see is a gradual thing.

After the surgery, I was bandaged up and sent home.

Dr. Ambati explained that if the procedure was successful, I'd gain vision as the days and weeks and months progressed. I trusted his ability, so I was very careful with my eyes as they healed. I slept with large shields over my eyes and bandages over the shields. Sleep was scary, because I had to ensure that my own fingers didn't touch my eyes at night while I slept. Every morning I'd carefully take off the shields and place them on my nightstand with the bandages. Then I'd sit in bed and survey my hands, waving them in front of my face. Everything was fuzzy, but gradually, week to week, I could begin to make out the outline and shape of my hands. Soon, I could count my fingers. I eventually moved to standing in the bathroom, where I surveyed the sink, the toilet, and the mirror.

I began to have hope that the KPros were going to allow me to get up and live my life. Finally, I grew confident enough to take a ride in the car with my new sight. Cars were fast and terrifying, but they also fascinated me; when a car zoomed by, I'd say, "Shit, did I just see that?"

One day, Tiffany and I pulled up to Aunt Louise's home. I was in the passenger seat when I adjusted the rearview mirror and saw my face at very close proximity. I was shocked to see for the first time how altered my face had become. Is this what I looked like now? This is how I had been walking around? No one told me my face was burned so badly. A flurry of questions raced through my head. *Why didn't someone tell me I looked like the damn Elephant Man?*

* * *

For the first time I saw not only my injuries, but even more hurtful, the damage I'd caused. The absolute worst of it was to my kids. Gazing at myself and seeing a body and face I didn't recognize was one thing, but seeing how my self-pity had negatively affected my children was a million times worse than staring at my altered reflection.

Over those three years in the bedroom, how many meals had I missed with my children, leaving them to fend for themselves as if they had no mother? Since the attack, Kesha's GPA had dropped dangerously low. I also had no idea that she'd been in an abusive relationship with a girl at school; things had gotten so out of hand that the police had been involved more than once. Where was I when Kesha needed help? Why couldn't I keep her safe and let her know that she wasn't alone, that she was loved?

Nuk was getting into trouble, too, doing things like beating up a boy who cussed at Shani on the school bus. Both Nuk and Shani had been suspended for three days. I never knew any of this. And Marcus, who was my quietest child, was close to failing out of school.

And who had I left in charge during all this? Mama. I left my babies in the care of a woman still addicted to crack, who stole money from me, who had proven over a lifetime of letdowns how unreliable she was. After surveying the mess that I allowed to happen during my self-imposed exile, I knew it was time for me to step up and be the mother I needed to be and get all my children in a position where I felt that they could thrive.

I didn't realize how hard that would be.

* * *

Kesha, my oldest child, had turned disrespectful at home. Her basketball coach at the school had turned against her, and I couldn't stand by and allow her mistreatment to continue happening. Like Shani years earlier, Kesha was another wake-up call, and I was not going to watch her fail.

Kesha had started looking at me differently when I began dating Blunt. She despised him and faded into the background long before he went to prison. But prior to Blunt, she didn't miss a beat. The boys credit Kesha for making them tough, pushing and knocking them down as they played hoops. And even though Kesha eventually started speaking to me in all kinds of disrespectful ways, she was crazy about Shani, and she made sure that the boys always had something to eat.

During this time, Kesha was dealing with a lot, which included having to adapt to living as a gay young adult while also dealing with a mom who lived in her room and had a boyfriend who'd walk in the house and not even acknowledge her or her siblings. Kesha looked at me as weak for not standing up to Blunt, and she started pushing against me, a tension that continued for years.

Kesha handled her frustrations and disappointments with me by not being home and was practically living with her girlfriend's family.

One day Kesha walked in my room with a challenge. "Do you get child support for me?" she asked pointedly.

I sighed. "Why, Kesha?" I was not in the mood for a fight.

"Because I feel like you need to start paying me child support."

I didn't have the energy. "Whatever, Kesha."

"I'll be back tomorrow to get it," she said, before walking out my room.

I started to despise when Kesha entered the house because I knew it was going to be something. We'd get into big arguments, and she never backed down. My boys gravitated to me. They'd come sit on the bed and talk, but I could never get a grip on Kesha. In fact, I couldn't discipline her. No one could say anything to her because she always had the last word.

Once Kesha called the police on me, claiming I hit her, which I had tried to do but missed. I wasn't intending to hurt my child, but she called me "a bitch." "Motherfucking bitch" and "This bitch" or that was all I heard.

My close friend Tiffany, who was there that day, stood between us as we went back and forth.

Eventually, Kesha ran out of the house and called the police, who arrived a few minutes later. The officers talked to Kesha outside before they stepped into the kitchen to question me.

"Ma'am, your daughter is wanting to press charges against you," one of the officers told me.

I sat down at the kitchen table. "I know, but let me ask you something," I said to him. "You got kids?"

"Yeah, I got a girl and a boy," he replied.

"What would you do if every time your child comes in the house, she was disrupting the home, and every time you turned around, she was calling you out your name? So yes, I did try to hit her, and if you going to take me to jail, then go ahead and take me now, because I don't regret it. I'd do that shit all over again."

"Ma'am, I totally understand," the officer said. "I'm going to go ahead and talk to her."

He left me at the table and went back to Kesha, who was waiting outside. A few minutes later he returned, informing me that he told her that if she pressed charges against me, I'd press charges against her. "I advised her to leave the house tonight and y'all figure this out tomorrow," he said.

Tiffany offered to take Kesha home to allow for cooler heads to prevail. Kesha returned about a day or two later, and we never talked about what happened.

Kesha was sixteen when all of this was going on, her behavior a result of a tumultuous school life. Her coach was giving her hell, accusing her of disrupting the team, calling her a "bad influence" for her teammates. Without the coach saying it, we knew the coach was basically saying: *Don't hang around Kesha because she's gay.*

I later found out that same coach had placed my smartest child in low-level classes to boost her grades to make her eligible to play for the school. How could I allow her to be used this way? After Kesha came to my room and informed me that she'd been accused by the coach of stealing a pair of shorts, I'd had enough.

I scheduled a meeting with the school administrators and listened as her coach sat there talking shit about my daughter. "Well, if she doesn't like basketball, tell her to quit," the coach said.

Quitting basketball was not an option. Besides, Kesha was the best point guard in South Carolina. She also had academic and career goals and loads of potential.

During the meeting, the school administrators proceeded to back the coach, telling me Kesha needed anger management classes.

I blinked slowly and shook my head. "She doesn't need anger management. If there's anyone who needs anger management classes, it's her coach."

They were trying to paint Kesha as the angry Black woman who was terrorizing the school and turning little straight white girls gay. Truth be told, I had encouraged her to be proudly gay, but these Bible Belt teachers and coaches saw that as a threat. While Kesha happily wore her rainbow bandana, other girls were dropping out of school because their parents had disowned them when they came out.

I wanted Kesha to live her best life. And while she took full advantage of that, the school thought she was the worst person in the world. Her coach was on a mission to have her expelled, but I went to school and stood up for her.

I realized she had a target on her back, so I had to get her out of there. I wanted to put her in a position where she could still be herself.

The pivotal point was when Kesha and her girlfriend got into a big fight.

One day, Kesha had gone to her girlfriend's mama's house to pick up some of her belongings, when the mama, the two sisters, and the girlfriend all jumped her. They also called the police after Kesha fought them all and won.

Meanwhile, laid-back Marcus sat in Kesha's car the entire time. As they recounted the events to me back home, I was astonished, and asked Marcus why he didn't jump in to help his sister.

He shrugged. "Mama, I didn't need to get out of the car. She had it," he said casually.

By the grace of God, the officer who came to my house this time was a former classmate of mine. She and I played basketball together at school, and now she was a sheriff's deputy. The moment she walked into 115, she said, "Miss Sabrina, girl, how you been doing?" She informed me: "I'm not pressing charges against your child. Though they want to press all kinds of charges."

After that, I did what I could to get her out of Clemson. I reached out to one of her favorite coaches at the AAU, the summer basketball league.

LaSheryl Smith loved Kesha. "Please, you got to help me get my child out of here," I begged.

LaSheryl listened and was thoughtful. "Let me call some connections and let me see what I can do."

When we presented Kesha with the idea of attending a boarding school, Oak Hill Academy, in Virginia (the NBA star Carmelo Anthony attended the prep school years earlier), she was all for it. She finished her eleventh grade in Clemson and started her new school for senior year. She had received a full basketball scholarship and was required to wear a uniform every day. However, just before she started, I learned she was arriving with a 1.9 GPA. Despite that, I insisted the school put her in all college prep classes because I knew she'd pass. In fact, I was sure of it because Kesha wanted to succeed.

She did better than that: she graduated in 2008 with a 4.0 GPA.

Three caravans of my family and friends drove up to see her walk across the graduation stage. Everybody was there: I had Shani all prettied up in a dress and ribbons. Destiny, Tiffany, Daddy, DeAndre, and Marcus all came. I screamed at the top of my lungs when Kesha accepted her diploma. When I hugged Kesha at the graduation, she said, "Thank you, Mama."

For me, those three words felt like a million dollars.

Before Kesha started at Robert Morris College in Pittsburgh months later, I asked her new basketball coach one thing. "Can she be herself?"

The coach turned to me and said, "Of course."

* * *

While I still dealt with depression and relied on people to help me get back and forth to my doctors' appointments in Georgia, I had developed a large degree of independence and achieved personal wins that at one time in my life I took for granted. One of the most exciting things about Kesha's graduation was that I could actually see her in her red graduation gown. That was an incredible gift to me.

Seeing Kesha move across the stage was, for me, miraculous. Did I see her like most parents there saw their children on that happy day? No, not at all, but I could *see* her—my life was no longer pitch black. Some days my sight would be good, other times it would be dark, but all of it was good enough for me. Even more, I was starting to see my children's faces again. I recall Marcus standing at the doorway of my bedroom.

"Why are you standing there?" I said, surprising him.

"Mama!" he gasped. "You can see me standing here?"

"Fool, you standing in my doorway."

He was struggling to believe me and couldn't contain his excitement. "For real, for real? You see me standing here? Mama stop playing. What color is my shirt?"

"Blue," I said.

"Oh, snap!" he said, drawing his hand to his face.

I will always recall having that moment with Marcus. Of all my children, Marcus looks most like me, and though his face was blurry that day, I knew it was him, and in him I could make out my own features, the face I had before the attack. As everyone came home that day, Marcus said, "Mama can see!" And the kids all jumped on my bed.

I pretended to be annoyed, but I was thrilled my babies were so excited for me. "I can't see nothing, get out of my room," I said, hiding my smile.

Despite the odds, my sight was improving, which also deepened my faith in God again and my self-confidence. I always feared returning to the darkness, but now I was determined to live every moment in the light.

Around 2008, that same year Kesha graduated from high school, I was going to my boys' football games at Daniel High School. Every Friday, I managed to go to my own closet and pick out my own outfit for the evening. I'd lay my clothes on the bed, making sure I was wearing the right colors—blue and gold.

I looked forward to every game. Now, with renewed confidence, instead of hiding from the public, I'd sit at the bottom bench and receive strangers who'd shake my hand and tell me how well the boys were doing on the field. Sometimes when they'd come off the field and get water, I could make out their numbers: Marcus was number 7 and DeAndre number 11. And if I'd strain my eyes a bit, I could make out their faces, too. Soon, no one had to tell me DeAndre snagged an interception or that Marcus made a touchdown, because I could make it out myself. I had to hold someone's arm to get to my car, but it was starting to feel like old times again.

* * *

As I was trying to find my way back to normalcy, I'd do anything to make sure my children got what they wanted, often, overcompensating for all the times in their lives I missed. I was determined that if they wanted it (not necessarily needed it), I'd make it happen. Marcus and Nuk decided they wanted to forgo wearing tuxedos for their prom, opting instead for the old gangsta look, so I reached out to a cousin of mine and asked to borrow his suits—oversized trousers and jackets, along with matching hats. As my sight improved a little more, I spent a lot of time in the kitchen whipping up big meals for the kids, practically creating entire feasts. I'd make fried chicken, meatloaf, barbecue pork chops, macaroni and cheese, fried cabbage, and cornbread, and simmer pinto beans in the Crock-Pot. I was imitating my grandma Frances, of course, but I did it in my own way.

Marcus, who loved to eat, especially loved my cooking, which encouraged me to cook even more. Soon, he began coming home early from school just to eat! No matter what I'd prepare, Marcus would always say, "Thank you, Mama, this food is so good." His siblings would tease him for always thanking me, but each time he did it meant so much to me.

I was trying to make up for lost time. In my own way, I stepped back into the mama role, but it was hard because, now, reality would soon set in. While cooking was my saving grace because it made me feel like I still got it, I often felt defeated, struck by anxiety and fear for doing something that used to come naturally. It took me a while to find my bearings in motherhood again. I was determined, but it was petrifying at times, because I had sat depressed in a room for so long.

This is when I knew I had to really start fighting, because depression would get the best of me most days, catching me as I tried to get up and vacuum or attempted to wipe the table or build my will up to cook another meal, all while still mostly blind. I was unwavering, though, and practice really did make perfect. The more I got up and worked in the house, the better I became at cleaning the floors or fixing the toilet; we had no money for repairs.

While I was still selling crack to make ends meet, my earning went to pay bills. I didn't have extra money like I did when I was stripping, though I was still able to give my children a daily stipend. So while I was trying to be a good mother by day, I was also dealing crack by night; I always had a pack of crack available and had a decent-sized clientele. But my biggest regret was selling to Mama, who always said she was copping the drugs for someone else. Deep down, I knew it was for her, which meant I was not only lying to myself, I was also contributing to her addiction.

Something I didn't regret, however, was selling drugs to Uncle Ottie. He had fallen on hard times, and I am sure he didn't want to come to my door for crack after killing Dilly. I knew he didn't want Daddy—his best friend—to know he was doing drugs, but then again, I didn't want Daddy to know I was selling them, either.

So if Ottie wanted a 100 slab, I'd give him a 200 slab, hoping he'd overdose and kill himself, not realizing I was hurting myself by giving away free dope. He only came to me three times, but the fact that he had come to me told me his demons had gotten the best of him. And at this time in my life, that satisfied me.

* * *

Truth be told, at first it was very tough to sell drugs, cook dinner every night, be a disciplinarian, and attend school functions, but I did it all with fervor. In fact, I overdid it all. Why couldn't I just cook one meal, instead of three different meals? Why did I have to give the kids *everything* they asked for?

I'd also overdo on the discipline. Marcus and Nuk were now teenagers and doing teenager things. Unconcerned about curfew, they would come back home well after our agreed-upon time. In turn, I'd show my ass and throw a complete tantrum. There were times I was screaming, cursing, and crying, just to get my point across. I realize now that I was adjusting, but I didn't know *how* to adjust to our collective new normal.

Once, when Marcus and DeAndre rang up a three-hundred-dollar cable bill watching something they knew they shouldn't have been watching, I unscrewed their bedroom door hinges and placed the door in *my* bedroom. I struggled, but finally I was able to slide the floor stereo with speakers out of their room and move the large television into the hallway. They came home from football practice and were shocked.

My thing was—they hadn't earned the right to freedom and privacy. I was less angry about them being curious and watching porn for the first time, but one of them had pressed the purchase button so many times that it added up to three hundred dollars—and they had lied about it, too. While I was spending the whole darn day taking the hinges off the door, someone might have looked at me and said "she's the one coming unhinged," but the truth is, I was only attempting to regain control of my house by any means necessary.

I also made sure the kids knew, number one, that they were not to let them white people at their schools call and tell me they had done something crazy; if so, we were going to have a problem. "I need good grades," I'd tell them, "and so when you go out, act like you got some common sense. When you get home, I will have your food cooked, your clothes washed, and your room cleaned." I also made sure to hold each child accountable in front of their siblings.

Once, the two boys got in trouble for selling their nasty sneakers to a mentally challenged boy. I was called in to school, as were five other parents. I thought I knew what I was walking into because I had been in the same office when I was younger and received "paddlings" from Mr. Wade and Mr. Jenkins years before.

This time, this meeting wasn't that. Now, I'm walking into a different situation: these white people had my Black boys, accusing them of something that they did do, but this time, the police were involved; the outcome of this situation could be far different from any I experienced when I was in trouble as a child. I knew I had to do something to distract them and ensure my boys didn't have to deal with the cops. I started cutting a fool, yelling at Marcus and DeAndre, "I told y'all! You know I didn't raise you like this!" I yelled. "And just *wait* till we get home!" Satisfied that I would discipline the boys, the principal ended the meeting. "Okay, take your boys home. We see you got this."

As punishment, I gave them two choices: cut your dreads or take an ass whooping. They both looked at each other, looked back at me, and said, "We're going to cut our hair." So off to the barbershop we went, and I stood there while the barber cut their hair, all those beautiful dreads completely falling, one by one, on the floor.

* * *

With bolts purchased from Ace Hardware, I had shut my room off from the rest of the world for years. I locked my children out, telling myself that it was for their own protection to not see me cry. Looking back, I was locking myself in. In my deep sorrow, I had withdrawn from my own family.

As much as I had hidden in my room and thought I was crying in silence, I now realized they heard me. They heard everything. I wasn't present, and they knew. With the courage I gained from my improved sight, I soon emerged from my room and declared it would no longer keep me captive. I decided my room would now be the "Get Right" room—actually it was the children who coined it. It was going to be the place where my kids and I could talk to each other openly and tell it like it is.

At first, the idea was met with resistance. "This is what white people do," one of the kids said. "Who do you think we are, the Partridge Family?"

They knew if I called them in the room, which I usually did, and said, "Shut the door," which I usually said, that meant that the kids and I would be in the room with me for about two hours. They would sit on the edge of the mattress, and I would talk and talk and talk. I'd later hear them mumbling, "I'd rather do anything then go in there and hear Mama talk for two hours."

DeAndre was the worst when it came to the Get Right room. He had a thing where if he was mad at me, he would sing loudly and tauntingly. "There is something called bipolar," he'd sing, or "The Get Right room ain't right."

I'd say, "I know you ain't talking to me."

Every last one of them had to come into the Get Right room at one point. To be honest, I didn't know what I was doing. I attempted to control my children from inside the house because my eyesight meant I couldn't keep up with them outside the house, but I didn't know what I was doing. I had to literally turn into what they perceived to be a crazy woman and hope they would do right before they did wrong, because otherwise they would have to face the consequences of a damn raging maniac.

Deep down, I was determined to make sure they didn't repeat my mistakes. Everything that had been done to me, I did the opposite to them. Nobody talked to me for hours or held me accountable for my mistakes or tried to understand how I felt about things so I could do the next thing differently. So what did I do? I kept making the same mistakes over and over.

I really didn't know if this was the correct approach or not, but I felt that giving them attention, talking to them a lot, was the right thing for my family.

* * *

Sometimes Marcus would come into my room and simply sit with me—he was a quiet child who'd rather draw or listen to music than talk, and his tenderness helped pull me out of myself. Despite all my setbacks, despite all the medicine I was constantly having to take, despite all the negative thoughts I would think, this child made me feel like I was a mom again—that he *needed* me, that all my children did, and that I still had a critical role to play in their lives.

Marcus never paid any attention in school, never cared about it, and I always had to stay on him about his grades, but he was artistic. The boy could sit there and draw your face, paint, sing his behind off, and produce beats; he just hated school. His grades became especially unimportant to him after I got hurt, but when I stopped living in the bedroom and tried to be a mother again, I made it a family mission to ensure Boodia graduated from high school. In order to do that, he had to pass two classes during summer school.

"Listen, this boy is going to graduate. Y'all gotta help me," I said to everyone.

During dinner at the big dining table, I turned to Marcus. "Boodia, I'm not playing with your ass. They told me you must pass two math classes, geometry and algebra." In fact, the school told me he couldn't even be a minute late to summer school.

Together, we all did our part to make it happen. I turned to DeAndre. "Nuk, your job is to take him to summer school. Kesha, your job is to pick him up."

Marcus passed his classes, and now I believed he could go to college, too. It was late in the game, and by this time, most schools had overlooked him because his grades were not where they needed to be, but I stayed on his football coach to make something happen.

I'd see him and say, "Coach Rob, what we're gonna do with Marcus?"

He'd say, "I don't know."

I would call Coach Rob in between surgeries so he knew I was determined to figure out a plan for Marcus. After my eyesight got even better, I started going to my boys' basketball games. I could see much better there than I could at the football games, because the audience was right on top of the action. I'd sit behind the bench, talking to strangers. This was a milestone period for me. My confidence was soaring.

At the games, I'd find Coach Rob, asking every single time, "What we going to do about Marcus?"

Finally, we came up with a solution. After making a highlight reel of Marcus's biggest plays, we sent it to Georgia Military, where they were interested and asked to see more footage. After much persistence and pressure from me, we got another tape made, and finally Marcus got accepted to the school. Out of all my children, I was especially proud of Marcus, who didn't have the drive to want to succeed in school, but somehow he did it.

*   *   *

Dr. Ambati's prosthetic corneas led me to ultimately have 20/50 vision with prescriptive glasses, which was outstanding for me, a person who couldn't see anything just a few years earlier.

One of the biggest milestones was me driving by myself, though it was a gradual thing. Before I conjured up the courage to drive, I'd sit behind the wheel of the Lexus when the kids were at school, rubbing my hand along the dashboard and imagining myself driving. I missed my car, but I really missed the power of sitting in the driver's seat.

One day I was cooking and needed something from Ingles grocery store a block away.

I said, "Shani, come go with me, you might have to guide me," I told her as I made my way the car. She sat on the passenger side while I got my courage to back out of the driveway. I drove slowly, so slowly that I had about six cars behind me honking, but I didn't care.

After that, I'd find reasons to drive to the grocery. "Oops, I better go pick up some more eggs. Oops, need more chicken." Thinking back now, I don't know how I didn't have a wreck. Instead, I experienced what I hadn't experienced in years—independence.

*   *   *

Around this time, I went to a routine medical visit, and my retina doctor told me my retina was detaching, which means the back part of the eye (or the retina) peels off the wall of the eye. I stayed in the hospital as the surgery team prepared me for the operation to fix it.

I had three surgeries within a three-week span. First, the doctor injected gas to get the retina to stick back to the wall of the eye. During a second surgery, they inserted a balloon to try to keep the retina stable. My last surgery during this time involved wrapping a band around the retina, hoping that would help the retina to reattach, but the doctors couldn't save my left eye. It was just too weak to withstand all the surgeries. And once I had a retinal detachment, that eye was truly gone.

Still, I had what I called "my good eye," which I could see out of, though it wasn't how most people could look at a coffee cup and think, that's a coffee cup. It was as though someone put a thin sheet of plastic up to my eyes, and that's how I could see, but I was thankful for that.

Meanwhile I continued to live my life. I could put on my reading glasses and get on my iPad and pull up Apple Music. For the first time in years, I could do anything.

This is when I started asking God for vision. I started praying, "Just give me vision." In hindsight, I didn't know what I was asking for, but I think I worried that my eyesight wasn't going to last. I was seeing everything, but my eyesight wasn't consistent—some days were better than others. I'd say, "God, if this is how it's going to be the rest of my life, I am cool with that."

To be honest, though, it was the most unnerving thing to have to go through. Every single day, I had one thought: *Is this the day I lose my sight again?*

* * *

From 2010 to 2013, the years DeAndre played college football, I was the most active since the attack. In fact, the day in 2010 when DeAndre decided to go to Clemson, I flushed all the drugs I was selling down the toilet. I didn't want anything to fall back on Nuk, because here was a child who really tried to make something of himself and build a legacy for the whole family.

His blind mother was not about to be arrested for selling drugs. I didn't care if I was broke, I didn't care if me and Shani had to eat tuna every day, I was not going to hurt his chances. He had worked so hard, and he deserved everything coming to him.

I attended all his home games at Clemson, where Nuk indeed became the big star. When I wasn't at the games or cleaning the house, I was constantly listening to gospel music, because the music gave me peace and stability, especially the song "Still I Rise" by Yolanda Adams, who'd eventually become a great friend of mine. I kept the song on repeat and even tattooed "Still I Rise" on my neck.

The song starts with the words: "Shattered but I am not broken. Wounded but time will heal." I'd listen to every word and equate it with the things happening in my life. It became my private testimony—that whatever I am going through, I'd press on. And that helped me do what I hadn't done in so many years—be out in public in front of hundreds, if not thousands, of people and not giving a hoot that someone might be staring at me.

* * *

I loved being back in Death Valley, among the eighty-five thousand fans, the cheers, the energy and noise. I loved it all, just as much as I did when Hummie was the biggest star at Clemson. Now, it was my son's turn. Somehow everyone knew I was the mother of the star player. Strangers would talk to me or come shake my hand. When Nuk ran down the hill just like his uncle did many years before, I'd jump up screaming at the top of my lungs.

During this period, I was still going back and forth to the doctors, but I was happy because I had DeAndre's games to look forward to every single week. And DeAndre never disappointed. Now a wide receiver, he made touchdown after touchdown and was one of the few players ever to break Hummie's records. I couldn't think of anyone who doubted that he was going to the NFL.

These wonderful years DeAndre was at Clemson gave me life. One of my favorite things to do was tailgate. And word was no one could tailgate like DeAndre's family! I'd get everyone together and we'd prepare for days, spending hours at night in Walmart buying food and drinks. Mama; all my children; DeAndre's godmother, Frances; and even Steve's mama, Shirley Ann, were always part of these events. Although we didn't all get along, we showed up for DeAndre those three years. Daddy was in charge of bringing a generator, a television, and a speaker because some people didn't want to watch the game inside the stadium. Every parent of a football player had an allotted space, and I'd make sure we used every inch of ours. We'd set up four tables and load them with chicken, fried fish, potato salad, drinks, and alcohol. Other tailgating families would come to our party, lining up like we had set up a buffet.

Mama, my friend Veronica, the kids, and everyone else would get there by 6:00 a.m. with coffee, but I'd arrive fashionably late, decked out in Clemson's orange and purple colors. In fact, tailgating became a fashion show for me. Mama would say, "What she got on now?" as I arrived. Once, I came in with an orange dress that fit like skin; it had a white faux-fur collar, and of course I wore purple earrings.

As much fun as it was, tailgating was a lot of work. I had to recruit people to be in charge. We'd cook all day and night. And it took a lot of energy to put everything up in the morning and break it down that night, but I didn't care. It was my way of saying to DeAndre: "We appreciate you." Then again, I've always been that way: you show me you're trying, and I am going to show you that I got your back. I might not tell you, but I am damn sure going to show you.

Although DeAndre decided to attend school in his hometown, he once warned me, "Mama, just pretend I went to school far away. I don't want you to be coming up on campus." And I didn't, but I viewed tailgating as a little piece of home I wanted to give him. After the games, he could walk out of the locker room and come to his tailgate party. He'd bring some of his teammates, and they'd feast on chicken and fried fish.

Once again, another child of mine was pushing me back to normalcy. I had a thousand excuses to stay depressed and lay around the bed, and honestly who could blame me? But each one of my children in their own way made me realize I needed to fight, whether it was Kesha's rebellion, DeAndre's sheer will to create a better life for all of us, or Shani's and Marcus's love of their mother's cooking. My babies, every single one of them, are the reasons I am standing, and they are the reasons I still rise every morning.

CHAPTER 20

Ending Generational Curses

The year 2013 was packed with so many highs and a few lows, so many tears and even more laughs. Even though I only had one "good eye" at the time, I knew this was the beginning of some good days ahead. De-Andre, who by his junior year had broken the Clemson University career records for receiving yards and touchdown receptions, had been drafted in the first round by the Houston Texans, and the family got together in our Texans blue-and-red jerseys to see his debut NFL game in San Diego.

Although I had a host of relatives and friends with us, one person was missing: Mama had decided months earlier she would enter rehab. It was actually DeAndre who came up with the idea. "Mama," he said to me one day, "I want to spend my first check on Grandma getting the help she needs."

And so I sat my mother down and shared DeAndre's offer, and she accepted. She stayed for only thirty days, but I saw it as her attempt for redemption, and I was grateful for that.

A year earlier, something I did set me on my own path, a path to end family secrets that have cursed and kept us spinning for generations: I gave myself a formal celebration to mark the ten-year anniversary of my attack. I spent months and months planning the event, which would be held in a ballroom in Clemson. I invited fifty women who each had been influential in my healing. On the day of the event, the women wore all white. My children and Hummie's two children wore black and marched me into the ballroom to the song "Still Standing," by Monica.

As the boys released my hand, I did a twirl and a little two-step. This was such a celebratory moment for me and a decade-long milestone. I had come so far but still had a ways to go. I remember how happy I felt among the people who showed me love through the darkest of times. That night, I realized if I could pull this many people together, I could have a good influence on so many others.

Next, I needed to tell my story from a place of healing: my first speaking engagement was at the public library in Easley, where about ten people showed up, five of them my family members, Mama, Daddy, one or two of my kids. I talked about an hour, crying the entire time.

Soon I began to give more talks, this time in Anderson, Clemson, and even Greenville. In the winter of 2013, I worked up the nerve to speak at Abel Baptist, our family church I'd attended as a child. I knew it would be a challenge because everyone in attendance not only knew me but would be expecting me to talk about the attack, but I had something else in mind for all of them.

I was no longer a child being made to keep a secret. I was now a forty-three-year-old woman with grown kids of my own, and no one could threaten, punish, or keep me quiet anymore. I now understood that violence and hurt had the power to transfer from generation to generation because it lived in the shadow of an even more powerful force: silence.

So much of what we've been able to do in my family, me and my kids, has everything to do with empowering each other to speak the truth and take the power away from silence. A big part of that is not turning a blind eye to what's really happening. It means that if you see violence, you call it what it is. You don't hide it. You don't excuse it. You don't repeat it. You don't pretend it away by acting like it doesn't exist, and you definitely don't accept what you know in your gut is wrong just because you're not sure how to make it right. The longer that kind of silence goes on, the deeper the damage runs.

What did Granny or Grandma Frances see when they were girls? How did their mamas and daddies behave with each other? Fuss and yell? Did they hit each other? As my mama grew up with my grandparents, watching her daddy hit her mom, and then pretending like it wasn't happening or even questioning whether it was right, what were the chances that she *wasn't* going to repeat the same behavior in her own marriage?

I'm the little girl hiding with her brothers under the bed to escape her parents' screaming. I'm also the woman whose own children tried to escape the same hollering coming from their mama's closed bedroom door. It doesn't take a lot to repeat a wrong when everyone's afraid to speak the truth. But I would not leave a legacy of silence to my children.

* * *

After I accepted the invitation to speak at Abel Baptist, the tough part began. A week prior to my speech, I called my father over to the house. I had to tell him what I intended to do. The moment he walked in, I said, "Daddy, I got to tell you something."

I looked him straight in the eye. "Reverend Lottie molested and raped me when I was ten years old. And I am going to talk about it and let everybody know what he did. I'm going to speak at Abel and wanted to let you know."

Daddy stood there shocked for a minute and finally said, "That motherfucker." Then he walked out the door. Daddy's response didn't shock me; in fact, I was relieved I didn't have to have a full conversation about it. Two things were accomplished by me speaking out to my daddy, and each of those things helped with my goal of breaking the generational curses: First, I told Daddy the truth instead of hiding it like we always do. And second, he immediately believed me and made no excuses for Lottie, which gave me the fuel I needed to go forward.

The next week, I entered Abel with my friends Veronica and Angela, ready to put a voice to the silence I had held within me for decades. I walked up to the pulpit and held on to the podium for dear life.

At the time, my sight was pretty good, at least for me: I could see movement in the church and even make out a few faces. Up there, though, I shivered like the scared little girl I was when I stepped out onto the porch to tell Mama and Grandma what Reverend Lottie had just done to me.

I now understand that childhood trauma stunts emotional growth, causing a woman like me to use childish antics as a coping mechanism. That ten-year-old girl had been present in every relationship, fought every fight, and dealt with every distressing ordeal. But I have begun to tell her: "It's okay now. You don't have to show your ass, you don't have to curse, you don't have to be angry because we're okay now." As I mature, I've developed the tools that ultimately help to heal my inner child.

I looked out from the pulpit into the congregation and saw with my restored sight my mama, aunties, and cousins sitting right there in the pews of Abel Baptist, where we had Dilly's homegoing service many years ago, and where both Dilly and Hummie are buried side by side in its cemetery. I began to speak.

In my head, I reminded myself to tell the story chronologically so that I wouldn't miss anything—especially the rape. I recall thinking that I had to speak up loudly so everyone could hear. I began with our childhood in Easley when Mama and Daddy were going through a divorce, and how all hell broke loose once we moved to the Hill in Clemson.

Soon, I could hear myself say the words I swore I'd never say out loud: "I was raped and molested by Lottie Davis, who most of you know as Reverend Lottie Davis."

I could hear gasps and people saying, "Oh my God." I took a breath. I saw a few people covering their mouths and others frozen in silence, but I was determined to let everyone know what this monster did to me. I didn't flinch or stutter. I had just told everyone in this church that a former leader of their community had violated a child.

What he did to me could no longer be denied. The more I spoke, the more I grew bigger than my secrets, and the more the memories lost the power they'd once had to hurt me. Despite having delicate vision that could still vanish at any time, I felt like I saw things clearer than I'd ever seen in my life.

* * *

Someone from the church escorted me away from the pulpit, and I sat there in a chair, gratified about what I just said, though nervous about who would welcome me with open arms and who would shun me. Not everyone appreciates the airing of truth, but that wasn't my concern anymore. I had done the unthinkable, and I knew there would be those who left whispering in disbelief that I would say such things about a man of the cloth. But there were also the church ladies who simply squeezed my hands, not uttering a word, letting me know in their own way that they, too, had been through something unspeakable.

But it wasn't until one of my cousins took me aside after church and said, "Girl, he did it to me, too," that I felt something else that was totally new: a sense of purpose.

Seeing her in myself and myself in her, I began to embrace everything that had happened to me. Maybe I had to suffer and go through all this to break the cycle of violence in my family so my children could become the remarkable people that they are today: if so, I'm at great peace with this. Even as I write this, and every time I say it, God reminds me that actually I'm not suffering. I'm at peace because my struggles made everybody go harder. They gave my family motivation and also were a lesson so that my kids wouldn't repeat the same mistakes. In the end, if I had to go through this so that my children wouldn't have to face what I did, then it was all worth it. But it's a long, hard road—a desperate road, truly—to transform victimhood into forgiveness.

You see, silence begets secrets. Generations and generations of secrets, secrets like the ones I kept for way too long that ate away at my self-esteem and started me on a path to choosing men whose ugly behavior I thought suited how ugly I felt on the inside, and what I felt at the time was what I deserved.

The same goes for alcoholism, drug addiction, and depression in my family: How would life have been different if our family hadn't ignored or excused Uncle Ottie's alcoholism? Would Dilly be alive?

How would life have been different for my mama, for my brothers and me, even for my daddy and the rest of our family, if we hadn't accepted Mama's drug addiction by not calling her on it for decades?

Would Hummie still be alive if one of us, any of us, had acknowledged that he was depressed, that he needed help? That he needed the intervention of a professional and that he may have needed medication? Whether together or apart, would Debra have had a stable partner to raise her children if Hummie had received treatment for his depression? Would his children, Daejha and Terrence Jr., have grown up with a daddy who protected them from harm rather than put them in harm's way?

How many others beyond our family needed one person to speak the truth out loud to let them know they weren't the only ones, that they weren't damaged or worthless—that they deserved better for themselves and had every right to expect others to believe them and believe in them?

* * *

DeAndre and I had become notable for a tradition in which he'd hand me the football immediately after every one of his touchdowns. It first happened during one of his early NFL games in Houston. I discovered my seat had been given away, so I was escorted to a seat in the first row of the end zone, at the far end of the football field. During each game, DeAndre always looked to see where I and the whole crew were sitting: Shani was usually to the right of me and Kesha to the left. That day he caught a touchdown and started moving toward me with the football, but I couldn't see him until he got close.

As he reached me, Shani and Kesha instructed me to bend down, and that's when I felt DeAndre's arms embracing me for a hug and him planting a deep kiss on my forehead. "I love you, Mama" was all he said as he placed the football in my hands.

Dramatically, I held the ball up in the air, which was photographed by the national media and started something big. I later told ESPN that the tradition of DeAndre bringing me the ball signified a bond between us that couldn't be broken. Soon, the media began to refer to DeAndre's and my relationship as "the unbreakable bond."

During his postgame interviews, DeAndre explained that while I couldn't see him, I could feel the ball and the energy it carried. At the time, I could actually see a little, at least in the way I could see in my good eye, but things were starting to get blurry again.

* * *

After DeAndre returned home that first year, having been selected for the NFL All-Rookie Team, we drove to downtown Greenville to have a massage and lunch by the water. DeAndre parked his new BMW, and I held on to his arm as we strolled along the recently restored area, which was now packed with all kinds of high-end restaurants, shops, cafés, and waterfalls. At the spa, we were greeted with thick white robes, and I could smell some sort of aromatherapy had been diffused into the air. As we were rubbed down with warm stones, DeAndre tried to convince me to leave 115 and let him buy me a new home.

"Nope, I'm not moving. You just paid off the house. I want to enjoy my house. Give me another year," I reasoned with him. Living at 115 had signified a lot in my life—some good and some bad—and I was hesitant to let it go.

"But Mama, I got it now," DeAndre cajoled. "You can move. It's okay."

Taking me out to eat was nothing new. I remember DeAndre taking me out to Chinese restaurants when he was in middle school. Even back then, strangers would come up to us, his local fans, and say how nice it was for him, still a child, to take his mother out to dinner.

After the massage was done, we walked over to the restaurant by the water. As we sat down, I got a call from Blunt—of all people. He had been released from prison, said he loved me and that he wanted to be with me.

DeAndre always called him by his first name: "Mama, you going to let Wayne come back?" he asked.

I had to be honest with him. I still loved Blunt. "What you think about it?"

"That's good, if he's going to come back and do right. I like that for you."

Unlike Kesha, DeAndre was crazy about Blunt. And by the time we got home, Blunt was sitting on the steps waiting for us.

Months later, Blunt and I would leave 115 and move into my new 6,000-square-foot home in Easley. We'd attend church together and hold hands, but one day I heard him on the phone talking to a woman. I particularly heard the word "ultrasound." After confronting him, he finally admitted he had gotten his ex-girlfriend pregnant with their third child. After getting out of prison, he went to her house first, but when I said I'd take him back, he wrote her a letter telling her he was gone and left it on the kitchen table. He hadn't done right by her.

Blunt and I became more distant. Here I was in the middle of healing, my life was on track, and my son was in the NFL and he had just purchased me a beautiful home, but now here comes Blunt and his drama trying to shake up my beautiful life. I did love Blunt, but I had had enough of his shenanigans. And once I started standing up for myself, he got pissed off.

Things only grew worse between us. Once after a party we argued, and in bed he kicked me, or I kicked him and the other kicked the other. We both jumped out the bed and stared at each other. I was done. I told him directly: "I'm not going through this with you again. This isn't working. You need to go be with your kids." He agreed, grabbing a few of his belongings around the room, and left. I called Kesha, who had just left the house a bit earlier, asking her to come back and stay with me for a while.

The next day, I called Pastor Ova and her prayer warriors, who included my close friend Veronica, to come to pray through the house where I had sex everywhere with a man. "I think y'all need to come and pray the sex demons out of here!" I told them over the phone.

And that's exactly what they did, anointing their prayerful, holy oil all over my new house, and finally cleansing Blunt from my life.

* * *

In late 2013 my good eye had become even more hazy and cloudy, and I was diagnosed with retinal hemorrhages.

For a year and a half, I was put on bed rest as to not exacerbate the bleeding in my eye. The only time I got up was when I would travel to go see DeAndre play, but even those travels soon became fewer and farther between. But when I did go, I'd return and get right back into bed, where I had to sit upright, never lying flat, trying to do everything I could to save my eye. I went to games holding people's arms; I was so disgusted with my situation, because I had come so far. But what was happening was really extremely serious: the retina was beginning to tear.

When the hemorrhages started, I knew that it was a possibility that I could lose my sight in my working eye. I'd pray and say, "Okay, Lord, well, if this is what I got to deal with, I'll sit up, I'll do whatever."

* * *

In 2014, in DeAndre's second year with the Houston Texans, I was invited to speak at a megachurch in Houston called Windsor Village. Between its two services and the congregants watching the live streams, I spoke to more than twenty thousand people that day. As I stood on the pulpit talking for thirty minutes, telling my story of survival and how I made it through, I noticed the room was silent. Veronica, who traveled there with me, would later tell me the pastor was literally at the edge of his seat. While I addressed the congregation, I realized two things. First, I was fulfilling Pastor Ova's vision years ago that one day I would be speaking before thousands. Second, I knew in my spirit and in my soul this is what I would be doing for the rest of my life. Long lines of women waited to talk to me. It felt like speaking at this event was something I was called by God to do.

Despite standing for hours until my knees felt like they were going to buckle, I spoke with every person who waited to speak with me. Several women in that line that day confided in me that they had been raped, too.

One woman leaned in and said about her partner, "He jumped me and now I am staying over my sister's house." Another whispered, "I'm going to go home and pack and leave him."

Another woman told me, "If you can get out, I can leave, too."

Inspiring hundreds of women who have also been through it allowed me to understand the power of my own story. Each one of us in some way or another is just waiting to hear that whatever it is that has happened to us, whatever we've done or whatever we're going through, that we're not the only one on Earth going through it. Sometimes that's all it takes to stop the hurt. And there are a great many of us: most studies estimate that at least one of every five American women alive today has been raped or suffered an attempted rape.

My cautionary tale was not only helping me end generational curses through my children but motivating strangers to end their secrets—and all of this inspired me.

There was no man in my life, but I was happy, and I had found my passion. Things were looking up, and I knew things were only going to get better.

* * *

My blood hemorrhages continued on, up until 2015. I started feeling there had to be more to do than sit upright in the bed—like this was the year 1840 or something—so I left my doctors in Augusta and started seeing an excellent doctor in Atlanta, who planned surgery on April 14 to stop the hemorrhaging.

Several days before the surgery that year, I had gone out to dinner with Marcus, DeAndre, Shani, and Montez, Poopie and Missy's youngest brother. I started experiencing sudden blurriness, closer to a darkness, while eating dinner at the restaurant. I nudged Shanterria, "Shani, my vision's getting blurry. My bandage contact must have fallen out."

This wasn't your regular contact lens but a large flexible one made to protect the plastic cornea. I had to wear it for twenty-four hours and change it every two or three months. I took out my solution and poured it on my eye right at the table, but it didn't get any better. "Mama, let's go to the bathroom," Shani urged, leading me to the restroom. There, I cleaned the contact and let Shani hold it, so I could wash my hands before touching my eye area. I put it back in my eye, but my sight was still dark.

"Oh my God," I said, beginning to cry. "I can't believe this is happening right now!"

We rushed back to the table. "Get the check, everybody," Shani said. "Mama's sight just went out." During the car ride to Easley, everybody was quiet while I sat sniffling in the front passenger seat.

When we got to the house, the children escorted me to my room to change my clothes, then Marcus and DeAndre rushed me to the hospital in Atlanta. Even though I didn't have sight in my good eye at the moment, I felt comforted that my two kings were there protecting their queen—Marcus on the right side of my hospital bed and DeAndre on the left. I tried to convince them to get a hotel room, but they refused and stayed the night, both of them sitting up in the chair until morning. Thinking about it now, I know my boys were scared and feeling helpless because there was nothing they could do but wait.

My new doctor still believed he could fix everything and sent me home, scheduling a surgery later, but when he went into my eye, he realized his efforts would be useless: a parasite had gotten into my eye and wreaked havoc, causing my retina to detach.

Eventually, the doctor said the words I never wanted to hear: "Your eye is inoperable."

My good eye was too damaged to repair.

I haven't had sight since 2015. That dinner was the last time I'd ever see my children's faces.

* * *

When the doctors told me that I'll never be able to see again—including a second opinion I sought from specialists in Miami—it was almost like a calm came over me. Nobody will ever know what it was like for me to wake up every day and wonder whether this would be the day that I would lose my sight.

Still, I cried all the time and would not come out of my bedroom. And I began to repeat behaviors I thought I'd abandoned for good. Shani, who never, ever gets in trouble, started acting out. On one day in particular, Shani walked out the door and still wasn't home by nightfall. I was beside myself with worry and called a friend to help me go out and find her. When I finally got her home, Shani broke down. She told me I was scaring her, and that she couldn't watch me disappear all over again. She told me she needed me to be her mama, and that she couldn't be mine.

The next morning, I got up, made the bed, and said: "God, if you woke me up and I'm still in it, I know you'll give me the strength to go through it." Now I say this every day. And each morning I remind myself that I'm not starting over, just picking up where I left off, having come a long, long way. I made a promise to myself that I wouldn't hide—not in my room, not in a bottle of Hennessy, not behind anger or self-pity or excuses.

Still, I am thankful for all the things I did see. I got to see my three oldest kids go to college, I watched DeAndre achieve generational wealth, and I saw my first grandbaby, DeAndre's daughter, come out of the womb in 2014.

CHAPTER 21

Beautifully Blind

It would be a few years until I finally began to embrace the notion that I would be blind for the rest of my life. For so many years, I carried the weight of fear that I would lose my sight. Until recently, I had no clue how much that fear had been a part of me. Now, with the fear behind me, I wake up every day pursuing peace on purpose—that's how I'm able to stay sane. I'm at greater peace now than I've ever been.

In the years after 2015 when I lost my sight for good, I began to be more courageous and more in love with who I was becoming. Even today, people think they need to tell me I'm still beautiful, but I don't crave that anymore because I *feel* it. The crazy thing is when I really was flawless, with beautiful brown eyes, a clear complexion, and long hair, I never felt beautiful. If anything, I felt ugly inside, tarnished and broken, but now? I feel beautiful through and through; my inside and outside finally match.

I say this knowing how I physically look. While I have an hourglass figure, I also bear a scar from my temple to my chin, and my eyes are distorted, inset a little because one eye has shrunk. I can sense this as well, because when I talk, I feel a pulling on my lip. And yet I believe I am the most beautiful blind person in the world.

I have done the work on myself, which is really where any effort needs to be focused. And what is this work? Learning to embrace who I am to move forward, which would not be possible until I could forgive myself. It's the hardest thing to do, but I had to do it: I had to do the work of forgiving myself before becoming comfortable in my own skin.

But before I could even start to forgive myself—which is the key to loving yourself—I had to first be held accountable. In my case, I had to be accountable to my children. And that was tough.

People talk about forgiveness as if it's as easy as flipping on a switch. "You've just got to forgive," they say. But you can't do it with a snap of the fingers. I'm here to tell the world that forgiveness is *a hard job*. And the deep, deep truth is, it's way easier to remain bitter and angry and blame others for what's happened to you. In order to learn how to forgive, I had to do it in stages. The first was seeing my past clearly, holding myself accountable for it, and expressing it out loud.

I sat each one of my kids down and told them I was sorry. My apologies were not general—they were specific. I believe that this is how real forgiveness must begin: by letting the person know that you're entirely and specifically aware of what you've done, showing them that you've come to them after long reflection and that you know the work that you have to do, and are prepared to do, to earn *their* forgiveness.

I also sat down with Kesha, Boodia, Nuk, and Shani together to create a circle of forgiveness, and I apologized for all of the broken promises and apologies I made over the years when they tried to intervene, tried to keep me from chasing after men who weren't good for me, who weren't good for us. I've apologized for telling them too many times that I wouldn't let another man into my life, into our home and our family, who hurt me, and then hurting them by doing it all over again.

I've apologized to my children for forcing them to be adults when they were children, because I didn't have the good sense to be the adult for them.

It's important to never make excuses for your behavior. There are no "buts" in real apologies. You can explain what you've learned about why you may have acted a certain way or done certain things, but only to create better understanding, not to get the people to whom you're apologizing to feel sorry for you. That's playing the victim, that's still seeing yourself as the wronged one. And as long as that's how you see yourself, you can't really take responsibility for the way you treat, or have treated, others.

Being specific about the things you've identified that you should be sorry for isn't the end of the conversation, either. What I tried to do with my kids after offering specific apologies was to ask them what it is that they feel I've done to hurt them—and to listen for as long as it takes for them to tell me. Once that's happened, I repeat what they've told me, and then offer an apology for those things as well. The hardest for me was to hear what hurt them and listen as they let me have it.

Then I made a promise that they're never again going to have a mother who says one thing on Monday and something different on Tuesday. I'm going to be the same mom every day, and that includes being a person who's constantly working on herself to grow.

Forgiveness is incomplete without redemption. The entire process is about growing and changing so that you are, and can continue to be, the person who doesn't repeat mistakes or fall into familiar patterns.

*　*　*

I'm in my fifties now. I can walk into a room and still turn heads, but I'm hardly perfect: I'm self-taught and had to learn to believe I belong in the room. And now I'm teaching myself that I also belong at the table, that I can be and should be part of the conversation, and I will be heard.

In 2017, I received a call from Congresswoman Sheila Jackson Lee of Texas. She asked if I would tell my story at the Congressional Black Caucus in Washington, D.C., later that year. I'd only have five minutes to talk, but it was in front of some of the most important people in politics. I asked Kesha and Shani both to come with me, because I wanted them to experience D.C. for the first time.

During the event, Kesha sat beside me while Shani watched from the audience. I told my story among a panel of speakers, but there were two panelists who stood out to me: Marissa Alexander and Ramona Brant, two Black women who talked about their experiences of being failed by the American justice system. Marissa's case had become well-known after she had fired a warning shot at her abusive husband in her state of Florida. After being denied her defense on the Stand Your Ground statute, she was sentenced to twenty years.

Ramona was sentenced to life in prison in 1995 without parole for drug conspiracy, even though she didn't deal drugs. Instead, she believed she spent twenty-one years in prison because of her relationship with her drug-dealing boyfriend. Her story had the entire room in tears. Fortunately, President Barack Obama commuted her sentence in 2017.

As I listened to each woman's extraordinary story of perseverance, I couldn't help but think that either of them could have been me. I probably sold more drugs, and I literally stabbed a man. I never stopped thinking about these ladies, but a year later Ramona died in her sleep. On my Facebook page, I wrote of her: "I will cherish the time I spent with this strong sister and continue to carry the torch for women like us. Rest in Peace."

That event was the beginning of a relationship I'd have with Congresswoman Lee, who now often calls on me to speak on issues of domestic abuse.

In 2019, Congresswoman Lee and I attended Houston's Project Prom Donation and Giveaway, an event providing five hundred homeless and disadvantaged high school students with attire for prom. When the congresswoman arrived onstage, she surprised me by asking me to come to the podium, where she said publicly that my story inspired her to fight for a reauthorization of the Violence Against Women's Act, a federal law providing housing for victims of domestic abuse. I turned to my staff as if I could see them. I was shocked as I realized everything I had gone through may help thousands of people I will never meet.

That same year, I sat on a couch across from Mina Kimes, a reporter for ESPN. I couldn't see Mina or the photographers and cameramen standing around me, but I could feel bright lights on my face. I was prepared more than ever to tell what I never felt comfortable saying, but now I had an obligation to DeAndre to reveal our story in the right way. I held nothing back, boldly explaining how I sold crack to put food in my children's mouths. I was far from a soccer mom, but my children loved me despite all I had put them through.

The reporter asked me questions about DeAndre, about my life and the attack, and I sat there like a queen, calm and collected, answering everything thrown at me.

DeAndre and I would be the subject of an ESPN cover story in both the magazine and a television episode. Everything that I had feared revealing about all these years was now out in the world. After the story was published, I could hear the whispers as I walked to my seat at DeAndre's games or even to the grocery store: "That's Sabrina, that's DeAndre's mom."

Strangers started walking up to me saying all sorts of things: "I read your story, and I think you're a hero," or "Your story is just like mine."

* * *

All this unfolded right before the Covid lockdown, but soon I'd be on my own like everyone else. I had been living in a new four-story, six-bedroom home in Anderson County. My house has several large fireplaces, a theater room, and a large swimming pool outside. My furniture is all white and black, and there are large photographs of me on the walls; these photographs are not me before the attack but beautifully blind me.

In the mornings, I devote ten minutes to thanking God, but I try to live in a state of gratitude throughout the day. After prayer, I instruct my virtual assistant Alexa to turn on some of my favorite singers, like Jessica Reedy and Tasha Page-Lockhart. As a blind person, I'm especially stimulated by sound, and the sound of gospel music is like drinking ten cups of coffee at one time! The music feeds my soul and wakes up my body. Then I maneuver through the kitchen, where I make myself turkey bacon, eggs, and toast, and drink my coffee before starting my day. I do this every morning because it gives me another chance to live in this amazing skin of mine.

After years of not wearing makeup, I do wear it now, but only to enhance my features—not to hide my scars. I want my scars to show: I was burned over 17 percent of my body, and so I don't want to hide it. My scars are part of who I am.

* * *

My large home may seem too grand for a blind woman to live in by herself. Sometimes it can feel like I'm walking a mile to get from my bedroom to the bathroom, and occasionally I might get lost in the closet or bump into a wall, but now I find humor in it. I tell the wall, "You weren't there yesterday."

On the other hand, I deserve this big house. When I began this journey of redemption, I was on a mission to stand in my truth. Now I'm on a mission to stand up for myself, to love myself, to advocate for myself, and to live—but to live not just for me but for those abused women who are not here today.

This is why I choose to be unapologetically myself whether I'm dancing in my bikini or singing out of tune; I am still here, somehow, and so I am going to live. I'm going to do whatever I want to do, whether it's making breakfast in the morning, or traveling to Cabo with my girlfriends or to one of DeAndre's games. I know I'm defying the odds, and I hope when people see me that I inspire every person with a disability or with a challenge to know that anything is possible.

I can do what everyone else can do except drive. I have a house cleaner who comes weekly, but most of the time I clean when something spills; I wipe my counters down and I wash my dishes and I cook my food. I listen to a lot of books electronically, which fills a great deal of time when I'm not traveling or on Zoom calls for work. When I'm not with my girlfriends or working to help save the lives of women who have been abused like me, I pride myself on getting my family together. Sometimes there's a house full of my kids and their kids, while I'm still cooking the meatloaf and a five-course meal. I get so excited about having everybody over that I can't sleep, and instead I get up at 4:00 a.m. to prep the turkey, my dressing, the mac and cheese, and the collard greens. I don't allow people in my kitchen because I like to put everything where it needs to be. I may bump my head or my leg or burn my finger, but I'm determined, because if I fail to live a normal life, that means the people who attacked me won.

To my grandchildren, I'm a very active GG. We do FaceTime, they call me, and on holidays we get everybody together at my house.

Still, as the saying goes, the more things change the more they stay the same: Despite not having sight, I still go to my same eye doctor in Georgia every six months in case technology catches up; until then, I must continue putting eye drops of steroids and antibiotics in my eyes for the rest of my life to maintain my eyeballs. And I must change the large bandage contact lenses every two months until I die.

Dr. Ambadi continues to be a friend, and I seek advice from him when I need it, but periodically we just talk on the phone to catch up with each other's lives.

I'm still the same hustler who used to babysit and sell dope, but my game now is much different. Instead of selling drugs, I spend that same energy now on helping women who were just like me.

In 2013, together with Kesha, I founded the nonprofit organization S.M.O.O.O.T.H.—Speaking Mentally, Outwardly Opening Opportunities Toward Healing. SMOOOTH is dedicated to helping women heal from domestic violence and to ending the cycle of abuse once and for all. We provide support—education, housing, and job assistance, among other services—to those who are rebuilding their lives and have faced adversity—and won. DeAndre started collaborating with us one year later. We like to say, "DeAndre knocks on doors, and then we walk through them."

* * *

As the CEO of SMOOOTH, I must look my best as I sit next to the likes of famous politicians or CEOs of big companies. There's a video of me, Kesha, and DeAndre standing in a room packed with a camera crew and people from the Houston shelter called Women's Home. That day, I'm wearing a long white blazer, and my hair is sleek and down my back. I tell the women, "I stayed in my room for three years. I know what it's like to be at my lowest, but I also know what it is to smile, and feel beautiful, and to walk in my boldness, and to be resilient."

The video shows me sitting next to Norm Miller, the CEO of a home goods company called Conn's HomePlus. He was the reason we were there. The man donated forty-five thousand dollars' worth of furniture and appliances to Women's Home, and he wanted us to collaborate with him.

Although I only have a high school education, I find myself standing beside giants, important people like NFL Commissioner Roger Goodell, people who have the compassion and means to help the type of women SMOOOTH is dedicated to supporting. So I carefully choose everything I intend to wear. Hazel, my travel assistant, who happens to be my stylist, too, literally walks in the door of my home, takes her shoes off, and we start what we call "maniac-ing."

She runs from room to room, pulling out pieces of clothing. I choose the outfits I plan to wear after Hazel describes things to me, and then I feel it and give a stamp of approval. It's the same way I decorated my home. I know what I like but I always say I have good "describers" around me.

In 2022, I was invited to the Root Institute in D.C., which I received a standing ovation after telling my story. Sharing the stage with the likes of Representative Stacey Abrams and actor Courtney B. Vance, I turned out in a sleek white suit, looking like the CEO I am; at least that's what everyone tells me. To get the professional look I wanted, I used my senses, but Hazel asked, "How you want to look? You want to look boss, or you want to look like a sexy mom?"

Truth be told, I am a visionary on many levels. On those days I'm home alone, I might read a book, or text my assistants, or prepare for my next speech or event. I'm doing better about texting my staff on the weekend. I used to randomly text, all day and night. Those are the times I'm putting my thoughts together and prepping my mind to be in these rooms with important people and in places where I try to encourage women to fight.

As I prepare for my speaking engagements, I try to future-proof everything. For instance, I will need to know how much time I have to speak and whether I'll be standing before a podium or using a lapel mic. I prepare by envisioning myself in front of a large audience. Although I might be nervous and unsure, imagining myself standing there only helps me to believe I belong on a stage, where I tell my truth as Pastor Ova predicted years ago.

From the moment I wake up until the second I lay my head on my pillow, I'm thinking of ways to help the next woman. I envision what a successful outcome looks like. After I see it in my mind's eye, I spend my waking days making it happen. As part of SMOOOTH's efforts to save lives, I work year-round speaking in churches and community centers to men and women; abuse isn't only a women's issue, after all. We make sure the attendees we help have everything from food to counseling, to mentoring and education about abuse and its effects on the family dynamic. We stock the kitchens of women who are getting back on their feet after leaving abusive relationships—whatever makes even the tiniest difference, me and my team are always there to make it happen.

In fact, I remember the day I got the call about a young woman named Katera. She had dropped her infant son off at the fire station in Houston and left him because she had gotten beaten by her boyfriend the night before and convinced herself that her baby would be better off without her. Her car barely made it to the fire station. If you can imagine the raggediest car, one with smoke coming out the back and could barely move five miles an hour, that was Katera's car.

Katera was an emotional wreck, but she knew that in the state of Texas, if you take your child to a hospital or a fire station, there's nothing the authorities can do to you because you're giving the child a better life.

But when she dropped her child off, she drove down the road and returned, deciding that she ultimately wanted her child back. By then, police were there, as were social workers and the emergency crews. They made this big fuss, which by right they should have. While in South Carolina, I received a call around 11:00 p.m. from someone in Houston, asking if I could help this young lady. By now, Katera's baby had been placed in protective custody. I was able to make a call and get the young mother into a shelter immediately because I had a SMOOOTH chapter in Houston.

But Katera was not happy. In fact, she believed because she went to the safe house, she'd get her son back immediately. When that didn't happen, she started showing her butt, cursing people out in the shelter, and demanding that someone bring her child to her.

On the phone, I corrected her. "No," I said, "you got to put the work in." I talked to the Department of Social Services, and they said the child could not be returned because of her car, which would be dangerous for her baby to be in.

I sent two women from SMOOOTH to get Katera whatever she

needed—women's products, food, even flowers to brighten her day. She started taking parenting classes for a month, but Social Services was close to throwing in the towel.

I flew to Texas to meet Katera because she was showing out again. Kesha met me at the airport and drove me to the shelter, where I talked to Katera. Then I called the Social Services agent who was considering taking permanent custody of Katera's son in order to put him in foster care. "Listen," I said, "this is a woman under my care. I'm sitting here with her now. I vouch for her." They listened, so I continued, ensuring them that Katera would do what was needed to get her son back, which would include taking anger management classes.

When I hung up the phone, I turned to Katera. "Let me tell you something. This is my first time meeting you, but you're going to stop showing your ass. We will get your child back. You made one mistake, and now the whole city of Houston knows about it."

Let me tell you how this story ended. With some financial help from DeAndre, my staff in Texas was able to get Katera a car and pay six months of her insurance. With a new car and completed anger management courses under her belt, Social Services gave Katera back her son and they are both doing well to this day.

* * *

One of my favorite SMOOOTH events is Pretty Scars into Stars, where women are selected from local shelters and transitional centers to receive beauty makeovers.

Everything I do is a reflection of what I went through at the time of my abuse. When I was going through hell with Mark, the last thing I could think about was my appearance or keeping myself up.

This day, however, is more than just pampering—it's dedicated to celebrating growth, transformation, and survival through external and internal restoration. We pick the ladies up from the shelters in limousines and take them to get facials, massages, teeth whitening, and professional hair, nail, and makeup services.

In 2019, the same year Katera participated, the famous Paul Mitchell

Salon did the women's hair, lashes, and makeup. David's Bridal donated beautiful dresses and a variety of shoe brands provided them with dress shoes. I always have my staff line up and applaud as the women enter the salon.

As they're getting gussied up, I schedule time to introduce myself to the women and encourage them to let us love up on them and show them we care about them.

When I was being abused, I had no support, and no one to tell me I was beautiful, and I deserved better, but now I know how important that is. All my relationships with men were abusive in one way or another, except for Steve, and when I was going through my abuse, I had no one. Understanding that these women have experienced the same thing, I tell them, "I know you're hesitant. I know life has beat you up, but this is the day it's going to end. And while life is still going to come at you, this day will give you the courage to know you're worth the fight."

After all the pampering, the women gather for a catered dinner accompanied by their close family or friends for an ultimate Purple Carpet reveal. This same year, forty-eight children came to see their moms be stars. Special guests, motivational speakers, and charitable sponsors also gathered for the evening.

Throughout most of the evening, I'm busy managing all the details, making sure everything is perfect and the ladies are not popping out of their dresses. Toward the end, though, I finally sit down, and that's when the children come over to talk. But it was the moment when Katera came over with her son that brought me the most joy. "Miss Sabrina," she said, laying his tiny hands on mine. "I want you to meet my son, and I just want to say thank you."

I'm proudest of SMOOOTH when we can help people like Katera, because these cases have real impact and can change a life. But I also love when we can bring some light to an entire community. During another SMOOOTH event called 100 Shades of Purple, we do a purple balloon release for all those who have fallen to domestic violence. Then we celebrate all the beautiful kings and queens and survivors that are still living.

DeAndre has worked with me on so many projects, but one of my favorite collaborations was a basketball tournament in Clemson, where three thousand people showed up. DeAndre and three other former Clemson football players signed autographs while Kesha orchestrated the entire tournament and SMOOOTH gave out four thousand backpacks. It felt like the entire town came out. Now I'm implementing that same thing in three other states.

* * *

I always say I was a blink away from being in a shelter myself, which is why I started SMOOOTH. At the time I kept praying, asking, "God, what can I do to help women like me?" One night it came to me. I believe it was God who spoke to me and gave me the word "SMOOOTH," with the three Os. It made no sense to me. And, I said, "God, what are you trying to tell me? How in the world does this word relate to domestic violence?"

I called one of my best friends, Veronica, one night, crying and frustrated that I didn't know what God was trying to tell me to do.

"Be obedient to God's vision," Veronica replied simply.

I followed faith and named the organization SMOOOTH, and soon I figured out why God gave me the word: everything I do involves helping women have a *smooth* transition from instability and uncertainty to a life of stability. Everything about SMOOOTH is about transition, and that brings me to Brittany, a young woman from Houston.

We were in the early days of the pandemic when I got a call again in the middle of the night about a woman sleeping in her car with her young daughter. She had been in an abusive relationship, and she couldn't keep up with her rent.

This was the very early days of the pandemic, when there was no government help, and many women were forced to stay in their homes with their abusers. During this time, domestic violence incidents not only went up, but skyrocketed. There were also a lot of people who got put out of their dwellings because they couldn't work and, therefore, couldn't pay their rent.

I agreed to pay Brittany's hotel fees for one week, which turned into two weeks, and then longer. I was in South Carolina, but I worked on her case from my home during those early pandemic months, assigning Kesha to her case in Houston. Before she stopped by to see them, she picked up a teddy bear for Brittany's little girl.

Kesha shared that Brittany and her daughter had all their belongings, everything they could call theirs, in two small plastic bags.

While Brittany and her daughter were in the hotel, we soon discovered the young woman had Covid. My staff brought food to her door, and we tried to keep the child away from her mother and reminded her to keep her mask on. Within a month, Brittany had healed, but the child had contracted a severe case of the virus. At one point we worried her daughter wasn't going to make it, but she survived. Eager to get Brittany stabilized during such an uncertain time, SMOOOTH worked closely with another organization called Twelve Days of Christmas. Collectively, we reached out to food banks and raised ten thousand dollars through a GoFundMe campaign. There's a video of Brittany and her daughter walking into their new apartment. Surrounded by Kesha and SMOOOTH members Hazel and Alanna, Brittany was shocked as she surveyed her beautiful new apartment, decorated with candles and bright new furniture. She moved over to a laptop where I was waiting for her on Zoom. When she sat down, I started talking. "Today your story has been changed," I said. "Hold your head up high. You have a second chance."

CHAPTER 22

The Promise

God gave me a second chance the day I was attacked, which is why I call the anniversary of that tragic day my "second birthday." The average person would never want to celebrate such a horrific event, but I have since the very first year.

In July 2022, DeAndre hired an event planner to coordinate and decorate my twenty-year anniversary, which I called my "My Celebration of Life." As much as I loved putting events together, this time there was little for me to do but to show up. And yet, the night before, I was all nerves. I called my makeup artist to be sure she'd arrive at my hotel on time, and I laid out my outfit on the bed: an elegant sleeveless Alice and Olivia diamond-beaded shirt and white sleek bell-bottom pants, diamond-beaded stilettos, and a matching clutch bag. My bone-straight extensions were already in and swinging down to my waist.

I took a breath and said to myself, "Okay, lady, you're about to embark on a new chapter in your life." It was that moment when I realized I was no longer a survivor. I had already done all the surviving I could do—now I was an *overcomer*.

The next day I rode in the back of a white Rolls-Royce to Juliet's, a fine-dining restaurant in Houston. I wondered if everyone followed my orders to wear white, and then I told myself, of course they did. I needed to settle down, because it was going to be a great night of celebration, a lot of crying, laughter, and hugs.

When I stepped out of the limo, my friends and some spectators surrounded the car flashing their cameras and cell phones. A crowd clapped and cheered me on as I walked into the venue. Kesha and Shani grabbed each arm. Shani whispered, "Mama, you can't imagine this room. There are big vases everywhere with hundreds of red roses in them."

I sat in my designated seat surrounded by my children as they continued describing the atmosphere of the event. "Mama, they have two big life-sized photographs of you," Kesha said.

The room was packed with about forty people, relatively new friends, mostly people I had met during the seven years DeAndre had been in Houston. They didn't know the broken me but only the beautiful-blind me, the visionary me, the love-me-some-Sabrina me, the country-bougie me, the boss me. One by one they delivered remarks about how I inspired them. There were the members of my team: Hazel, Tashia, and Alanna; then there was Lo London, who was my social media editor and a reality TV star before she became a great friend; and Humble, my financial adviser, who had traveled from Los Angeles to be part of the festivities.

When I stood up and raised my champagne glass to all these friends, and my children, it was my way of telling my attackers: *You didn't take anything from me.*

*   *   *

Hearing my children speak was likely the greatest part of the celebration that day. Marcus was the first to the podium. He was my quiet one, which made me lean into his words more. "Mama is my twin, and all my children look just like her." He paused, and a moment later continued.

"I was there the night Mama lost her sight forever. I was also there when she hit rock bottom, but she got up and started all over again." He paused again. "Mama is the strongest woman I know. She just doesn't give up."

Next, Shani approached the front of the room with the microphone in hand; I could tell by her voice that she was turned toward me. Her voice trembled, but my baby held it together. "I feel everything you feel. We go through everything together," she said, setting off more sniffles. "When you're sad, I'm sad, and when you are happy, I am happier. To see you smile, that's the only thing I ever want to see. Anything to see you happy."

Then I could hear her voice shifting to the front of the room. "I want to thank you all for all the things y'all have done for my mama, those little things, sending her emails, doing her makeup, anything to make her feel like a regular person."

DeAndre was next. I wanted to get out of my chair to protect him, because he spoke from the heart that night, and he seemed so vulnerable. People told me later that he had kept his head low and tears were streaming down his face as he revealed the secret that he and I had kept since he was twelve years old. No one in the room knew about my suicide attempt and him saving my life.

"It had to be three in the morning," he reflected. When he finished the story, with him stopping me from jumping into the highway and leading me back to 115, he admitted the truth: "She was trying to kill herself." Then he said that's why he now realizes God put him on Earth, to save his mama's life. I swear there couldn't have been a dry eye in the room.

After that, DeAndre read a beautiful poem that he wrote on the plane coming back into Houston, a poem about me being a young mother, working at Dayco, and dancing, his words blending almost like a rap song. Some words rhymed and some did not. He wrote about him and Marcus rubbing my aching feet after a night at Godiva's, and how he decided as a young boy to never ask anyone for nothing but instead to challenge himself to the tenth degree to change our lives forever. Kesha got up and was all Kesha. "Stop all this crying shit," she said, setting off loud roars of laughter.

Being the oldest, she revealed that she saw the most. Then she added, "I'm incredibly proud of the strength she displays every day. It's why I try to be excellent. How dare I complain when she literally goes through what she must go through every day from the time she wakes up till the time she goes to sleep? She doesn't have a normal life."

Then she sparked laughter again. "If you around her," she said, "you better know how to describe some shit."

These are my beautiful, winning children. I thought that I was the one who gave them life, but in truth they returned to me my own.

* * *

I attempted to break generational curses with my children through open dialogue, talking about the past, apologizing for everything that I had done, but I had no idea I would also be faced with breaking the generational curse for Hummie's children, my niece and my nephew, and really, for the entire family.

Months after the party, I was sitting on the couch in DeAndre's home while the production crew of HBO's *Hard Knocks*, the reality sports documentary series, was setting up around me. They were to feature DeAndre for the ongoing documentary. That's when DeAndre came over and mentioned that I needed to speak to Daejha, Hummie's daughter, who was in the back room.

I was surprised that she was even there. Although Hummie's son, Terrance, had become close to DeAndre, spent summers with our side of the family, and become an NFL player himself, Daejha hadn't been around much. I heard from the kids that she had grown tired of her job as a lawyer in Atlanta and was now traveling the country to find herself. So, after the TV crew had completed their film work and was packing up, I sought out Daejha, hugged her, and invited her to come visit me. A few weeks later, she called. "Auntie, I want to take you up on your offer and come visit with you for a few weeks before I head back to Georgia."

Of course I said yes.

"I'll let you know when I'm on my way. It's just me and my fur babies." My promise—that our generational curse of holding painful family secrets stopped with me—had to extend to Hummie's daughter, I realized, who was obviously emotionally lost. I knew in my heart I would have some answers to her questions, I'd help her find a missing piece of her puzzle, and I'd provide a safe place for her to ask those questions. About three weeks later she arrived. I was so impressed with how she openly talked about her travels, and how at each place she visited she found hints of what she needed to heal.

We had a little routine—every morning she'd take her dog and cat for a walk, and then we'd catch up over coffee. Sometimes we'd go out for dinner, and sometimes I'd cook. Every day I was around her, I noticed she had my brother's quiet tendencies—the way she would stop and start her words, her serene demeanor, and other similarities, gave me chills.

I knew in my heart I was going to fulfill my promise. I was going to talk to her about her father and provide her with the last missing link to her journey. A few days before she planned to leave, I decided to begin the conversation during our coffee time.

"I got something I want to talk to you about," I said. "I'm sure you heard the story about your father before, but you've never heard my version."

I told her about our childhood, about Dilly's fatal accident, and how none of us were the same after his death—especially her father. I shared with her how outstanding her father had been in high school and college, but she had no idea what I was about to say next. "I want you to know your daddy never made one bad decision in his entire life but that one day."

She touched my hand. "I know. I want to hear all about it."

I revealed that her mom and dad were having problems, and it was tough for Hummie because divorce, for him, was not an option. I stated that something else was going on in his brain, because he just wasn't himself.

She grew very quiet as I continued.

"I knew the police's bullet grazed your arm when you were only two years old."

She lifted her shirt and took my hand and put it on her stomach.

I felt a large keloid that stretched across her belly. I did not know the police had shot her in the stomach, too. "My God, I had no idea!"

Then I told her I had something I wanted to show her, too. I had her walk with me to the closet, and I latched on to her arm, pointing to a safe. I told her to bring it to the kitchen island and open it. I started pulling precious items out of the safe, including Steve's rings, which I had taken out to touch a million times. But then I produced Hummie's Oakley sunglasses. One of the lenses had popped out of the frame by now. "These are your father's glasses," I said. "They were in his car the day your grandfather went to retrieve it after his death."

Then I pulled out a news article about Hummie's funeral and slid it over to her. There was a photograph of me on the front page being carried out of the church by Richard, who was taking me to the hospital.

Since going blind, I had had Shani read me the article so many times. I gave Daejha a minute to take everything in, but finally I handed her the tape recorder.

"Auntie, what is this?"

"That's the tape your father left behind. Not too many people know about it, but it's where he tells everybody . . ."

She burst out crying before I could utter the word "goodbye."

"Come here," I said and held her tight as she cried in my arms.

"Nobody said he left it," she continued to cry.

"Almost nobody knew, honey. I was told never to talk about it. But I don't want to die without letting you know it exists."

After I finished telling her my version of the story, she asked to go to her room to process everything. I had held on to the items because it was a way of holding on to my brother, but I had realized over time I had to sacrifice what I had left of him for his daughter, my niece. All these years I'd sneak over to the safe, listen to the tape recording, and cry, but now I had not one single possession of his.

But I had broken our family curse for my niece and her brother.

She deserved the information that would set her free.

Sometimes in life, until the time comes, we retrieve things we never realize could be the missing links to someone's burning questions.

By giving her these objects, I was breaking a generational curse of silence that had been tearing our family apart for years. I wanted her to break the emotional stronghold I imagined had been binding her and her brother.

* * *

Back when I was hurting and recovering from the attack, an older woman, a friend of a friend, had come into my bedroom. She told me at that time, "Honey, you got to forgive them." And I was like, "Yes, ma'am. Yes, ma'am, I do." But in my mind, I was thinking how the heck can she tell me this? But she was right. The only way I was ever going to be able to move on from the attack was to forgive Savannah Grant, my attacker, and Antonne—and this was just about the hardest thing I ever had to do. But it wasn't just my attacker. I had to forgive all those people who I was still angry at for the wrong they had done to me. It's never-ending—all these people are still in my face. It's a process. I'm constantly processing all that happened whenever I'm in their presence.

Even forgiving my father was very difficult. Daddy reentered my life after the attack. He took me to doctors' appointments and sat with me after surgeries. Over time, I've learned how to see his humanity, especially when it comes to the circumstances that led him to divorce Mama and to his absence from *our* lives. He doesn't make excuses for his part in the ugliness and violence. When he talks about how desperate he was to get himself out of the toxic dynamic he was in with my mama, I now have a more sympathetic understanding of where he was coming from. I understand what it means to be in situations where, unless one person leaves, the cycle of ugliness just won't stop. I've also come to understand that even though my daddy's choices hurt me to the depths of my being and made me feel worthless for so long, he did what he had to do for him and not because he didn't love and value me.

After all these years, the kind of relationship Daddy and I have now is a model not only for talking honestly, no matter how difficult or uncomfortable it may be, but also for what it means to forgive. When someone is showing you what they're doing every day to set things right, you must release them from the prison of how they've wronged you—for both of your sakes. That's because forgiveness, of course, extends to our own selves, too.

* * *

Deep down there's likely only one reason I was able to forgive Savannah, Antonne, and also Uncle Ottie, who killed Dilly. It's a selfish reason, I suppose, because I did not do it for them, but for me: the Bible says that you can't hate somebody and expect for breakthroughs or blessings to come. So I can't hate anybody, because I have two people waiting on me in heaven. I do believe that there's a heaven and a hell and that my brothers are in heaven, so then how can I hate someone on Earth and expect to be with them again? And from what the Bible says, I will literally get a whole new body. I will get brand-new eyes. I will have a mansion in heaven, and most of all, I'll be able to laugh and sing and hug my brothers again. This life has been pretty fucked up, but dying is like starting over. Don't get me wrong, I am going to live this life to the fullest, but I am not afraid to die when I know Dilly and Hummie are waiting for me.

So how did I start to forgive the woman who blinded me? The thought of it made my stomach turn.

But once I'd learned to hold myself accountable, I was able to see the chain of decisions that I'd made, which set off the row of falling dominoes in my life. Instead of blaming Savannah Grant for throwing acid in my face, I began to ask myself about all the choices I'd made that put me in front of Savannah at that place at that moment in time. That's what opened the door to forgiving her.

Every morning I woke up and said these words out loud: "I forgive. I forgive. I forgive."

I said them even when I didn't fully mean them. I couldn't really mean them because in the beginning I didn't fully believe them. But I was repeating them over and over and over, as sure as I was drinking coffee every morning. Somehow, just repeating those words aloud opened the door to empathy.

Truth be told, I needed to wrap my head around how could somebody be so cruel, and the only way to do that is to normalize her. It allowed me to put myself in Savannah's shoes. She was a young black woman who'd been manipulated and deceived by the same guy. She had a four-year-old child, just like me. We even had the same initials. What if our roles had been reversed? What if I'd been manipulated into throwing the acid? That could've been me in jail and her blindly trying to take care of a young child at home.

Empathy for Savannah opened the door to the hardest part of my journey. I began to pray for her. My stomach cringed the first time I did. The last thing you want to do is pray for anyone who's wronged you, let alone someone who left you blind. But I repeated these words every day until they were imprinted in my mind: "I pray for Savannah and her child. I pray that everything she touches turns to gold. I pray for prosperity and health and wholeness over her life."

That was as far as I could get, but it was a long way from where I started, and it opened the door to the next stage. Soon, my prayers grew longer and longer, for they began to include all the people who'd hurt me throughout my life. These prayers became something like a ritual. As they grew longer, my forgiveness kept expanding. And over time, I found that missing piece of my soul that been pulled out of me by Reverend Lottie and stomped on when I was ten years old.

I now had faith.

* * *

One day, Kesha finally got so sick and tired of me carrying on about all the ways that my mama was falling short that she looked me square in the eye. "You can't keep expecting something from her that she can't give you. You have to love her where she is."

Mama is still fighting her demons, and my relationship with her remains the biggest challenge in my life on my journey of truth and forgiveness. Although my mom and I are in a good place now, I've chosen not to be her mother anymore, not to be her friend, but to be her daughter. I now understand that I must heed Kesha's sage advice and meet my mother where she is, not where I want her to be. I shouldn't expect so much from her, because that's when people let you down. When I am around my mother, I expect her to be just who she is, my mother. If she never says she's sorry, my job is not to transform her into something that she may never be.

When I began to understand that my mama is exactly who she is, I started healing. For years, I was the mother and she was the daughter, and I was mad and angry, and I had every right to be. But when I made the choice to allow my mother to be the mother, whatever that looked like is whatever that looked like. However she shows up, it is not my job to chastise and raise her. When you no longer try to chastise your parents, that is when the disrespect stops.

Loving people where they are, not turning them into someone you want them to be, also suggests that we're learning how to love ourselves. And learning how to love yourself includes learning how to be alone, which is something I'm still working on to this day.

I'm open about the fears I have of being in a relationship with a man, not quite trusting myself to choose the right person, being afraid that I'll fall into old habits. Part of me still loves, and will always love, Steve. DeAndre says his dad is still with me, and I believe that. There are things that I feel and sense. We once met a lady with psychic abilities, and she told us that Steve's not only protecting Nuk but also walking with me, back and forth with his arms folded. She said he's ready to go when I find a man to treat me right, a man that truly loves me. But I haven't found anyone yet.

Still, the more I grow and the more I surround myself with people I trust, the more I learn that love isn't meant to fill the holes in your heart. The people who love you most and best are those who stand alongside you while you bind up your own wounds. They aren't happiest when you feel small, but when you're standing tall. They stand at your back when you need support, and they give you a push when you're too afraid to take the next step forward.

* * *

It still amazes me how different each of my children's experiences were, the things they remember that I have no memory of but that I have to accept. Because even though the truth hurts, it's their truth, and I will never take their truth away from them simply because it makes it easier for me to ignore the pain I caused. I won't take my kids' voices away from them or damage their ability to trust themselves by saying I don't believe them when they're speaking their truth. They will always know that I'll listen to them, and that I'll believe them, no matter what they have to say. They will not feel the need to hide anything about themselves or be anyone other than who they are. Not from me, and not for me.

I remember when DeAndre was drafted by the NFL, and I was already out there speaking in the community, which I had started doing even before my testimony about Reverend Lottie at Abel Baptist Church. I figured that he was on a national stage and maybe would feel differently about how open I was in telling my story—our story, including talking about his father. I asked him, "Do you mind me saying that your daddy was a drug dealer?"

"Mama," he said, "if that's your story, tell it."

Not only has Nuk encouraged me to keep talking, but he has chosen to be totally open as well. From the moment he was drafted, in every interview Nuk gave—from the local papers in Houston to national papers, like *USA Today*—he included his whole story, my story, and what our family has been through. He knows that he has the power to help a lot of people by speaking the truth, too.

* * *

I am still here to experience all that life still has for me. As my eyes water and I struggle to hold back tears because I don't want to mess up my makeup, I reflect on all the blood, sweat, and tears I shed to be where I am. Kesha is now a Realtor in Houston and is the owner of a women's football team. Marcus is a proud father of four who produces music for various artists in South Carolina. DeAndre has now been in the NFL for ten years, becoming a better player every day. Shanterria, my baby girl, has modeling contracts in three states and never misses a day calling her mama. I am so proud of my family, but most of all I am proud of my resilience and perseverance to be the strong mother I am today. I now know that putting in the work to forgive others also changed my life for the better. I realized that everything had to happen just as it did so that my story could be this amazing gift to the world, because there are still millions of women out there who are struggling to find themselves, and I want to be that woman who meets them where they are and shows them there is life after death.

* * *

Around the time of the party and Daejha's visit, I recall Shanterria and I had decided to go to dinner one evening. The moment Shanterria entered the house, I could feel something was wrong.

"Shani, what's going on?" I said.

"Mama," she began, "I am still upset at how they did you, and it bothers me when I see you walking around blind. I know it's been twenty years, but it hurts me to see you like this."

"Shanterria, sit down," I instructed. "Baby, do you know your mother is a living testimony? What if God allows things to happen to some people in order to get the attention of other people? If that is the case, I am not going to question God or my purpose. You need to realize that if I had to do everything all over again, I wouldn't change one single thing." I told her I needed her to understand I was okay and would continue to be okay.

*   *   *

The stronger I get, the more I realize that the purpose I found once upon a time remains the same today, and that sight never had, and still doesn't have, anything to do with my ability to serve that purpose. My vision does—a vision for my life that I'd never appreciated until I lost my ability to see.

And so, I ask myself every day:

Would I trade my vision if I could have my sight?

Every day, the answer is no.

Because the reason I'm still here is my vision. That's what's inspired me to change my life, and I've no doubt it's why I'm still alive.

Don't get me wrong—I don't want things to be this way. I don't want to have to relearn how to put one foot in front of the other while trying to push away the fear that I'm going to fall, and I don't want to have to rely on others for even more help than I needed before. To make it sound like everything's peaches and cream would be untrue. To say that every day isn't a battle would be false.

The difference is that now I'm prepared for the battle, and I know I have the strength to stay in the fight. Everything I've been through led me to face my demons, face myself and the people I've hurt, cultivate the courage and develop the tools for changing my life—all of it has prepared me for this moment.

*   *   *

I used to wake up every morning wondering if that would be the day my sight disappeared again and lay down at night not grateful for all that I'd seen, but worried that I was just one tomorrow away from blindness. I never was able to just breathe into it, trusting that all would be well.

But when I wake up now my first thought—the same one I'd had since 2015—isn't about what I might lose. And that is a win. I feel free in a way I never had before, at liberty to dedicate my whole self to making my vision a reality—to only look ahead, not over my shoulder.

I spend every day trying to keep rising, keep holding on to the positive changes I've made, to keep walking my talk, helping as many people as I can for as long as I can because I still can and have no excuses not to.

I hope to leave you all with the awareness that no matter who you are, where you come from, or what your story is, there are things that can be taken from us, and there are things that can only be taken if we give them away.

I know from experience that people can rob you of your innocence, that death can take the people we love, and that the physical abilities we take for granted can disappear in the blink of an eye.

Yet I've also learned that self-respect, dignity, hope, inner strength, courage, compassion, commitment, determination, and faith—these are only lost to us forever if we willingly surrender them to someone or something, or if we don't do everything we can to reclaim them when we lose our way.

The poem DeAndre reads at the twenty-year celebration:

The Strength of My Mama

I remember when I was ten
And I came home to a yard full of people crying
Heard whispers of Sabrina Greenlee dying
They pulled me in the room
And said your mom is fighting for her life
I thought they was lying
Realizing it was true because if you know her
She don't allow anybody in her room

The first thing I did was call her phone a hundred times
To hear her voice on the ring back
My dad died when I was six months
So the only thing I knew was to keep calling
And hope that God would give me a ring back

True story, can't make it up
I called her phone just to hear her voice
That day I made a vow to myself
If it's only us in this world
I'm going to take care of my little sister Rejoice

I found myself as an adult thinking
About what could've or should've
But God didn't make a mistake
Because my mama spirit never break
It gave its toughest battle
To its most loyal soldier

She took care of her two brothers when she was a kid
The Lord been chose her for this moment
She pushed and pushed
And never stopped moving that mountain

Dayco job, dancer at night
The Sabrina I know
Is going to make sure her kids
Have an even chance in life to fight

Whatever it took for us to have a better upbringing
Than what she knew
My brother Marcus and I rubbed her feet at night
From the soreness of her high-heeled shoe

Everything that happened to our family
Was part of God's plan
And I thank my mama for everything she did
Right or wrong
Because if you were raising four kids
How would you write your song

Her song is beautiful
And it's still going
Y'all say twenty years since being assaulted
But I say twenty years of her still glowing

DEANDRE HOPKINS

Acknowledgments

First and foremost, I want to thank my Lord and Savior, Jesus Christ, who is the head of my life. To God be all the glory. I now walk by faith and not by sight.

For everyone who has helped grant me vision:

Terry Allen Smith Sr. and Rosa "Nett" Smith: Here's to my two heroes, who showed me how to turn life's pain into power and taught me the true meaning of still standing.

Terry "Hummie" Smith Jr. and Russell "Dilly" Smith, my two eternal kings, you will always be the driving force that motivates me to prosper. Because of you, I stood in my truth and fought to live to tell our story.

Harris Steve Hopkins, my soulmate, you made loving me look easy. Thank you for being my partner in crime, my best friend, and my everything. I will always love you.

Kesha "Smitty" Smith, Marcus "Boodia" Greenlee, DeAndre "Nuk" Hopkins, and Shanterria "Shani" Cobb, my four champions: My desire to change because of you outweighed my desire to stay the same. I'm a better version of myself today because you never gave up on me.

My grandchildren, may you carry this torch of liberation into the future, crafting a legacy of resilience and writing a new narrative that represents who I am—"Gigi"—and what we stand for.

Terrance Smith and Daejha Smith, I dedicate these pages to breaking generational curses and creating boundless possibilities for the two of you.

Allen "Justin" Smith and Christopher Smith, my loving brothers: This book is a tribute to the enduring strength and the unbreakable bond we share as siblings.

Zona Ladd and Frances Austin, a special dedication to my heavenly grandmothers for their unconditional love and guidance.

Auntie Louise Greenlee, your unique style, confidence, and creativity taught me how to embrace my beauty and capture the essence of a true diva.

Montez Greenlee, my cousin and counselor, thanks for never skipping a beat and always being there for me. In your words, "I don't play about that one right there!"

The HarperCollins team, thank you for a life-changing opportunity and for providing a platform for a memoir that is unapologetic and a true reflection of me—and a special thanks to Adenike Olanrewaju for her tenacity in driving this process and seeing it through.

Jane von Mehren, thanks for bringing us all together. Your expertise has been instrumental in shaping this work.

Tatsha Robertson, I am forever grateful for your unwavering support and guidance throughout the making of this masterpiece. It would not have happened without you.

Humble Lukanga, thank you for walking this journey with me. Without you believing in my vision, none of this would be possible. Cheers to many more Moscow mules and five-hour conversations! I especially also want to thank my Lifeline Financial family. Thank you for allowing me to flow. It is because of you that I sleep with ease each night.

Angela Hicks, Tiffany Garrison, Destiny Wilson, Veronica Parker, and Lauren Lima, my best friends, thank you for always holding me accountable and never allowing me to give up on myself. Each of our relationships is different and incredibly unique, but the one thing that remains constant is my love for all of you.

My SMOOOTH ladies, a heartfelt thanks to my incredible team, who work effortlessly behind the scenes to uplift and empower survivors. Your dedication and loyalty make our mission possible to promote the growth and evolution of women worldwide.

Team All Things Sabrina: Alanna "Boss Lady" Murray, you wear many hats. Your loyalty, support, and dedication to me and the SMOOOTH organization is unmatched. Hazel "OG" Brown, thank you for all of the many maniac moments and always making sure that I am fashionably on point. Tashia "TT" Taylor, for the years of dedication; it doesn't go unnoticed. Loren "Lo London" Jordan, thank you for introducing me to the world of social media and allowing me always to be my unapologetic self.

Mr. and Mrs. Larry and Shirley Greenlee, Mr. and Mrs. Rodney and Jackie Blunt, Tyleek Hopkins, Kerry Jordan, and Latasha Young, a special thank-you. I feel incredibly fortunate to have you all in my life.

A'Lores "Sugar Foot" Norris and Joseph "Jocasso" Smith: your passion for your craft is evident. Our beauty bond goes beyond brushes and combs and speaks to a stronger connection of vulnerability and trust that you will always ensure I look my absolute best—and thank you to every makeup artist, hair stylist, videographer, photographer, and fashion expert who has worked tirelessly and been the driving force behind my confidence.

There is no way that I could have finished this book without acknowledging two influential figures in my life: Dr. Bala Ambati, who showed me compassion and restored my hope when I needed it the most; and Pastor Ova McCauley, who lifted me up and revitalized my faith in God.

To all my beautiful queens who were told or made to feel like you were never enough: This memoir is not just my story; it's our collective anthem of perseverance. May these pages be a mirror reflecting your strength, a reminder of your worth, and a source of inspiration for every woman who has faced adversity.

Finally, I want to thank anyone who invested time and shared a space with me and my children. Whether it was by praying, picking up the phone to say, "Girl, you got this," or attending one of my fabulous parties, I want you to know that your gesture did not go unnoticed. From the bottom of my heart, I love you on purpose—THANK YOU!

About the Author

SABRINA GREENLEE is a South Carolina native, celebrated community activist, nationally recognized inspirational speaker, life coach, and domestic violence survivor who has dedicated her life to facilitating the transformative power of healing. As the founder and president of the nonprofit SMOOOTH, Sabrina uses her voice, wisdom, and unique experiences to inspire healing, promote transcendence from hurt, and encourage women to *Take Their Power Back*.

To book Sabrina for a speaking engagement, go to her website at www.sabrinagreenlee.co.

To make a contribution to Sabrina's 501(c)(3) nonprofit, go to www.smooothinc.org.